LEARNING FROM EXPERIENCE: Evaluating Early Childhood Demonstration Programs

Jeffrey R. Travers and Richard J. Light
Editors

Panel on Outcome Measurement in
Early Childhood Demonstration Programs

Committee on Child Development Research
and Public Policy

Assembly of Behavioral and Social Sciences

National Research Council

NATIONAL ACADEMY PRESS
Washington, D.C.   1982

Library of Congress Cataloging in Publication Data

Main entry under title:

Learning from experience.

    Includes bibliographical references.
    1. Child development--United States--Addresses, essays,
lectures. 2. Education, Preschool--United States--Addresses,
essays, lectures. I. Travers, Jeffrey R. II. Light, Richard
J. III. National Research Council (U.S.). Panel on Outcome
Measurement in Early Childhood Demonstration Programs.
LB1115.L33   370.15'2   81-22595
ISBN 0-309-03232-6   AACR2

Available from

NATIONAL ACADEMY PRESS
2101 Constitution Avenue, N.W.
Washington, D.C.   20418

Printed in the United States of America

Panel on Outcome Measurement in Early Childhood Demonstration Programs

Richard J. Light, (Chair), Graduate School of Education
    and J.F.K. School of Government, Harvard University
Rochelle Beck, Children's Defense Fund, Washington, D.C.
Joan S. Bissell, Employment Development Department,
    Sacramento, California
Urie Bronfenbrenner, Department of Human Development and
    Family Studies Cornell University (member until 1980)
Geraldine Kearse Brookins, Department of Psychology,
    Jackson State University
Anthony S. Bryk, Graduate School of Education, Harvard
    University
Dennis J. Deloria, Administration for Children, Youth,
    and Families, U.S. Department of Health and Human
    Services
William S. Hall, Center for the Study of Reading,
    University of Illinois
Robert W. Hartman, The Brookings Institution, Washington,
    D.C.
Pablo Navarro-Hernandez, Department of Anthropology,
    Inter-American University of Puerto Rico (member until
    1980)
Barbara Heyns, The Center for Applied Social Science
    Research, New York University
Melvin D. Levine, Department of Pediatrics, Children's
    Hospital Medical Center, Boston, Massachusetts
Garry L. McDaniels, General Accounting Office,
    Washington, D.C.
Samuel Messick, Educational Testing Service, Princeton,
    New Jersey
David P. Weikart, High/Scope Educational Research
    Foundation, Ypsilanti, Michigan

Lee J. Cronbach (ex officio), Member, Committee on
    Ability Testing, School of Education, Stanford
    University

Staff

Jeffrey R. Travers, Consultant/Study Director
Janie Stokes, Administrative Secretary

Committee on Child Development Research and Public Policy

Wayne Holtzman (<u>ex officio</u>), Chair, Panel on Selection
and Placement of Students in Programs for the Mentally
Retarded; Hogg Foundation for Mental Health, University
of Texas

Sheila B. Kamerman (<u>ex officio</u>), Chair, Panel on Work,
Family, and Community; School of Social Work, Columbia
University

Contents

Preface

Late in 1978 the National Research Council, with
support from the Carnegie Corporation, established the
Panel on Outcome Measurement in Early Childhood Demonstration Programs, to operate under the aegis of its
Committee on Child Development Research and Public Policy.
The panel was established in response to a widely perceived need to review and reshape the evaluation of demonstration programs offering educational, diagnostic, and
other services to young children and their families. The
panel's mandate was to examine the objectives of contemporary demonstration programs; to appraise the measures
currently available for asssessing achievement of those
objectives, particularly in light of their relevance for
public policy; and to recommend new approaches to evaluation and outcome measurement.

The members of the panel construed their mandate
broadly. Recognizing the increasing diversity of programs
aimed at young children and their families, we examined
programs providing a wide range of services--not just
preschool education (probably the predominant focus of
demonstrations in the past) but also day care, health
care, bilingual and bicultural education, services to the
handicapped, and various family support services. Because
we wanted to contribute to the future of evaluation more
than to comment on its past, we deliberately included
services and issues that have not been heavily studied
but are likely to be salient in the 1980s and beyond.
Rather than confine our attention to relatively small-
scale, carefully controlled demonstrations, such as the
preschool programs that were precursors of Head Start in
the 1960s, we also examined larger, less controlled,
policy-oriented demonstrations of novel service delivery
systems. We paid explicit attention to the problem of

ix

implementing successful demonstrations on a large (state or national) scale. While we tended to focus on publicly funded programs for children from low-income families, we also examined privately funded programs and programs that serve children without regard to income.

The panel examined questions that went considerably beyond "outcome measurement" as that term is usually conceived. We paid relatively little attention to the metric properties of particular instruments, concentrating instead on the broader context of outcome measurement--on the kinds of information that would be most useful in shaping policies and program practices. This inquiry led to consideration not only of outcomes but also of the services delivered by programs, of day-to-day transactions between program staff and clients, and of interactions between programs and their surrounding communities. Finally, we found it impossible to discuss outcome measures without also considering the kinds of research designs and evaluation processes in which measures might most usefully be embedded.

The panel itself was a diverse group, including persons trained in psychology, sociology, anthropology, economics, medicine, and statistics--some of them from the academic community, some from state and federal governments, and some from private research organizations. Although there were, of course, differences in emphasis and differences of opinion about specific points, it is significant that these diverse members agreed on the panel's basic message.

An important part of the panel's message involves programs themselves: the diversity of services they render, the clients they serve, and the policy issues they raise. As members of the panel pooled their knowledge about particular programs, we began to see that systematic examination of the characteristics of contemporary demon- stration programs, and of their attendant policy issues, would go a long way toward pinpointing the inadequacies of existing measures and designs as well as point toward needed improvements.

Our emphasis on program realities and policy concerns is not intended as advocacy for specific programs or policies; it is intended solely to highlight issues of design and measurement. In this connection, we attempted to balance attention to the benefits of children's programs with attention to measurement of their costs, administrative burdens, and unintended consequences. We by no means want to imply that evaluators must confine themselves to questions posed by program managers and policy makers. On the contrary, one of the most important functions of evaluation is to raise new questions, and one of its major responsibilities is to reflect the concerns and interests of children, parents, and others affected by programs. Nonetheless, sensitivity to issues of public policy and program management, in addition to professional expertise in child development, family functioning, or research methodology, will probably increase the evaluator's ability to identify significant questions that have previously escaped notice.

Existing evaluations have tended to focus on how programs influence the development of individual children. Although the underlying concern of many programs has been long-term effects, in practice most evaluations have had to measure immediate impact--the "short, sharp shock," as one member of the panel put it--often by means of standardized measures of cognitive ability and achievement. A panel composed primarily of researchers might be expected to urge a search for new measures in the "socioemotional" domain and to recommend design and funding of long-term, longitudinal studies of program effects. Although we recognize the value of such measures and studies for addressing certain scientific and practical questions, we see them as part of a larger mosaic of potential measures and designs, addressing a much wider range of questions.

No single evaluation can examine every aspect of a program's functioning. On the contrary, resource constraints and the burden that evaluation imposes on programs and clients necessitate careful selection of questions to be answered and methods to be used. However, the choice of measures and of research designs should be based on rational assessment of the full range of possibilities, in light of the goals and circumstances of the particular program and evaluation in question--not on grounds of convention or expediency. To this end the panel urges that evaluators give careful consideration to several types of information that lie outside the domain of developmental effects but that can potentially illuminate the working of programs as well as program outcomes in the broadest sense. Specifically we call attention to the importance of:

• characterizing the immediate quality of life of children in demonstration programs, particularly day care and preschool education, in which they spend a large part of the day;

• describing how programs interact with and change
the broader social environment in which a child grows or
a family functions--the web of formal and informal
institutions (extended families, schools, child welfare
agencies, and the like) that can potentially sustain,
enhance, or thwart growth and change; and
        • documenting the services received by children and
families and describing the transactions between clients
and program staff. This information is essential for
determining whether programs are operating in accordance
with their own principles and guidelines and those of
their funding agencies and sponsors. It is also
essential for understanding variations in effectiveness
within and across programs.

More generally, we believe that the most useful evaluations are those that show how and why a program worked or
failed to work. To understand which aspects of a demonstration program can be applied in wider contexts, tracing
the interactions among programs, clients, and community
institutions is more valuable than merely providing a
scorecard of effects. For this purpose, a mix of research
strategies may be needed--qualitative as well as quantitative, naturalistic as well as experimental.
    This report bears the burden of amplifying and justify-
ing the position outlined above. In preparing the report
the panel drew on a group of papers on outcome measurement
for specific types of programs, prepared by panel members
and consultants. Although the papers stimulated our
thought and discussion, the report does not simply summarize the papers nor are its conclusions a compilation of
conclusions presented in the papers. Rather the report
identifies common themes and overarching ideas that do
not necessarily appear in any single background paper.
    The papers vary widely in scope and emphasis. The
paper on health programs, by Melvin Levine and Judith
Palfrey, covers a range of issues in health measurement
that have arisen from the authors' experiences with a
particular program, the Brookline Early Education Project.
The paper by Jeffrey Travers, Rochelle Beck, and Joan
Bissell offers a taxonomy of measurement approaches to day
care. The paper on family service programs, by Kathryn
Hewett and Dennis Deloria, concentrates on special issues
raised by the unique and comprehensive characters of
several federal and private programs. The paper on compensatory preschool education, by David Weikart, discusses
the short- and long-term effects of some of the earliest

and most important demonstration projects, concentrating particularly on the High/Scope Foundation's Ypsilanti Perry Preschool project. The paper on programs for the handicapped, by Mary Kennedy and Garry McDaniels, focuses on the concerns of federal policy makers. Finally, the paper on communication and dissemination of research results, by Dennis Deloria and Geraldine Brookins, discusses a cross-cutting issue outside the domain of outcome measurement per se, but one that is highly relevant for the use of evaluation results.

Several people were particularly helpful in the preparation of this report, and I would like to acknowledge their contributions. Barbara Finberg of the Carnegie Corporation made constructive suggestions throughout our work. Early drafts of the report were reviewed in detail by Robert Boruch and Alison Clarke-Stewart as well as by members of the Committee on Child Development Research and Public Policy. John A. Butler developed the original plan for this panel, helped organize the study, and was study director at the beginning of the project. Janie Stokes, administrative secretary for the project, typed drafts of a number of the papers and kept things generally in order.

I am fortunate to be associated with a panel that was both hard working and enthusiastic. Many members worked beyond the call of duty, and the individual papers that panel members volunteered to coauthor were helpful in guiding our discussion and presenting issues. Finally, my special thanks go to Jeffrey Travers, who wrote the report. Originally a panel member, then study director for the project, he produced draft after draft with both grace and humor. This report has benefited enormously from his substantive insights about children's programs and his ability to organize a complex mass of information.

Richard J. Light, Chair
Panel on Outcome Measurement in
   Early Childhood Demonstration
Programs

Part 1:
Report of the Panel

Evaluating Early Childhood
Demonstration Programs

INTRODUCTION

During the last two decades, public and private
programs for young children and their families have
undergone profound changes. Programs and philosophies
have proliferated. Program objectives have broadened.
Federal support has increased: Projected expenditures
for child care and preschool education alone neared
$3 billion several years ago. Target populations have
expanded and diversified, as have the constituencies
affected by programs; such constituencies reach beyond
the target populations themselves.

A sizable evaluation enterprise has grown along with
the expansion in programs. Formal outcome measurement
has gained increasing acceptance as a tool for policy
analysis, as a test of accountability, and to some extent
as a guide for improving program practices. Programs have
been subjected to scrutiny from all sides, as parents,
practitioners, and politicians have become increasingly
sophisticated about methods and issues that once were the
exclusive preserve of the researcher. At the same time,
evaluation has come under attack--some of it politically
motivated, some of it justified. Professionals question
the technical quality of evaluations, while parents,
practitioners, and policy makers complain that studies
fail to address their concerns or to reflect program
realities. Improvements in evaluation design and outcome
measurement have failed to keep pace with the evolution
of programs, widening the gap between what is measured
and what programs actually do.

This report attempts to take modest steps toward
rectifying the situation. Rather than recommend specific
instruments, its aims are (1) to characterize recent

3

developments in programs and policies for children and
families that challenge traditional approaches to evaluations and (2) to trace the implications for outcome
measurement and for the broader conduct of evaluation
studies. We have attempted to identify various types of
information that evaluators of early childhood programs
might collect, depending on their purposes. Our intent
is not so much to prescribe how evaluation should be done
as to provide a basis for intelligent choice of data to
be collected.

Two related premises underlie much of our argument.
First, policies and programs, at least those in the public
domain, are shaped by many forces. Constituencies with
conflicting interests influence policies or programs and
in turn are affected by them. Policies and programs
evolve continuously, in response to objective conditions
and to the concerns of constituents. Demonstration
programs, the subject of this report, are particularly
likely to change as experience accumulates. Consequently,
evaluation must address multiple concerns and must shift
focus as programs mature or change character and as new
policy issues emerge. Any single study is limited in its
capacity to react to changes, but a single study is only
a part of the larger evaluation process.

Second, the role of the evaluator is to contribute to
public debate, to help make programs and policies more
effective by informing the forensic process through which
they are shaped. Though the evaluator might never
actually engage in public discussion or make policy
recommendations, he or she is nevertheless a participant
in the policy formation process, a participant whose
special role is to provide systematic information and to
articulate value choices, rather than to plead the case
for particular actions or values.

Note that we distinguish between informing the policy
formation process and being co-opted by it--between
research and advocacy. Research is characterized by
systematic inquiry, concern with the reduction and
control of bias, and commitment to addressing all the
evidence. Nothing that we say is intended to relax the
need for such rigor.

There are many views of the evaluator's role. Relevant
discussions appear in numerous standard sources on evaluation methodology, such as Suchman (1967), Weiss (1972),
Rossi et al. (1979), and Goodwin and Driscoll (1980).
Some of these views are consonant, and some are partially
contrasting with ours. For example, one widely held view

is that the role of the evaluator is, ideally, to provide definitive information to decision makers about the degree to which programs or policies are achieving their stated goals.[1] Though we agree that evaluation should inform decision makers (among others) and should strive for clear evidence on whether goals are being met, we argue that this view is insufficiently attuned to the pluralistic, dynamic process through which most programs and policies are formed and changed.

Sometimes the most valuable lesson to be learned from a demonstration is whether a particular intervention has achieved a specified end. Often, however, other lessons are equally or more important. An intervention can succeed for reasons that have little import for future programs or policies--for example, because of the efforts of uniquely talented staff. Conversely, a demonstration that fails, overall, may contain successful elements deserving replication in other contexts, and it may succeed in identifying practices that should be amended or avoided. Or a demonstration may shift its goals and "treatments" in response to local needs and resources, thereby failing to achieve its original ends but succeeding in other important respects.

By the same token, a randomized field experiment, with rigorous control of treatment and subject assignment, is sometimes the most appropriate way to answer questions salient for policy formation or program management. In such situations, government should be encouraged to provide the support necessary to implement experimental designs. There are situations, however, in which experimental rigor is impractical or premature, or in which information of a different character is likely to be more useful to policy makers and program managers. Preoccupation with prespecified goals and treatments can cause evaluators to overlook important changes in the aims and operations of programs as well as important outcomes that were not part of the original plan. If demonstrations have been allowed to adapt to local conditions, thoughtful documentation of the process of

---

[1]Strictly speaking, this view applies only to "summative" evaluations, as distinguished from "formative" evaluations, which are intended to provide continuous feedback to program participants for the purpose of improving program operations.

change can be far more useful in designing future programs
than a report on whether original goals were met.

Even if change in goals and treatments is not at
issue, understanding the mechanisms by which programs
work or fail to work is likely to be more helpful than
simply knowing whether they have achieved their stated
goals. These mechanisms are often complex, and the
evaluator's understanding of them often develops
gradually. To elucidate mechanisms of change, it may be
necessary to modify an initial experimental design, to
perform post hoc analyses without benefit of experimental
control, or to supplement quantitative data collection
with qualitative accounts of program operations.

In short, we believe that evaluation is best conceived
as a process of systematic learning from experience--the
experience of the demonstration program itself and the
experience of the evaluator as he or she gains increasing
familiarity with the program. It is the systematic
quality of evaluation that distinguishes it from advocacy
or journalism. It is the need to bring experience to
bear on practice that distinguishes evaluation from other
forms of social scientific inquiry.

A Word on Definitions

This is a report about the evaluation of demonstration
programs for young children and their families. Each
word or phrase in the foregoing sentence is subject to
multiple interpretations. The substance of this report
is intimately bound up with our choice of definitions.

By evaluation we mean systematic inquiry into the
operations of a program--the services it delivers, the
process by which those services are provided, the costs
of services, the characteristics of the persons served,
relations with relevant community institutions (e.g.,
schools or clinics), and, especially, the outcomes for
program participants.

By outcomes we mean any changes in program participants
or in the contexts in which they function. The latter is
a deliberately broad definition, which includes yet
extends far beyond the changes in individual children
that are usually thought of as program outcomes. We
believe that the definition is appropriate, given the
nature of contemporary programs, and we endeavor to
support this claim in some detail.

By demonstration programs we mean any programs
installed at least in part for the purpose of generating
practical knowledge--such as the effectiveness of
particular interventions; the costs, feasibility, or
accessibility of services under alternative approaches to
delivery; or the interaction of a program with other
community institutions. This definition goes beyond
traditional concerns with program effectiveness. We
believe that it is an appropriate definition in light of
the policy considerations that surround programs for
young children today.

Finally, by young children we mean children from birth
to roughly age eight, although some of our discussion
applies to older children as well. We take very
seriously the inclusion of families as recipients of
services; we emphasize the fact that many contemporary
programs attempt to help the child through the family and
that outcome measures should reflect this emphasis.

Plan of the Report

We begin by tracing the historical evolution of
demonstration programs from 1960 to the mid-1970s, and of
the evaluations undertaken in that period. Although
children's programs and formal evaluation have histories
beginning long before 1960, the programs and evaluations
of the early 1960s both prefigure and constrain our
thinking about outcome measurement today. Following this
historical overview is a section that examines in some
detail the policy issues and programs that have evolved
in recent years and that appear to be salient for the
1980s. The next section--the heart of the report--
identifies some important implications of these programs
and policy developments for outcome measurement and
evaluation design. The final section points to
implications for dissemination and utilization of
results, for the organization and conduct of applied
research, and, finally, for the articulation between
applied research and basic social science.

PROGRAMS FOR CHILDREN AND FAMILIES, 1960-1975

Programs for children and families have come a long
way since 1960, but it is fair to say that the earliest
demonstration programs of the 1960s, precursors of Head

Start, still have a hold on the imagination of the public as well as many researchers. It is perhaps an oversimplification—but nevertheless one with a large grain of truth—to say that outcome measurement, which was reasonably well adapted to the early demonstrations, has stood still while programs have changed radically.

To illustrate, let us consider the experience of a "typical" child in a "typical" demonstration program at various points from 1960 to the present, and let us briefly survey the kinds of measures that have been used at each point to assess the effects of programs. In the early 1960s it would have been easy to characterize a typical child and a typical program. Prototypical demonstrations of that period were primarily preschool education programs, designed to enhance the cognitive skills of "culturally disadvantaged" children from low-income families, in order to prepare them to function more effectively as students and, ultimately, as workers and citizens. It was only natural to measure as outcomes children's school performance, academic ability, and achievement. Some practitioners had misgivings about the fit between available measures and the skills and attitudes they were attempting to teach, and many lamented the lack of good measures of social and emotional growth. There was fairly widespread consensus, however, that preacademic instruction was the heart of early childhood demonstrations. (Horowitz and Paden, 1973, provide one of several useful reviews of these early projects.)

By 1965 the typical child would have been one of more than half a million children to participate in the first Head Start program. Despite its scale, Head Start was and still is termed a "demonstration" in its authorizing legislation. Moreover, Head Start has constantly experimented with curricula and approaches to service delivery, and it has spawned a vast number of evaluations. For these reasons it dominates our discussion of demonstrations from 1965 until very recently. (A collection of papers edited by Zigler and Valentine, 1979, reviews the history of Head Start. See in particular Datta's paper in that volume (Datta, 1979) for a discussion of Head Start research.)

The program originally consisted of eight weeks of preschool during the summer and was soon extended to a full year. Proponents had stressed "comprehensive services," and many teachers viewed socialization rather than academic instruction as their primary goal. Many of the federal managers and local practitioners did not

conceive Head Start exclusively as a cognitive enrichment
program. Nevertheless, Head Start was widely perceived--
by the public, by Congress, and by many participants--as
a way to correct deficiencies in cognitive functioning
before a child entered the school system. Early Head
Start programs involved many enthusiastic parents, but
the educational mission and direction of the program was
set by professional staff and local sponsoring organizations. Programs and developmental theories were numerous
and diverse; no uniform curriculum was set. Yet there
seems to have been consensus and a high level of
confidence with respect to one key point--that early
intervention would be effective, regardless of the
particular approach.

In some quarters this confidence was severely shaken
by the first national evaluation of Head Start's impact
on children, the Westinghouse-Ohio study (Westinghouse
Learning Corp. and Ohio University, 1969). The study
reported that Head Start graduates showed only modest
immediate gains on standardized tests of cognitive ability
and that these gains disappeared after a few years in
school. However, for others the results testified only
to the narrowness of the study's outcome measures and to
other inadequacies of design. Some partisans of Head
Start and critics of the Westinghouse-Ohio study, claiming
that the program was much more than an attempt at compensatory education or cognitive enrichment, argued that the
study had measured Head Start against a standard more
appropriate to its precursors. These advocates argued
that Head Start enhanced social skills (to which the
Westinghouse-Ohio study paid limited attention) and
provided food, medical and dental checkups, and corrective
services to children who were badly in need of them.
Thus its justification lay in part in the provision of
immediate benefits to low-income populations, not solely
in expected future gains. Furthermore, argued advocates
of Head Start, many local programs had mobilized parents
and become a focus for community organization and
political action. To be sure, some of the criticism of
the Westinghouse-Ohio study was rhetorical and politically
motivated. However, many of the critics' points were
supported empirically, for example, by an evaluation by
Kirschner Associates (1970), which documented the impact
of the program on services provided by the community.

By 1970, Head Start had begun to experiment with
systematic variations in curriculum. Now the typical
preschool child might be served according to any of a

dozen models, ranging from highly structured academic
drill to global, diffuse support for social and emotional
growth. Models were viewed as fixed treatments, to be
applied more or less uniformly across sites. Parallel
models were also put in place in elementary schools that
received Head Start graduates, as part of the National
Follow Through experiment. Under most models, treatment
was still directed primarily to individual children, not
families or communities. Some models made an effort to
integrate parents; others did not. Noneducational program
components, such as health, nutrition, and social services, had expanded but were still widely viewed as
subordinate to the various developmental approaches.
Comparative evaluations continued to stress a relatively
narrow range of educational outcomes. As a result, programs with a heavy cognitive emphasis tended to fare
better than others, although no single approach proved
superior on all measures, and there were large differences
in the effectiveness of a given model at different sites.
Dissatisfaction with the narrowness of outcome measures
continued to grow, as programs broadened their goals and
came to be seen as having distinctive approaches and
outcomes, not necessarily reflected by the measures being
used.

By 1975, Head Start had changed and diversified
significantly. Program standards were put in place,
mandating comprehensive services and parent involvement
nationwide. In 1975 more than 300 Head Start programs
were gearing up to provide home-based services as supplements to, or even substitutes for, center-based services.
The home-based option was permitted in the national
guidelines following an evaluation of Home Start, a
16-site demonstration project (Love et al., 1975). The
evaluation, which involved random assignment of children
to home treatment and control conditions, found that the
home treatment group scored significantly above the
control group on a variety of measures, including a
standardized cognitive test, and that the home treatment
group did as well as a nonrandom comparison group of
children in Head Start centers. In addition, several
offshoot demonstrations, some of them dating from the
1960s, began to get increased attention, notably the
Child and Family Resource Program, the Parent-Child
Centers, and Parent-Child Development Centers. These
projects extend services to children much younger than
age three or four, the normal age for Head Start entrants.
These programs work through the mother or the family

rather than serving the child alone. They combine home
visits with center sessions in various mixes. Although
these programs even today serve only about 8 percent of
the total number of children served in Head Start, they
represent significant departures from traditional
approaches. We have a good deal more to say about these
programs below.

Thus by 1975 the experience of the typical Head Start
child had become difficult to characterize. The child
might be served at home or in a center; he or she might
receive a concentrated dose of preacademic instruction or
almost no instruction at all. In the face of this diversity, it is apparent that standardized tests, measuring
aspects of academic skill and ability, capture only a
part of what Head Start was trying to accomplish.
Evaluations of Head Start's components, such as health
services, and offshoot demonstrations, such as the Child
and Family Resource Program, have been conducted or are
currently in progress. Head Start's research division in
1977 initiated a multimillion-dollar procurement to
develop a new comprehensive assessment battery that
stresses health and social as well as cognitive measures.

By the late 1970s other programs, mostly federal in
origin, were beginning to take their places beside Head
Start as major providers of services to children. In
addition, federal evaluation research began to concentrate
on other children's programs, such as day care, which had
existed for many years but had begun to assume new
importance for policy in the 1970s. In the next section
we attempt to characterize some of the recent program
initiatives as well as the policy climate that surrounds
programs for young children and their families in the
early 1980s.

THE PROGRAM AND POLICY CONTEXT OF THE 1980s

Public policy both creates social change and responds
to it. The evolution of policies toward children and
families must be understood in the context of general
societal change. Demographic shifts in the number of
young children, the composition of families, and the
labor force participation of mothers in recent years have
increased and broadened the demand for services. They
have also heightened consciousness about policy issues
surrounding child health care, early education, and
social services. Policy makers and evaluators in the

1980s are coping with the consequences of these broad
changes. Contemporary policy issues and program
characteristics constitute the environment in which
evaluators ply their trade, and they pose challenges with
which new evaluations and outcome measures must deal.

To understand the policy context surrounding demonstration programs for children in the 1980s, it is useful to
begin by outlining some general considerations that affect
the formation of policy. These generic considerations
apply to virtually all programs and public issues but
shift in emphasis and importance as they are applied to
particular programs and issues, at particular times, under
particular conditions. The most fundamental consideration
is whether the program or policy in question (whether
newly proposed or a candidate for modification or termination) accords with the general philosophy of some group
of policy makers and their constituents. Closely related
is the question of tangible public support for a program
or policy: Can the groups favoring a particular action
translate their needs into effective political pressure?

Assuming that basic support exists, issues of access,
equity, effectiveness, and efficiency arise. Will a
program reach the target population(s) that it is intended
to affect (access)? Will it provide benefits fairly,
without favoring or denying any eligible target group--for
example, by virtue of geographic location, ethnicity, or
any other characteristics irrelevant to eligibility? And
will its costs, financial and nonfinancial, be apportioned
fairly (equity)? Will it achieve its intended objectives
(effectiveness)? Will it do so without excessively
cumbersome administrative machinery, and will cost-
effectiveness and administrative requirements compare
favorably with alternative programs or policies
(efficiency)?

Two related concerns have to do with the unintended
consequences of programs and policies and their interplay
with existing policies and institutions. Will the policy
or program have unanticipated positive or negative
effects? Will it facilitate or impede the operations of
existing policies, programs, or agencies? How will it
affect the operations of private, formal, and informal
institutions?

Programs for children and families are not exempt from
any of these concerns. Some have loomed larger than
others at times in the past two decades, and the current
configuration is rather different from the one that
prevailed when the first evaluations of compensatory

education were initiated. The policy climate of the early 1960s was one of concern over poverty and inequality and of faith in the effectiveness of government-initiated social reform. The principal policy initiative of that period directed toward children and families--namely, the founding of Head Start--exemplified this concern and this faith. Head Start was initially administered by the now defunct Office of Economic Opportunity (OEO), and many local Head Start centers were affiliated with OEO-funded Community Action Programs. Thus, while it was in the first instance a service to children, Head Start was also part of the government's somewhat paradoxical attempt to stimulate grass roots political action "from the top down." The national managers made a conscious, concerted effort to distinguish Head Start from other children's services, notably day care. The latter was seen as controversial--hence, a politically risky ally.

The early 1960s was a time of economic and governmental expansion. Consequently, questions of cost and efficiency did not come to the fore. The principal concerns of the period were to extend services--to broaden access--and to demonstrate the effectiveness of the program. As noted earlier, effectiveness in the public mind was largely equated with cognitive gains. Despite the political character of the program, studies documenting its effectiveness as a focus for community organization and political action received little attention or weight-- perhaps because the political activities of OEO-funded entities, such as the Community Action Programs and Legal Services, were sensitive issues even in the 1960s. Yet it was precisely the effectiveness of Head Start at mobilizing parents (together with the political skills of its national leaders) that saved the program when the Westinghouse-Ohio study produced bleak results and a new administration dismantled OEO.

During the 1970s the policy climate changed markedly. Economic slowdown and growing disillusionment with what were seen as excesses and failures of the policies of the 1960s brought about a concern for accountability and fiscal restraint, a concern that is still present and growing. Head Start responded by establishing national performance standards in an effort at quality control. Expansion was curtailed as the program fought to retain its budget in the face of inflation and congressional skepticism. (In fiscal 1977 only 15-18 percent of eligible children were actually served by Head Start.) Policy makers and program managers began to demand that evaluations focus on management information and cost accounting.

At the same time, other policies and programs for children and families were gaining national attention. Economic pressures, the increased labor force participation of women, and the rise of feminism brought day care into prominence. Federal investment in day care increased under Title XX of the Social Security Act and numerous other federal programs for the working poor, backed by a curious alliance of feminists, liberals, child advocates, and "workfare conservatives." Although anti-day-care, "pro-family" forces remained strong, public subsidy of day care was gradually, if sometimes grudgingly, accepted as a reality. Most of the policy controversy surrounding day care in the 1970s centered on the trade-off of cost and quality: Should day care be viewed primarily as a service designed to free (or force) mothers to work--and therefore be funded at minimum levels consistent with children's physical and psychological safety? Or should it be viewed as a developmental service, akin to Head Start, or as a vehicle for delivering other services, such as health care and parent counseling, with attendant increases in cost? The controversy took concrete form in the debate over the Federal Interagency Day Care Requirements-- purchasing standards that specify the type and quality of care on which federal dollars can legally be spent.

As we move into the 1980s, new, or more precisely latent, issues are likely to become prominent with respect to day care. The financing of day care is likely to become an ever more pressing problem, as the service becomes increasingly professionalized. Day care workers, among the nation's lowest paid, are likely to seek higher wages. Informal, low-cost care by friends or relatives may absorb less demand than it has in the past, as women who have heretofore provided such care either enter the work force in other capacities or begin to seek increased recognition and compensation for their services. At the same time, the importance of relatively informal care arrangements, such as family day care, have come to be recognized in policy circles. Informal arrangements are in fact the most prevalent forms of out-of-home care, especially for children of school age and for children under three. With this recognition will come new debates about the proper role of government: Should it regulate? Provide training? Invent new subsidy mechanisms? Major demonstrations examining alternative funding and regula-

tory policies for both center and family day care have
already been undertaken by the state of California.
Novel ways of funding child care, such as "tuition"
vouchers, have been urged and studied, and a child care
tax credit has already been legislated.

Day care is of course not the only type of children's
program that underwent major change in the 1970s.
Important new initiatives arose in the areas of child
health and nutrition. For example, the Department of
Agriculture established the Supplementary Food Program
for Women, Infants, and Children and the Child Care Food
Program; these provide low-cost nutritional supplements
to low-income families and to the child care programs
serving them. The Early and Periodic Screening,
Diagnosis, and Treatment program was established to
ensure that children from low-income families would be
examined for problems of health, vision, hearing, etc.

Another initiative, sweeping in its implications, was
the federal mandate under the Education for All
Handicapped Children Act of 1975 (P.L. 94-142) that
handicapped children be provided with a "free, appropriate
public education," interpreted to mean education in the
"least restrictive environment" feasible given their
handicaps. The consequences for public schools have been
enormous, and federal programs for younger children have
also responded by building in provisions for the handicapped. The Head Start Economic Opportunity and Community
Partnership Act of 1976 requires that 10 percent of Head
Start slots in each state be set aside for handicapped
children.

Although P.L. 94-142 is linked to federal funds to aid
the handicapped, the law has the character of an entitlement rather than being a service program per se. The law
establishes very broad rights and guidelines, not particular machinery for service delivery. Entitlements greatly
broaden the constituencies affected by federal policy,
for they extend far beyond the children of the poor. They
highlight questions of access and equity for those
charged with enforcement at the federal level. In the
case of P.L. 94-142, questions of effectiveness and
efficiency have largely been delegated to the local
level: Local experts and practitioners are confronted
with the task of devising programs that work at reasonable
costs under local conditions. Questions having to do with
overall effects of the policy on children, schools, and
families have not been addressed at a national level.
However, federal funds have been made available under

other legislative authorization for the establishment and
evaluation of small-scale model programs for serving
handicapped children.

Another major development with profound consequences
for the schools is the bilingual education movement. The
movement has been reinforced by the courts, most notably
by the case of Lau v. Nichols, in which a California
federal district court, later upheld by the U.S. Supreme
Court, declared that it is discriminatory for schools to
provide instruction only in English to students whose
primary language is not English. Although the case was
brought on behalf of Oriental children, its primary
effects are being felt in those states where Hispanic
children constitute a large and growing segment of the
student population. And, like P.L. 94-142, the bilingual
education movement has generally trickled down to the
preschool level, where bilingual programs are rapidly
being established in Head Start and other programs. The
bilingual movement poses basic questions about federal
and state policies toward minority subcultures--questions
of pluralism versus integration that have never been fully
addresssed. At the local level, these highly controversial issues are fueled with additional controversies over
what are seen as federal rights of encroachment and the
responsibilities of local governments.

Concurrent with these specific legislative and judicial
initiatives, more diffuse but no less important policy
issues have arisen in connection with certain federal
demonstration programs. Two characteristics of these
programs are particularly salient: an emphasis on the
family and the community institutions with which it
interacts, rather than on the child in isolation, and a
stress on localism--on the diversity, rather than the
uniformity, of programs and on their adaptation to local
values and conditions. Programs exemplifying these
emphases include Head Start's spinoff demonstrations,
such as the Parent-Child Development Centers and the
Child and Family Resource Program. These projects have
acquired new strategic importance, in part as a result of
a recent General Accounting Office report (General
Accounting Office, 1979) that holds them up as models for
future delivery of services to children from low-income
families. Some nonfederal programs also emphasize
multiservice support for families; an example is the
Brookline Early Education Project, a privately funded
program within a public school system. Other important

examples are day care programs funded under Title XX of
the Social Security Act, which provides grants to states
to purchase social services. These programs often
provide a wide range of services that go beyond direct
care of the child. And Title XX itself represents an
attempt to decentralize decision making by allowing
states considerable latitude in the use of federal funds.

These policy emphases have multiple roots. In part
they stem from a reaction against what has been seen as
an intrusive, excessively prescriptive federal posture
vis-a-vis local programs and their clients. In part they
represent an assertion of the family's central role and
responsibility in child rearing. In part they have a
theoretical base and reflect an ecological perspective on
child development--one that sees changes in the child's
immediate social milieu, the family, and family-community
relations as the best way to create and sustain change in
individual children. In part they arise from practical
experience with and applied research on earlier programs,
which repeatedly showed dramatic differences in practices
and effects from site to site, even when they were
allegedly committed to implementing some prescribed
treatment or model.

Family support programs raise issues that have not
been prominent with respect to earlier demonstrations.
They focus attention on the relationships between
children's programs and other service agencies in local
communities. They also focus attention on relations
between programs and informal institutions, such as
extended families, which in some subcultures have
traditionally provided the kind of global support that
some demonstration programs aim to provide. They raise
basic questions as to whether ecological approaches in
general are more effective than interventions aimed at
the child alone. Finally, they highlight issues having
to do with the prerogatives and responsibilities of
different levels of government and of government vis-a-vis
private program sponsors, service providers, and clients.
A tension is created by pressures for accountability at
the federal level and conflicting pressures for delegation
of responsibility to the state or local level. Evaluation
often plays a role in struggles among the various levels
of government, usually as a device by which federal
program managers attempt to exert some control over local
practices.

In short, the policy context surrounding early childhood demonstration programs in 1980 has become very complex. Old issues have remained, and new or resurgent issues have been overlaid on them. The need to measure program effects on children has not diminished—witness the current effort by Head Start to develop a new, comprehensive battery of outcome measures. Concerns about cost, efficiency, and equity have become acute, as the federal government has expanded the scope of its responsibilities. Broad entitlements and new initiatives have increased the competition for finite resources in the face of widespread resistance to further taxation and bureaucratic expansion. There is increased pressure for centralized accountability and cost and quality control. At the same time there has been a broadening of the constituencies affected by early childhood programs as well as increased emphasis on pluralism of goals and values; decentralized, local decision making; and the individualization of services. Fortunately, no single evaluation will ever have to address all of these policy concerns simultaneously. Nevertheless, their complexity and antithetical value premises pose staggering challenges for the evaluator who hopes to influence policy. Although evaluators can address only a small subset of these concerns, they must constantly be aware of the larger picture or run the risk that the information they provide will be irrelevant or misleading in light of the full configuration of issues bearing on the future of a particular program.

These last observations lead to a final point about the policy climate of the 1980s: the role of evaluation itself in policy determination. An evaluation industry was born with the Great Society programs of the 1960s, which often included evaluations as integral parts. That enterprise has continued to grow and its audience has expanded, as clients, advocacy groups, and practitioners as well as policy makers and social scientists have learned to use evaluation results for their own diverse purposes. Congress has explicitly written evaluation requirements into the authorizing legislation for major programs, such as Title I of the Elementary and Secondary Education Act and the Education for All Handicapped Children Act.

As evaluation has grown in prevalence and importance, some of its limitations have also become apparent. By their very nature, evaluative studies must be restricted in scope and therefore can address broad policy issues only in a partial and fragmentary fashion. The injection of rational, systematic, analytic perspective into policy formation does not dispense with value conflicts; the choice of questions in evaluations is partly a matter of values, and findings are always subject to interpretation from multiple perspectives. Evaluation itself has costs, not only financial but also in terms of respondent burden and potential invasion of privacy. There are concrete manifestations of resistance to evaluation, in the form of increased restrictions on data collection.

Despite these limitations we believe that evaluation can contribute to policy. Particular findings may mesh with the immediate information needs of policy makers and thus affect decisions directly. Boruch and Cordray (1980) provide some striking case studies illustrating this sort of direct contribution. Perhaps more typically, findings from many studies over time can create a general climate of belief, for example, belief that early intervention in some sense "works," which in turn subtly and gradually shapes the questions that policy makers ask, shifting their attention, for example, from questions of effectiveness to questions of access, equity, and efficiency. Evaluation can also reveal unintended consequences of programs and point to new policy questions and new directions for program development. Sophistication about the multiple concerns of policy makers and their own limited roles in the process of policy determination may breed in evaluators a salutary humility, but it should not breed despair. And awareness should make their contribution even greater.

IMPLICATIONS FOR OUTCOME MEASUREMENT AND EVALUATION DESIGN

The programs and policy issues that have evolved over the past two decades, particularly in the late 1970s, pose serious challenges for evaluators. However, experience in performing evaluative studies has been accumulating since the early 1960s, and that experience offers contemporary evaluators some lessons about how to deal with at least some of these challenges. In this section we discuss specific characteristics of contemporary programs for young children that confront evaluators with problems of design and measurement and lessons drawn from past experience that may help improve future evaluations.

Challenges to the Evaluator

Many of our concepts of outcome measurement and
evaluation design were, as already suggested, shaped by
the compensatory education and cognitive enrichment
programs of the early 1960s. These programs were
initiated under private auspices, often with government
funding, at one or a few sites. While these programs
were to become models for public policy and in many cases
were consciously intended as such, they were not
immediately concerned with issues of administration and
implementation on a large scale or with links to other
public service delivery systems, such as nutrition or
health care. Nor were they much concerned with questions
of cost or cost-effectiveness. The question on everyone's
mind was, will preschool education work? That is, will
it improve the school functioning and test scores of
low-income children?

The early programs were new and relatively small,
their goals were relatively clear and circumscribed, and
comparable services were not widely available. The
individual child was typically the recipient of treatment,
and the programs were implicitly conceived as operating
in relative isolation from other social institutions and
forces. Consequently, it was possible to devise simple
evaluations, in which test scores and school performance
of children in the program were compared with those of
similar children in the same communities who received no
services. The program itself was viewed as a unitary
"treatment," and children in the control or comparison
group were assumed to receive no treatment. Such
evaluation designs were straightforward extensions of
laboratory paradigms, although the children in control
groups were often selected by post hoc matching rather
than random assignment, thus making many evaluations
designs quasi-experiments rather than true experiments.
Of course, not all early programs were rigorously
evaluated, and not all evaluations were as limited as we
have suggested; for example, diffusion of effects to
siblings and neighbors was a topic of interest in some of
the early evaluation studies.

As suggested earlier, experimental designs are ideal
for answering certain kinds of evaluation questions,
because they provide the most direct means of establishing
linkages of cause and effect. Children's academic skills
and performance are often important program outcomes, and
standardized tests, properly interpreted, measure aspects

of these skills. However, experience with the demonstrations that have evolved over the past two decades has made three points clear: First, a wider range of outcome measurement is necessary to do justice to program goals. Second, measurement of outcomes alone does not show _why_ a program achieved or failed to achieve its intended goal-- often the most significant lesson to be learned from a demonstration. Third, the conditions necessary for successful experimentation are often not met when demonstrations are conducted on a relatively large scale. Treatments tend to be multifaceted and variable. Often the pairing of client and treatment is beyond the experimenter's control. Extremely complex designs may be needed to tease out complex chains of causation.

We amplify these points in the pages that follow. It should be clear, however, that we are not opposed to experimental approaches, controlled assignment, or formal designs. We discuss program characteristics that pose barriers to formal experimentation in order to make a case for supplementing, not supplanting, experimental approaches with other scientifically defensible forms of investigation. Similarly, we recognize the value of outcome measures focused on individual development, including academic skills and achievement. However, we emphasize program characteristics that point to the need for other kinds of data--measures of outcomes that go beyond the individual child and measures of context and process that illuminate why and how a program works or fails to work. We discuss below eight program characteristics that are particularly salient.

Diversity of Target Groups

In contrast to most earlier demonstrations, the programs of the 1980s are aimed at a broader range of client populations. Programs aimed at physically normal, English-speaking children from low-income families still predominate. The sweeping entitlements mandated by legislatures and courts, however, have created many programs to meet the special needs of handicapped children and children of limited English-speaking ability, not all of them from low-income families. Of course, these children themselves form extremely heterogeneous populations with diverse needs. Accompanying increased public attention to day care has been a concern about the effects of prolonged out-of-home care on children from all social backgrounds, including the middle class and well-to-do, and of all ages, from infancy through school age. Increased diversity in the children served by public and private demonstration programs calls for increased diversity in measures to address the needs and characteristics of the populations in question.

Diversity of Services

Closely related to the breadth of client populations is breadth in the range of services offered. Again, services to meet the special needs of handicapped children and children of limited English-speaking ability provide striking examples. In addition, preschool education, once the predominant service for children of low-income families, has been joined by health care and nutrition, referrals to a wide variety of social services, and training and counseling of parents in child care, in dealing with schools and other public institutions, in family relations, and in more peripheral areas such as employment and housing. This breadth of services obviously requires a commensurate breadth of measures-- not only better measures of children's physical, intellectual, social, and emotional growth but also measures of the quality of the child's life in the program itself (as programs increasingly become a large part of the child's daily environment); the quality of parent-child relations; the strengths and cohesion of families; and the family's adaptation to its social, economic, and institutional environment.

Emphasis on the Social Environment

In many programs there has been a widening of focus, from the child in isolation to the child in the family and the family in the community. Strengthening families and improving family-community relations are seen as ways to create social environments for children that foster growth--as well as ends in themselves. This emphasis on the child's social milieu creates a need to reexamine existing measures of individual development and family functioning, with an eye toward their appropriateness in assessing the effects of programs and policies aimed at reaching the child through the family. It may of course also create a need to modify existing measures or to

develop new ones. Similarly, it draws attention to
measures of linkage between families and institutions--
such as schools, courts, churches, voluntary organizations, social service and health care agencies--and
informal sources of support--friends, neighbors, and
relatives. There is an overarching need to test the
basic assumption of these programs: that the most
effective way to create and sustain benefits for the
child is to improve his or her family and community
environment. This assumption is well grounded in theory
and basic research, but whether it can be translated into
effective programs is an open question. Clearly, such a
test is not the task of any single study, but must arise
from a gradual accumulation of data on the effects of
many such programs.

Support Versus Intervention

Accompanying the focus on families and communities is
an emphasis on support rather than intervention. Intervention implies an initiative from outside the family, a
"treatment" whose goals and methods are prescribed by an
external agency, governmental or private. Support implies
shared goal setting and initiative on the part of the
family in selecting the services it or the child receives.
Though often merely rhetorical, this emphasis has potentially profound consequences for evaluation design and
measurement, since it implies that the goals of a program
and the treatment provided cannot be predefined, except
in a broad manner. In effect the client plays a role in
selecting both dependent and independent measures. An
additional, equally important implication of this emphasis
on support is that support itself should be measured.
There is a need to know whether family-oriented social
programs in fact strengthen the family or inadvertently
weaken it by creating dependence on government and cutting
ties to informal supports such as friends, neighbors, and
the extended family.

Even participation in a program may be hard to define
or interpret when contacts between family and program are
wholly or partially voluntary, as is the case with many
support programs. A family may choose not to contact a
program because it is doing well on its own, yet it may
also fail to make contact when it is most in need of help.
A family may remain out of contact for long periods, then
renew the relationship in time of stress. Thus participa-

tion is an ambiguous indicator of need and of program effectiveness. It may be difficult just to know at any time how many families are participating and difficult to determine who should be counted as participants when the program is evaluated.

It is important to note that certain key assumptions of support programs are embodied in far-reaching policies as well. P.L. 94-142, for example, establishes an advocacy process by which parents play a major role in the educational placement of their children. Like support programs, the law assumes that parents are rightful advocates for their children, that they can identify the child's needs and can and will act effectively in the child's best interest. In part, of course, this emphasis on parent involvement stems from basic value premises about the rights of parents. In part it also embodies empirical assumptions, which are subject to test through a gradual accumulation of information about the effects on children of programs and policies in which parental involvement plays a major role.

Individualization of Services

For many programs of the 1980s, services for a particular child or family are selected in light of that child's or family's needs; individualization of services has become a watchword. Individualization tends to characterize support-oriented programs, in which clients participate in decision making. It can also occur when the locus of control rests with the program. Individualization is required by law in educational programs for the handicapped. It occurs naturally as part of health programs—medical and dental services are provided in response to patients' complaints and diagnosed problems—although health programs may also provide uniform services, such as screenings and immunizations.

Nonuniform treatments challenge evaluation designs in fairly obvious ways. Although it is inappropriate to lump clients into a single treatment group to probe for common outcomes, it is equally unsatisfactory to treat individualized programs simply as a series of case studies. There is a need to find some middle ground that permits aggregation of effects across clients yet does justice to the diversity of treatments and outcomes. There is a complementary need to devise new techniques for "profiling" effects—for summarizing what the program has done for the individual child or family across a range of outcome domains, which may vary from client to client. Finally, there is a need to test the underlying assumption that individualization is a viable approach, through gradual accumulation of data on a variety of individualized programs.

Individualization of services also raises a related value issue: how to reconcile legitimate and desirable individual differences with the need to identify a manageable set of outcome measures that are consistent with program goals. Early childhood programs run the risk of attempting to homogenize certain characteristics of their participants. The need for relatively clear, consistent program goals can shade imperceptibly into an assumption that what is good for one is good for all. The process of evaluation, assuming that it is based on outcome criteria known to the program, may foster or exacerbate pressures for conformity and penalize children who are constructively different.

Decentralization and Site Variation

In part because of increased philosophical emphasis on local initiative and primarily because programs inevitably adapt to local needs and resources, even when federal program guidelines exist, decentralization of control and site-to-site variation are facts of life for the program evaluator of the 1980s. In multisite evaluations, site variations cannot be viewed as nuisance variables, to be quashed through insistence on rigid adherence to a treatment recipe or to be adjusted away after the fact by statistical manipulation. They are integral features of large-scale programs, to be examined in their own right. Evaluations must be designed to accommodate them, and outcome measures must be chosen to highlight rather than obscure them.

Indefinite Time Boundaries

Many demonstration programs of the 1980s are likely to be ongoing rather than time bounded. Classical interventions typically involve strict age guidelines; for example, preschool compensatory education programs normally serve children from age three to age five. In contrast, some contemporary support programs imply an indefinite

period of relationship between program and family;
programs continue to provide assistance as long as the
family wants it, lives in the area, and meets eligibility
criteria. This open-ended quality makes it difficult to
know when to measure a program's outcomes. Different
measures may be appropriate at different points in a
family's relationship with a program, yet these points
are defined not chronologically but by the juxta-
position of a need expressed and a service provided.

Integration of Services

Finally, the programs of the 1980s are likely to be
characterized by increased emphasis on the integration of
services. Head Start and Title XX day care attempt to
provide a wide range of services in a single facility.
Demonstrations such as the Child and Family Resource
Program try to capitalize on existing services in the
community, providing referrals and, if necessary, assistance and advocacy in securing services to which clients
are entitled. In part this emphasis on service integration arises from considerations of efficiency. In part
it arises from a felt need to present client families
with a coherent image of the social service system rather
than a fragmented one, with a sense of accessibility and
rationality, rather than one of obstruction and confusion.
Service integration raises questions that have heretofore
been largely ignored in evaluations of early childhood
programs, although they have been central in policy
analyses of social programs generally: Under what conditions is the referral approach more appropriate? The
answer depends in part on the services already available
in a given community. If services are available elsewhere
in a community, how should the convenience of service at
a single facility, such as a Head Start center, be
weighed against the efficiency of using existing services
outside the facility? If referrals are used, how is
demand for existing services affected? Is the system
structured so that the referral agency does not overload
the provider agencies? How do federal programs, such as
the Child and Family Resource Program, affect demand for
state and local services? These and other systemic
questions demand a different order of outcome measures
from those usually thought of in connection with programs
for children and families.

Lessons for Future Evaluations

There are no all-purpose solutions to the problems posed for evaluators by contemporary programs for children. Nor is there an all-encompassing list of widely accepted outcome measures from which evaluators can choose to suit their purposes. However, children's programs have been among the most heavily studied of all social programs, and considerable experience in the art of evaluation has accumulated. This section draws on that experience to make a series of broad suggestions about the kinds of information that evaluators might collect in order to make their results useful in shaping future policies and program practices. These suggestions should not be construed as implying that any single evaluation must make use of all of the kinds of measures mentioned. On the contrary, the panel is acutely aware of the constraints imposed by resources and by the need to avoid burdening programs and clients. Our suggestions are offered not as a recipe for the ideal evaluation but as a framework for choice. We have tried to provide some salient reminders about factors that should be considered in designing evaluations of children's programs, based on our review of program characteristics and contemporary policy issues.

Rethinking Developmental Measures

By choosing too narrow a range of outcome measures, the evaluator may forego opportunities to discover important effects of a program and thus misdirect policy or fail to address some of the many constituencies affected by a program. In this regard the limitations of traditional outcome measures, especially standardized tests of cognitive ability and achievement, have long been recognized. Because the goals of many early childhood programs lie in socialization, rather than cognitive enrichment, calls for better measures of self-concept, social skills, prosocial behavior, and the like have been frequent and forceful. (For some proposals regarding the measurement of social competence in young children, see Anderson and Messick, 1974; Zigler and Trickett, 1978.) While we are prepared to add our voices to the chorus, we argue that some important distinctions, qualifications, and additions must be kept in mind.

One can conceptualize socioemotional outcomes in terms
of enduring changes in the personality traits of children,
traits that are exhibited in other contexts and preserved
in later life. Or one can conceptualize such outcomes as
indices of the child's immediate well-being. For example,
one could speak of a day care program making a child more
cooperative with other children, with the presumption that
increased cooperativeness will manifest itself in the home
or in school, not just in the day care center. Or one
could simply speak of a day care center in which a cooperative atmosphere prevails, or in which a particular child
behaves cooperatively, with no presumption about cross-
situational generality or longitudinal persistence of
cooperativeness. We suggest that this distinction is a
crucial one, for the two interpretations raise different
measurement issues. This section discusses some of the
issues surrounding the "trait" interpretation. The
immediate well-being of the child is discussed later.

If the worth of a program is to be judged by its
ability to produce enduring changes in individual traits,
then a heavy burden of proof is placed on it. Despite
the progress that has been made in developmental psychology, basic researchers in the field are still struggling
with the question of how to conceptualize social behavior
and to sort it into portions attributable to the enduring
traits of the child and portions attributable to the
immediate situation. Similarly, a great deal remains to
be learned about which early behavior patterns are likely
to persist into later childhood and adulthood. Thus we
are currently ill equipped to choose or develop measures
that capture important, lasting traits of children and
that are also responsive to intervention. The evaluator's
problem in choosing social measures is not merely a
technological one that can be solved by straightforward
investment in instrument development. In fact, there are
already hundreds of instruments for measuring social
development in young children. These instruments are
reviewed, for example, by Goodwin and Driscoll, 1980;
Johnson, 1976; Walker, 1973; and Johnson and Bommarito,
1971. Unfortunately, the few that have been used in
evaluation have had disappointing histories. Developing
better social measures is a problem of basic research
that cannot fairly be handed to evaluators. Until such
measures are available, the limitations of our understanding should not be allowed to work to the detriment
of programs; programs should not be judged on the basis
of available measures, without regard for their actual

goals and practices. On the other hand, programs should
not be allowed to use ill-defined goals in the realm of
social development as a smokescreen to avoid accountability. Program planners should be specific and concrete
about their goals, so that the programs can be evaluated
as thoroughly as possible within the limits of existing
technology.

Paralleling the need for enriched psychosocial measurement is a less widely recognized need for measures of
physical development and health that are likely to be
sensitive to program interventions. Available measures
of physical status, ranging from height and weight to
presence or absence of a wide variety of diseases, are
unlikely to show such sensitivity for most children.
Height and weight are likely to be measurably affected
primarily in children who enter a program in a state of
malnourishment or physiological disorder. Ameliorating
these serious cases is of course a program effect of
major importance; however, detecting program effects on
children in the normal growth range may require more
sensitive measures. Incidence of serious diseases is
likely to be so low that any program effects could be
detected only with huge samples. More common diseases
tend to be less serious and/or self-terminating; the
incidence of such diseases may therefore be of secondary
importance as an outcome measure. Thus there is a need
for measures of "wellness" and normal development that
vary with nonextreme differences in environments.

Even for a measure that is well established in basic
research, there are numerous hurdles to be cleared in
adapting it for use in evaluation. Field conditions may
rule out some of the control that characterizes use of
the measure in the laboratory. Economic constraints in
large-scale studies may preclude recruitment of highly
educated field staff or extensive staff training.
Sometimes measures may lack the degree of face validity
they need if they are to be accepted by parents and
program staff. Even in small-scale studies, researchers
are often tempted to cut corners when a particular
instrument requires a heavy investment of time and
effort. For example, the "strange situation" developed
by Ainsworth (Ainsworth and Wittig, 1969) to measure an
infant's attachment to its mother has been shown to be a
reliable, valid measure that predicts social adjustment
up to age five (Sroufe, 1979). However, although many
researchers have been concerned with the impact of early
day care on mother-infant attachment, few have used

Ainsworth's demanding coding scheme, and few have confined
their research to the age range (12 to 18 months) for
which the instrument is known to work. Instead, even
basic researchers working with small samples have used ad
hoc modifications of Ainsworth's procedure, with the
result that much of the literature on day care and
attachment must be viewed as ambiguous (Belsky and
Steinberg, 1978).

Other important questions surround the adaptation of
individual developmental measures for use in evaluation.
One such question has to do with the expected timing of
effects--an issue on which current theory and research
give little guidance. Different outcomes may have very
different time courses: Some effects may be transient
and contemporaneous with the program itself; some effects
may be at a maximum on completion of treatment and may
diminish in size thereafter; and some effects may not
become apparent until long after participation in the
program. Preschool education, for example, has shown
both of the latter two patterns of effects. Scores on
standardized tests of ability or achievement tend to show
maximum differences between treatment and control on
completion of the program, diminishing afterward
(Bronfenbrenner, 1974). However, as discussed below,
there are recent reports of sleeper effects, in the form
of better school performance, years later, for some
programs. Assessment of program effects may thus depend
critically on the timing of outcome measurement. Without
a clear theory or at least a well-formulated hunch about
relationships between treatment and outcome, it may be
necessary to probe for effects at multiple time points.

Another such question has to do with the match between
the quantitative form of outcome measures and the goals
of the program in question. Some programs are designed
primarily to shift a distribution upward--for example,
the distribution of academic achievement scores of
low-income children. Some are designed to set a floor
under a distribution--for example, to guarantee that all
children in a program receive a certain minimum nutritional intake or achieve minimal literacy. Some are
designed to lower the prevalence of undesirable conditions
in the immediate present, such as dental caries, or in
the future, such as adolescent delinquency. Some are
designed to prevent relatively rare but catastrophic
events, such as child abuse. In some cases the variance
rather than the central tendency of a distribution may be
important. For example, mainstreaming of handicapped

children may not change their mean performance from that
of handicapped children in separate classes, but some
children might be doing much better and others much worse
when integrated with nonhandicapped children.

A program may look successful or unsuccessful, given
precisely the same distribution of individual outcomes,
depending on how the individual scores are aggregated and
analyzed. For example, a reading program may produce an
upward shift in the group mean by increasing the scores
of the children who read best already, while having no
effect on the skills of nonreaders. Whether the program
is deemed a success or a failure depends on whether the
evaluator emphasizes the mean shift or the lack of change
at the bottom of the distribution. The choice of quantitative summary measures is thus not a purely technical
matter; it is intimately linked to the substance of the
evaluation and the goals of the programs.

There are encouraging recent reports of lasting individual effects of some early preschool demonstrations of
the early 1960s (e.g., Lazar and Darlington, 1978). These
reports are significant not only for what they suggest
about the time course of the effects of intervention but
also for the nature of the long-term measures they use.
Reviewing a number of longitudinal studies, Lazar and
Darlington conclude that graduates of these programs were
much less likely than control or comparison children to
be placed in special education classes, to be held back
one or more grades in school, and to score poorly on tests
of academic achievement. The authors also conclude that
children's participation in preschool programs elevated
mothers' aspirations for their children's educational
achievement and increased the children's pride in their
own achievements. The panel has not reviewed these
studies in detail and offers no judgment about the
accuracy of their findings. What is significant for our
purposes is their attempt to use certain highly practical
indicators, which combine academic motivation and skill
(such as grade retention, placement or nonplacement in
classes for the retarded or learning disabled) as
indicators of long-term program effects on individuals.
These measures are clearly attractive for their direct
social and policy importance. They sidestep many of the
theoretical issues and value controversies that surround
most cognitive and social measures. However, they do need
careful scrutiny, since they are likely to be affected by
school policies and other external factors that might
cloud their interpretation as measures of long-term
individual success.

The foregoing remarks are not meant to imply that measures of long-term individual development have no place as outcome measures for early childhood programs. On the contrary, such measures have been and remain central. We take this to be a position that requires no elaboration or defense. We have chosen, however, to focus the remainder of our comments elsewhere because we believe that other measures have been neglected.

Measuring Quality of Life

In view of the fact that some programs, notably day care and preschool education, consume a significant portion of the child's waking life, a case can be made for considering the quality of life to be an outcome in itself. We are accustomed to thinking of programs for children primarily as investments in the child's future. Often, however, social programs, such as some programs for the elderly, are justified on the grounds that they provide a decent environment in the here and now for people whose welfare is the concern of the citizenry as a whole. Our intent is not to advocate that the citizenry or government accept such responsibility for children. Rather, our point is that once such responsibility is taken, immediate quality of life becomes an appropriate standard by which programs may be judged. The same consideration applies to the evaluation of services financed by nongovernment agencies or purchased privately by parents.

Clearly, measuring the quality of life is no easier than measuring socioemotional development, except insofar as the former phrase carries no implication of enduring effects. Equally clearly, quality of life and development are intertwined; patterns of behavior that indicate immediate engagement, stimulation, self-confidence, etc. on the part of the child are at least good bets to relate to longer-term socioemotional growth. In urging a shift of attention to the here and now, we are under no illusion that there exists a readily available, widely accepted technology for assessing children's social environments. There are examples, however, of influential studies that have focused on the child's immediate well-being. One is the National Day Care Study, a large-scale study of center day care, designed to inform federal regulatory policy (Ruopp et al., 1979). The study used natural observations of care givers and children to characterize the social experiences of children in groups of different sizes, with different staff/child ratios and different configurations of care givers' qualifications. The study found that cooperation and creative, intellectual activities by children were more frequent in small groups and that aimless wandering and noninvolvement were less frequent. This study also found that care givers with training specifically related to young children (e.g., in child development or early childhood education) provided more social and intellectual stimulation than those without such training. The study's results had a direct influence on the day care regulations subsequently proposed by the federal government (Federal Register, March 19, 1980), suggesting that the study's outcome measures had some weight for policy makers.

Assessing Effects on the Child's Social Milieu

Earlier we pointed out that ecological influences have gained increasing prominence in the rationales underlying contemporary programs. Some practitioners have come to believe that the best way to produce lasting effects on the child is to reshape the "ecosystems" in which the child grows--the immediate family and the larger web of relationships between families and external institutions, such as schools, the health care system, and social service agencies. Family support demonstrations, such as the Child and Family Resource Program, provide an obvious example of this ecological approach.

Our earlier discussion also pointed to some of the measurement requirements of family-oriented programs--the need to assess program effects on parent-child inter- action, family functioning, and family-community relationships as well as the larger need to test the assumption that the best way to help the child is to work through the family and the community. Fortunately, it is possible to go beyond mere exhortation in this regard. There is a massive literature on parent-child interaction that can be tapped to identify desirable and undesirable patterns of mutually contingent behavior of parents and children. For example, there have been studies of the effects of day care on parent-child interaction using as outcomes laboratory paradigms for measuring the quality of parental teaching (e.g., Ramey and Mills, 1975; Farran and Ramey, 1980). An evaluation of the Child and Family Resource Program, currently under way, assesses the

program's impact on parent-child interaction by video-
taping natural situations in the home (Connell and Carew,
1980). Similarly, there exist many measures of family
functioning that have been used in evaluation studies
supported by the Office of Child Development, now the
Administration for Children, Youth, and Families (see
Lindsey, 1976, for a review). There is a literature on
the effects of parent education programs (Brim, 1959;
Goodson and Hess, 1978), which can also be drawn on to
identify parental behaviors likely to be both significant
for the child and susceptible to influence by programs.
Finally, there is promising new theoretical work on the
ecology of human development, which offers both a
conceptual framework and specific suggestions about
variables and relationsips that might be examined in
real-world contexts, such as day care (Bronfenbrenner,
1979). Bronfenbrenner's work has been applied by others
in attempting to understand other practical problems,
such as child abuse (Belsky, 1980).

In general, we are in a fair position to identify
intrafamilial variables and measures that affect children;
however, while there are many measures describing the
interface between families and communities, published
work tying these measures to the well-being of the child
is just beginning to appear. This is an important area
for development, and existing intrafamilial measures have
certain problems. Most of them have been developed for
specific basic research purposes and adapted for use in
evaluation research. Little is known about the psychometric properties of various questionnaires, interviews,
and laboratory-based procedures when applied under field
conditions quite different from those under which they
were developed. In addition, when evaluations of early
childhood programs move beyond measures of the child into
areas of parent-child interaction and family functioning,
issues of privacy and confidentiality may inhibit
in-depth investigation.

Assessing Effects on the Service Delivery System

As suggested earlier, systemic effects are crucial for
policy. By systemic effects we mean effects on the
formal and informal service delivery system as a whole,
which can be intentional or unintentional. For example,
a voucher demonstration, allowing eligible parents to
purchase day care services as they choose, might draw new

providers into the business of family day care, as they
began to see a stable source of income for their
services--an intended systemic effect--or it might lead
to the purchase of substandard care in unregulated
facilities--an unintended systemic effect. Similarly,
federal regulatory policies might raise the quality of
subsidized day care but might also raise costs and drive
parents and providers into informal, unlicensed day care
arrangements. Or family support programs may benefit
children and parents but simultaneously increase their
dependence on government and displace private support
systems, such as the extended family. There are no
hard-and-fast rules for mapping the universe of potential
systemic outcomes. However, as a preface to evaluation
it is necessary to think broadly and systematically,
perhaps drawing on case studies in which unintended
effects were discovered, in order to identify as fully as
possible the range of such outcomes that might result,
particularly if a program is implemented on a large scale.

Fairly simple types of data can often shed a great
deal of light on systemic issues. Evaluators of early
childhood demonstrations often collect a limited amount
of basic information on the numbers of individuals served
by a program, the frequency or amount of participation,
the services received, and the like. Such information,
however, is usually accorded only subordinate status in
reporting results and often is not analyzed in detail.
We urge a fresh look at such descriptive data, and we
suggest that from some points of view such data can
legitimately be treated as measures of program effectiveness. Atheoretical indicators of services rendered and
of contacts between clients and programs can be invaluable
in program management, both on site and at the level of
the funding agency. Moreover, from a policy maker's
point of view, delivery of service is often an end in
itself, particularly when the value of the service is
known or assumed. Health services, such as immunizations,
are paradigmatic examples of services whose intrinsic
value has been independently demonstrated, i.e., by
medical research. Special education for the handicapped
is an example of a service whose general value is in
effect presumed by existing federal policies, and the
choice of specific approaches is left to state or local
discretion. The policy maker's concerns with issues of
access, equity, and efficiency of services are addressed
by descriptive data on types of services provided, numbers

of persons served, costs of service, and the like. For
example, these are the types of data included in reports
to Congress on the implementation of P.L. 94-142, prepared
by the Bureau of Education for the Handicapped (1979).
Another example of the utility of such data is provided
by demonstrations of service delivery mechanisms,
e.g., vouchers for day care, for which head counts of
persons served are obviously relevant as outcome measures.

Defining "Treatments"

A key problem in understanding the effects of a
demonstration is specifying the nature of the "treatment"
received by individual children or families within a
program. Some of the difficulties involved in describing
treatments were identified earlier. For example, we have
seen that treatments are often individualized to match
the needs of children and families. In the case of
support programs, clients have an active voice in
deciding what services they receive. As a result,
treatment is not standardized and is distributed across
clients in nonrandom fashion, complicating conventional
experimental design and statistical analysis. If the
program itself is defined as the treatment, and "treated"
subjects are compared with controls without regard for
actual variations in type and amount of service, important
information could be lost. For example, a program may
appear to have no overall effect, whereas closer examination may suggest that certain treatment strategies,
confined to a subset of the treatment group, were in fact
effective. Precisely this situation occurred in national
evaluations of Head Start and Follow Through (Smith and
Bissell, 1970; Stebbins et al., 1977). If actual services
received are measured within both treatment and control
(or comparison) groups, and measured service rather than
group assignment becomes the independent variable, the
simplicity of the analysis is sacrificed. Further
complicating the definition of treatment is the fact that
the time boundaries of a program may be fuzzy, and the
temporal relationship between treatment and effects may
be uncertain. When a program has no clearly defined
temporal endpoint, it is difficult to say when treatment
is complete.
Still another complication in many evaluations is that
control subjects may themselves receive treatment. For
example, low-income children not in Head Start may be

served in Title XX day care, which resembles Head Start in many respects. Children without access to an experimental health program may be treated at a local clinic. Depending on the purpose of a particular evaluation, these alternative sources of service may be either nuisance variables or highly relevant. If the purpose is to determine whether the program "works" in comparison to no treatment, they obviously cloud the issue. If the purpose is to determine whether a particular program confers an advantage over existing service systems or agencies, alternative sources of service may provide a useful comparison. In general, experimental designs presume that the treatment/no treatment comparison is the relevant one, but for many policy purposes comparison with the preexisting configuration of services is more relevant.

These observations make it clear that if the results of an evaluation are to be intelligible, it is crucial to document the precise nature of the treatment received by children or families in the experimental program as well as those in any control or comparison groups that might be involved. For this purpose, so-called process measures are needed--both gross measures of services provided and fine-grained measures of transactions between staff and clients. Such measures might be of many types--systematic observations using a coding system, participant observation, in-depth interviews, etc. Such measures have the potential to document what actually transpires in a program, as opposed to what is prescribed in the program's guidelines or self-description. Thus they can tell us whether a program is living up to its stated ideals; see, for example, Stallings' (1975) monograph on the relationship between program ideologies and program practices in Follow Through. They can help us distinguish between the delivery and the receipt of services--i.e., between what the program provides and what the child or family experiences.

More importantly, process measures have the potential to illuminate the connection between means and ends--to tell us why a program worked or failed to work. As argued earlier, this information is critical. A demonstration can succeed for idiosyncratic reasons that preclude wider use of its results. Similarly, a demonstration that fails to achieve its intended effects may nonetheless contain valuable lessons for the future.

Numerous examples could be adduced to illustrate the potential usefulness of process measures in clarifying the connection of treatments with outcomes. To cite just a few cases: An early evaluation of the Child and Family Resources Program failed to include such elementary process data as frequency of home visits or regularity of attendance at center sessions. When no effects were found on children's development or family functioning after two to three years in the program, no precise explanation could be given for the lack of program effects. In a current evaluation, detailed process data are being collected, and tentative relationships have been found between participation measures and children's performance on developmental tests. Similarly, staff of the Brookline Early Education Project kept logs of their contacts with client families, and contact frequency has been found to be related to positive outcomes. While correlational data such as those just cited cannot distinguish selection effects from genuine causal linkages between program participation and outcomes, they at least suggest plausible hypotheses for further exploration.

Understanding Site Differences

A related reason for giving careful attention to process measures is to understand the site differences in effects so often found for children's programs. Umbrella programs are likely to vary from site to site with respect to such features as scope of services, the role of parents, philosophy or curriculum, nature of the sponsoring agency, links to the school system, etc. In some cases, notably family service programs such as Parent-Child Centers and the Child and Family Resources Program, this diversity is deliberate: Such programs are intended to respond to local needs and to make use of local resources. Even when programs or models operate under uniform guidelines, however, studies have repeatedly found great diversity in actual practices and in effects from site to site. When site variation is great, it seems inappropriate to think of a program as a single treatment that is implemented at many sites or that varies unidimen- sionally from site to site in "distance" from national program specifications; rather, such a program is a collection of treatments, each of which applies to a single site or a few sites at most.

Large-scale comparative studies in the past, such as the evaluations of Head Start Planned Variation and Follow Through, have struggled against this reality, first by trying to enforce uniformity of program models

across sites, then by grouping programs or performing
various statistical adjustments in order to compare
"models." In our view such efforts are often misplaced.
We must learn to deal with site variations through innovations in design and analysis and through measurement of
program characteristics that allow us to understand site
differences. With respect to measurement, process data
can help the evaluator understand site variations in a
given program or model. With respect to design, it makes
sense not only to avoid comparative designs that presume
or require sites to be alike but also to capitalize on
site differences. By studying how programs adapt to their
settings, the evaluator can provide the policy maker with
useful information about the potential generalizability
of a locally successful approach and can provide practitioners with some indication as to whether a successful
innovation is likely to work well under their particular
circumstances. Investigation of site effects can also
give the policy maker some indication of which program
characteristics can and should be mandated at the federal
or state level and which are best left to local
initiative.

Measuring Costs and Cost Increments

Program cost has continued to be a concern of program
sponsors; it is one for which entire methodologies for
cost accounting and cost-benefit analysis have been
developed. While the panel has not directly concerned
itself with issues of cost measurement, it recognizes a
need for much more attention to the relationship between
costs and program outcomes. With the notable exception
of High/Scope Foundation's Ypsilanti-Perry Preschool
Project, early childhood demonstrations have made almost
no attempt to examine their total costs in relation to
long-run benefits. The Perry project claimed substantial
long-run cost-effectiveness, largely due to the fact that
its graduates were far less likely than control children
to require expensive special education during the school
years (Weber et al., 1977).
Furthermore, almost no attention has been paid to
variations in cost that are linked to variations in
program configuration. In the evaluation of early
childhood programs, variations in program philosophies
and curricula have frequently been studied, and variations
in delivery strategies or program structures have

occasionally been studied, but little attention has been
paid specifically to cost-relevant variations in programs.
Cost-relevant variations may include, for example, staff/
client ratios, economies that may derive from large-scale
provision of services, or transporting staff to families
rather than families to program centers. To the extent
that such variations are related to program effectiveness,
the nature of these relationships needs to be understood.
An example of the usefulness of findings linking cost to
quality of service is provided by the National Day Care
Study, mentioned in an earlier section (Ruopp et. al.,
1979). This study examined the costs associated with
different grouping and staffing patterns and concluded
that the most costly program elements are not the ones
most closely linked to quality of care--a finding that
influenced the day care regulations proposed in 1980 by
the federal government.

Such issues become even more important when one
considers that demonstration programs are often designed
as prototypes to be refined and made more cost-efficient
later, so that they may be implemented on a larger scale.
Dissecting such prototype demonstration programs, in order
to identify the components that are most closely related
to both outcomes and costs, is the best way to ensure that
later efficiencies will be accomplished without risk to
the effectiveness of the program.

Generalizing From Successful Demonstrations

Even when a program has proven to be highly effective
at one or a few sites, numerous factors may limit its
wider implementation. By being aware of these factors
and addressing them explicitly, the evaluator can provide
guidance as to where and how the program's lessons can be
put to use.

The kind of information necessary to make a reasonable
projection of the generalizability of a demonstration is
not typically collected in evaluations of programs for
children, but it is very much in line with our earlier
recommendations. Examples of relevant questions include:
To what degree are participants in the demonstration
typical of the populations that might potentially be
served? How feasible is it to recruit appropriate staff
in large numbers? To what degree are the program's
effects limited to particular sites with unique
characteristics? How much does the program cost? Are

there economies or diseconomies of scale? How complex,
costly, and burdensome is the administrative machinery
necessary to operate the program on a large scale? To
what degree would widespread implementation disrupt,
facilitate, or overlap with existing programs? An evaluation that focuses solely on the effects of a program on
children or families furnishes indispensable but insufficient information. An evaluation that incorporates
information about processes, costs, and the interaction
of the program with its setting is in a far better
position to address the concerns of those who would build
on the experience of the successful demonstration by
adapting it for a wide range of settings.

Rethinking Evaluation Designs

The challenges posed by contemporary programs for
children and the suggestions we have made for addressing
at least some of them require a broader view of alternative measurement techniques and evaluation designs than
is commonly maintained. In this section we distinguish a
number of different configurations of designs and measures
that might be considered, depending on the evaluator's
particular purposes.

The first distinction is between experimental and
observational approaches. The difference is highlighted
by characterizing the former as learning through manipulation. While suitable control is important for either
approach, the static nature of observational studies
heavily burdens the inferences that are drawn from them.

The concept of control leads to a second distinction--
that between randomized and nonrandomized designs. While
we make a plea for breadth, to have a rigorous demonstration of program effects there is no substitute for a
completely randomized study. Although they do not predominate, randomized designs have been used in the evaluation
of children's programs. For example, the Home Start
Evaluation (Love et al., 1975) produced particularly
clear-cut evidence of the effectiveness of home-based
intervention. Another example is provided by the
National Day Care Study (Ruopp et al., 1979), which
addressed the same set of questions through a large,
quasi experiment and a smaller randomized study.
The randomized study produced results generally similar
to but stronger than those of the quasi experiment.

One must, however, study the program and not the experiment. Ideally, randomized experiments should be combined with observational studies that focus on the natural setting(s) in which the program is intended to operate. In addition to checking the reactivity of the experimental design, such observations may elucidate the "why" of observed effects (and, in the absence of them, the "why not").

The quantitative/qualitative distinction is the third distinction to consider. Furthermore, we distinguish between qualitative assessment and qualitative research. The former denotes the use of qualitative techniques, such as clinical judgments, to gather data; the latter is exemplified by such approaches as grounded theory and analytic induction. Qualitative research relies primarily on three data collection techniques: document review, in-depth observation, and interviewing. It should be noted that both qualitative assessment and research may occur in experimental designs. A qualitative approach can provide a rich description of cases, which can broaden our understanding of the situation and the setting and answer the "why" of program effect or lack of it. Such description may also educe theory and provide a basis for subsequent research.

We find a great deal of promise in combining both qualitative and quantitative types of studies in the evaluation of early childhood programs. One approach would be to do both and see if they tell the same story. Another approach uses qualitative data to enrich and support quantitative findings. Especially promising seems to be a reciprocal strategy in which qualitative insights are treated as a challenge for the development of quantitative measures, and statistical findings are used as guideposts for more intensified and differentiated qualitative analysis.

At an entirely different level, that of the administering or funding agency, multiple approaches may also be useful in constructing an overall evaluation strategy. Many of the best-known evaluations have been large, multisite studies. Alternatives are possible, however, even when the agency's intent is to understand a large-scale program. Small studies often permit greater experimental rigor than large ones, and they avert the risk of catastrophic failure. Although each study yields only a partial picture, collectively they may permit a gradual accumulation of knowledge about the program as a whole. This cumulative approach is especially likely to be effective when the evaluation program as a whole is specifically designed to permit integration of findings-- rather than relying on after-the-fact integration in the manner of traditional literature reviews.

While this brief discussion of issues is not exhaustive, it does suggest the wide variety of approaches available. The choice of methods is, however, far from arbitrary. That choice should be linked to the questions to be answered, the state of knowledge, and the real constraints under which the research will be enacted. There are some questions, such as those addressing the issues of access and equity, that do not lend themselves to, nor are illuminated by, manipulation, and so are best addressed through observational studies. Again, the matching of design alternatives to the problem at hand is critical.

IMPLICATIONS FOR THE EVALUATION PROCESS

Some of our suggestions about design and measurement have indirect implications for the way in which applied research is organized and conducted, for the way in which its results may be presented most effectively, and even for the relationship between applied research and basic social science.

Involving Multiple Constituencies
in Selecting Outcome Measures

Given that demonstration programs affect many constituencies that have a stake or a say in the program's future, ways must be found to involve these groups or at least take account of their concerns in selecting outcome measures. Actual involvement is preferable, because it creates a commitment to the evaluation process, which may not otherwise be present on the part of some constitutent groups, even if the outcome measures used in an evaluation are relevant to their concerns.

To say that constituents should somehow be involved in identifying salient concerns or potential program outcomes of course does not mean that the outcomes can or should be selected on the basis of a survey. Constituencies differ in the salience that they accord to different outcomes. In some cases, outcomes valued by different constituencies may conflict. For example, when parents

of handicapped children exercise their rights to change
their children's educational placement, there is no
guarantee that the educational experiences of the child
will in fact be improved, either by the lengthy process
of appeals that may be involved or by the ultimate
outcome. In such a situation, legitimate values compete:
Is it more important for parents to have such rights or
for children to have steady, uninterrupted, and relaxed
educational experiences? Such conflicts create delicate
situations in which evaluators, sponsors of evaluations,
practitioners, and clients must negotiate the choice and
weighting of outcomes. Our point is that the scope of an
evaluation, the breadth of the audience for which it
provides at least some relevant information, and the
likelihood that its findings will be put to use will all
be enhanced if the perspectives of the various
constituencies are considered.

Communicating with Multiple Audiences

We have argued consistently that if evaluation is to
accomplish its goal of helping to improve programs and
shape policies, it must be attuned to practical issues,
not only to the interests of discipline-based researchers
and methodologists. Beyond this first and most important
step, evaluators can, by virtue of the way in which they
present their work, take further measures to ensure the
dissemination and utilization of their results.

Basic researchers are usually trained to speak only to
other researchers. Buttressed with statistics and hedged
with caveats, their reports typically have a logic and an
organization aimed at persuading professional critics of
the accuracy of careful delimited empirical claims.
However, applied researchers must address many audiences
who make very different uses of their findings. Policy
makers, government program managers, advocacy groups,
practitioners, and parents are among their many audiences.
Each group has its own concerns and requires a special
form of communication. However, all these groups have
some common needs and aims, quite different from those of
the research audience. They all want information to guide
action, rather than information for its own sake. They
have limited interest and sophistication with respect to
research methods and statistics.

This situation poses practical and ethical problems
for the evaluator. The practical problem is simply that

of finding ways to communicate findings clearly, with a minimum of jargon and technical detail. One strategy that has proved effective in this regard is organizing presentations around the questions of concern to non-technical audiences, rather than around the researcher's data-collection procedures and analyses. Adoption of this strategy of course presumes that the research itself has been designed at least in part to answer the questions of policy makers and practitioners. In addition, the impact of a report, however well written, can be enhanced by adroit management of other aspects of the dissemination process--public presentations, informal discussions with members of the intended audience, and the like--which can help create a climate of realistic advance expectations and appropriate after-the-fact interpretation.

The ethical problem is that of drawing the line between necessary qualification and unnecessary detail. One can always write a report with a clear message by ignoring inconsistent data and problematic analyses. The difficulty is to maintain scientific integrity without burying the message in methodological complexities and caveats. There is no general formula for solving this problem, any more than there is a formula for writing accurately and forcefully. It is important, however, that the problem be recognized--that researchers do not allow themselves to fall back on comfortable obscurantism or to strain for publicity and effect at the price of scientific honesty.

Building in Familiarity and Flexibility

The considerations about design and measurement discussed above have practical implications for the way in which applied research is conducted. One implication is that both researchers and the people who manage applied research--particularly government project officers and perhaps even program officers in foundations--need to develop intimate familiarity with the operations of service programs as well as basic understanding of the policy context surrounding those programs. Technical virtuosity and substantive excellence in an academic discipline do not alone make an effective evaluator. Over and above these kinds of knowledge, a practical, experiential awareness of program realities and policy concerns is essential if evaluation is to deal with those realities and to address those concerns. When third-party evaluations are conducted by organizations other than the service program or its funding agency, a preliminary period of familiarization may be needed by the outside evaluator. Moreover, that individual or organization should remain in close enough touch with the service program throughout the evaluation to respond to changes in focus, clientele, or program practices.

A second, related implication is that the evaluation process must be flexible enough to accommodate the evolution of programs and the researcher's understanding. Premature commitment to a particular design or set of measures may leave an evaluation with insufficient resources to respond to important changes, ultimately resulting in a report that speaks only to a program's past and not to its future. Such a report fails disastrously in meeting what we see as the primary responsibility of the evaluator, namely to teach the public and the policy maker whatever there is to learn from the program's experience.

There is danger, too, in the evaluator's being familiar with programs and flexible in responding to program changes as we have advocated. Too much intimacy with a program can erode an evaluator's intellectual independence, which is often threatened in any case by his or her financial dependence on the agency sponsoring the program in question. (Most evaluations are funded and monitored by federal mission agencies or private sponsors that also operate demonstration programs themselves.) We see no easy solution to this serious dilemma, but at the same time we can point to mechanisms that limit any distortions introduced by too close a relationship between evaluator and program. Most important among them are the canons of science, which require that the evaluator collect, analyze, and present data in a way that opens the conclusions to scrutiny. The political process can also act as a corrective force, in that it exposes the evaluator's conclusions to criticism from many value perspectives. Finally, as some researchers have urged, it may sometimes be feasible to deal with advocacy in evaluation by establishing concurrent evaluations of the same program, perhaps funded by separate agencies, but in any case deliberately designed to reflect divergent values and presuppositions.

This report does not discuss in detail the institutional arrangements that might lead to more effective program evaluations nor does it examine current arrangements critically. Such an examination would be a major

report in itself. Relevant reports have been written
under the aegis of the National Research Council, e.g.,
Raizen and Rossi (1981). However, we observe that many
major evaluations are funded by the federal government
through contracts with universities or private research
organizations. The contracting process is rather tightly
controlled. Subject to the approval of the funding
agency, the contractor is typically required to choose
designs, variables, and measures early in the course of
the study, then stick to them. It is rare that contrac-
tors are given adequate time to assimilate preliminary
information or to develop and pretest study designs and
methods. Sometimes the overall evaluation process is
segmented into separate contracts for design, data
collection, statistical analysis, and policy analysis.
It is perfectly understandable that the government is
reluctant to give universities or contract research
organizations carte blanche, especially in large evaluations, which may cost millions of dollars. Even the
fragmentation of evaluation efforts may be partially
justifiable, on the grounds that it allows the government
to purchase the services of organizations with complementary, specialied expertise. Whatever the merits of these
policies, it seems clear that in some respects the
contracting process is at odds with the needs we have
identified for gradual accretion of practical understanding and for flexibility in adapting designs and
measures to changes in programs.

Drawing on and Contributing to Basic Social Science

In some respects, evaluation stands in the same
relationship to traditional social science disciplines as
do engineering, medicine, and other applied fields to the
physical and biological sciences. Evaluation draws on
the theories, findings, and methods of anthropology,
economics, history, political science, psychology,
sociology, statistics, and kindred basic research fields.
At the same time, evaluation "technology" can also
contribute to basic knowledge. The approach to the
evaluation of children's programs set forth in this
report has implications both for the kinds of basic
social science that are likely to give rise to the most
useful applications and for the kinds of contributions
that evaluation can make to fundamental research.

Traditionally, evaluation has borrowed most heavily
from basic research fields that emphasize formal designs
and quantitative analytic techniques—statistics,
economics, experimental psychology, survey research in
sociology, and political science. The approach to
evaluation we suggest implies that quantitative
techniques can usefully be supplemented—not supplanted—
by ethnographic, historical, and clinical techniques.
These qualitative approaches are well suited to formulating hypotheses about orderly patterns underlying
complex, multidetermined, constantly changing phenomena,
although not to rigorous establishment of causal chains.
There is nothing scientific about adherence to forms and
techniques that have proved their usefulness elsewhere
but fail to fit the phenomena at hand. Science instead
adapts and develops techniques to fit natural and social
phenomena. When a field is at an early stage of development, available techniques are likely to have severe
limitations. But the use of all the techniques available,
with candid admission of their limitations, is preferable
to Procrustean distortion of phenomena to fit preferred
methods in pursuit of spurious rigor.

Our proposed approach also suggests that global,
systemic approaches to theory, of which the ecological
approach to human development is an example, are
potentially useful. Ad hoc empirical "theories" that
specify relationships among small numbers of variables,
whatever their merits in terms of clarity and precision,
simply omit too much. Theories that explicate relationships among variables describing individual growth,
family dynamics, and ties between families and other
institutions have greater heuristic value, even if they
are too ambitious to be precise at this early stage in
their development.

It should be clear that we favor precision, rigor, and
quantitative techniques. Each has its place, even given
the present state of the evaluation art, and that place
is likely to become larger and more secure as the art
advances. We argue, however, that description and
qualitative understanding of social programs are in
themselves worthwhile aims of evaluation and are
essential to the development of useful formal approaches.

We have indicated some of the directions in which we
think evaluation technology is likely to lead social
science. Because understanding social programs requires
a judicious fusion of qualitative and quantitative
methods, evaluation may stimulate new methodological work

49

articulating the two approaches. We may, for example, learn better ways to bring together clinical and experimental studies of individual children or ethnographic and survey-based studies of the family. Because understanding programs requires an appreciation of interlocking social systems, evaluation may contribute to the expansion and refinement of ecological, systemic theories. Thinking about children's programs may lead to a deeper understanding of the ways in which individual development is shaped by social systems of which the child is a part. Finally, because programs are complex phenomena that cannot be fully comprehended within the intellectual boundaries of a single discipline, evaluation may open up fruitful areas of interdisciplinary cooperation.

We are well aware that science often proceeds analytically rather than holistically; for example, it is useful for some purposes to isolate the circulatory system as an object of study, even though it is intimately linked to many other bodily systems. Nevertheless it is also useful now and then to examine interrelationships among previously defined systems to see if new insights and new areas of study--new systems--emerge. It is our hope that evaluation research can play this role vis-a-vis the social sciences. By focusing on concrete, real-world phenomena that do not fit neatly into existing theoretical or methodological boxes, evaluation may stimulate the development of both theory and method.

REFERENCES

Ainsworth, M. D. S., and Wittig, B. A.
  (1969)   Attachment and exploratory behavior of one-
           year-olds in a strange situation. In B. M.
           Foss, ed., Determinants of Infant Behavior,
           Volume 4. London: Methuen.
Anderson, S., and Messick, S.
  (1974)   Social competency in young children.
           Developmental Psychology 10:282-293.
Belsky, J.
  (1980)   Child maltreatment: an ecological integration.
           American Psychologist 35(4):320-335.
Belsky, J., and Steinberg, L. D.
  (1978)   The effects of day care: a critical review.
           Child Development 49:929-949.

50

Boruch, R. F., and Cordray, D. S.
 (1980)   An Appraisal of Educational Program
          Evaluations: Federal, State and Local
          Agencies. Report prepared for the U.S.
          Department of Education, Contract No.
          300-79-0467. Northwestern University (June
          30).
Brim, O. G.
 (1959)   Education for Child Rearing. New York:
          Russell Sage Foundation.
Bronfenbrenner, U.
 (1974)   A Report on Longitudinal Evaluations of
          Preschool Programs. Vol. II: Is Early
          Intervention Effective? U.S. Department of
          Health, Education, and Welfare, Publication
          No. OHD 75-25. Washington, D.C.: U.S.
          Department of Health, Education, and Welfare.
 (1979)   The Ecology of Human Development. Cambridge,
          Mass.: Harvard University Press.
Bureau of Education for the Handicapped
 (1979)   Progress Toward a Free, Appropriate Public
          Education. A Report to Congress on the
          Implementation of Public Law 94-142: The
          Education for All Handicapped Children Act.
          HEW Publication No. (OE) 79-05003. Washington,
          D.C.: U.S. Department of Health, Education,
          and Welfare.
Connell, D. C., and Carew, J. V.
 (1980)   Infant Activities in Low-Income Homes: Impact
          of Family-Focused Intervention. International
          Conference on Infant Studies, New Haven, Conn.
          (April).
Datta, L. E.
 (1979)   Another spring and other hopes: some findings
          from National Evaluations of Project Head
          Start. In E. Zigler and J. Valentine, eds.,
          Project Head Start: A Legacy of the War on
          Poverty. New York: Free Press.
Farran, D., and Ramey, C.
 (1980)   Social class differences in dyadic involvement
          during infancy. Child Development 51:254-257.
General Accounting Office
 (1979)   Early Childhood and Family Development
          Programs Improve the Quality of Life for
          Low-Income Families. Report to the Congress
          by the Comptroller General. HR-79-40
          (February).

Goodson, B. D., and Hess, R. D.
  (1978)   The effects of parent training programs on
           child performance and parent behavior.   In B.
           Brown, ed., Found: Long-Term Gains from Early
           Education. Boulder, Colo.: Westview Press.
Goodwin, W. L., and Driscoll, L. A.
  (1980)   Handbook for Measurement and Evaluation in
           Early Childhood Education. San Francisco,
           Calif.: Jossey-Bass, Inc., Publishers.
Horowitz, F. D., and Paden, L. Y.
  (1973)   The effectiveness of environmental programs.
           In B. Caldwell and H. D. Ricciuti, eds.,
           Review of Child Development Research. Vol.
           3: Child Development and Social Policy.
           Chicago, Ill.: University of Chicago Press.
Johnson, O. G.
  (1976)   Tests and Measurements in Child Development:
           Handbook II. Vols. 1 and 2. San Francisco,
           Calif.: Jossey-Bass, Inc., Publishers.
Johnson, O. G., and Bommarito, J. W.
  (1971)   Tests and Measurements in Child Development: A
           Handbook. San Francisco, Calif.: Jossey-Bass,
               Inc., Publishers.
Kirschner Associates, Albuquerque, N.M.
  (1970)   A National Survey of the Impacts of Head Start
           Centers on Community Institutions. (ED045195)
           Washington, D.C.: Office of Economic
           Opportunity.
Lazar, I., and Darlington, R. B.
  (1978)   Lasting Effects After Preschool. A report of
           the Consortium for Longitudinal Studies. U.S.
           Department of Health, Education, and Welfare,
           Office of Human Development Services,
           Administration for Children, Youth, and
           Families.
Lindsey, W. E.
  (1976)   Instrumentation of OCD Research Projects on
           the Family. Mimeographed report prepared
           under contract HEW-105-76-1120, U.S.
           Department of Health, Education, and Welfare.
           Social Research Group, The George Washington
           University, Washington, D.C.
Love, J. M., Nauta, M. J., Coelen, C. G., and Ruopp, R. R.
  (1975)   Home Start Evaluation Study: Executive
           Summary—Findings and Recommendations.
           Ypsilanti, Mich., and Cambridge, Mass.:
           High/Scope Educational Research Foundation and
           Abt Associates, Inc.

52

Raizen, S. A., and Rossi, P. H., eds.
  (1981) Program Evaluation in Education: When? How?
          To What Ends? Committee on Program Evaluation
          in Education, Assembly of Behavioral and
          Social Sciences, National Research Council.
          Washington, D.C.: National Academy Press.
Ramey, C., and Mills, J.
  (1975) Mother-Infant Interaction Patterns as a
          Function of Rearing Conditions. Paper
          presented at the biennial meeting of the
          Society for Research in Child Development,
          Denver, Colo. (April).
Rossi, P. H., Freeman, H. E., and Wright, S. R.
  (1979) Evaluation: A Systematic Approach. Beverly
          Hills, Calif.: Sage Publications.
Ruopp, R., Travers, J., Coelen, C., and Glantz, F.
  (1979) Children at the Center. Final report of the
          National Day Care Study, Volume I. Cambridge,
          Mass.: Abt Books.
Smith, M. S., and Bissell, J. S.
  (1970) Report analysis: the impact of Head Start.
          Harvard Educational Review 40:51-104.
Sroufe, L. A.
  (1979) The coherence of individual development:
          early care, attachment and subsequent
          developmental issues. American Psychologist
          34:834-841.
Stallings, J.
  (1975) Implementation and child effects of teaching
          practices in Follow Through classrooms.
          Monographs of the Society for Research in
          Child Development 40(7-8), Serial No. 163.
Stebbins, L. B., et al.
  (1977) Education as Experimentation: A Planned
          Variation Model. Vol. IV. Cambridge, Mass.:
          Abt Associates, Inc. Also issued by the U.S.
          Office of Education as National Evaluation:
          Patterns of Effects. Vol. II of the Follow
          Through Planned Variation Series.
Suchman, E. A.
  (1967) Evaluation Research: Principles and Practice
          in Public Service and Social Action Programs.
          New York: Russell Sage Foundation.
Walker, D. K.
  (1973) Socioemotional Measures for Preschool and
          Kindergarten Children. San Francisco,
          Calif.: Jossey-Bass, Inc., Publishers.

53

Weber, C. U., Foster, P. S., and Weikart, D. P.
  (1977)   An economic analysis of the Ypsilanti Perry
           Preschool Project. Monographs of the
           High/Scope Educational Research Foundation.
           Series No. 5.
Weiss, C. H.
  (1972)   Evaluating Action Programs: Readings in
           Social Action and Education. Boston, Mass.:
           Allyn & Bacon, Inc.
Westinghouse Learning Corporation and Ohio University
  (1969)   The Impact of Head Start: An Evaluation of
           the Effects of Head Start on Children's
           Cognitive and Affective Development.
           Executive Summary. Report to the Office of
           Economic Opportunity (ED036321). Washington,
           D.C.: Clearinghouse for Federal Scientific
           and Technical Information.
Zigler, E., and Trickett, P.
  (1978)   IQ, social competence and evaluation of early
           childhood intervention programs. American
           Psychologist 33:789-798.
Zigler, E., and Valentine, J., eds.
  (1979)   Project Head Start: A Legacy of the War on
           Poverty. New York: The Free Press.

Part 2: Papers

To facilitate the panel's discussion of the evaluation of children's programs, panel members together with outside consultants prepared a number of background papers. Each paper covers a specific type of program: health, day care, family service, and preschool compensatory education programs and programs for the handicapped. In addition, two panel members wrote a paper on the communication and dissemination of the results of evaluation.

These supporting papers were commissioned by the panel to provide a basis for discussion and serve as a reference source for the panel's report. Views represented in the papers are those of the individual authors. The panel as a whole did not approve each formally, although all papers were discussed by the panel and modified by their authors in light of this discussion.

The Health Impact of Early Childhood Programs: Perspectives from the Brookline Early Education Project

Melvin D. Levine and Judith S. Palfrey

In the evaluation of early childhood programs the
health status of the children enrolled is often a
prominent issue. Planners and policy makers are likely
to ask whether participation in such programs enhances
children's health and, if so, whether the gains are
substantial enough to justify the costs. In early
childhood programs for which improved health is not a
primary objective, program planners may want to know if
the addition of a health-monitoring component would be
cost-effective. As evaluators survey early childhood
programs and their impact on health, they may consider
the possibility of modifying the content of traditional
preventive health care. They may examine the feasibility
of collaborative service models that include the consoli-
dation of early education and preventive pediatrics, so
that communities can shape and upgrade simultaneously the
health care and developmental monitoring of children.

At first glance it might seem that the health of
children is easily amenable to evaluation and measurement.
Accurate numbers, however, are difficult to obtain and are
often misleading. In this paper we outline some salient
clinical and methodological issues that have become apparent to us in working at the Brookline Early Education
Project analyzing the health impact of a comprehensive
early childhood project.

The first section of the paper delineates a number of
critical issues facing evaluators. The second section
discusses the scope of "health" by detailing the various
background and process factors that need to be considered
during evaluation. The third section outlines specific
questions evaluators can ask as they measure the impact
of health. Finally, drawing on our experiences with the
Brookline Early Education Project, the last section

58

reviews seven evaluation prototypes and discusses
matching alternative evaluation strategies to specific
questions.

RELEVANT ISSUES FACING EVALUATORS

Defining Health and Its Borders

Health is more than the absence of disease. It is the
absence of handicap, social and emotional discord, and
environmental stress as well as the presence of resiliency, stamina, and homeostasis. There is growing awareness that traditional pediatric health cannot be viewed
apart from psychosocial, behavioral, developmental, and
educational status (Richmond, 1975; Rutter et al., 1970;
Haggerty et al., 1975). Functional health and its
promotion have increasingly become the purview of the
pediatrician working in conjunction with professionals
from other disciplines (Levine, Brooks, and Shonkoff,
1980).

Health issues are likely to involve other areas. For
example, it is essential for those managing children with
musculoskeletal defects to address the functional (i.e.,
gross and fine motor and psychosocial) impacts of such
handicaps. Professionals helping neurologically impaired
children must involve themselves in the assessment of
higher-order cognitive function, self-esteem, behavioral
adjustment, and related family issues. Health maintenance
must include anticipatory guidance and counseling, for
patterns of behavior are as much within the domain of
child health as are infectious diseases and specific
organ disorders. Table 1 samples the broad spectrum of
child health disorders. So many factors are involved
that it is easier to describe what should be included
under the rubric of "health" than to isolate issues
irrelevant to health maintenance.

Describing Health Status

Characterizing the health status of groups of children
is even more difficult than characterizing individual
health. Since universally acceptable scoring and
weighting systems do not exist, the health evaluation of
a cohort enrolled in an early childhood project can be
costly to obtain and difficult to interpret.

TABLE 1   Some Negative Health Outcomes Whose Effects
Early Education Projects Are Intended to Minimize

---

1. Poor growth and/or nutrition

2. Sensory deficits

3. Chronic illness and symptoms

4. Poor utilization of health services

5. Recurrent trauma

6. Neurological disorders

7. Neurodevelopmental dysfunctions

8. Psychosocial mobility

9. Mental retardation/multiple handicapping conditions

10. Life-threatening diseases

A group's health status cannot be presented as a simple inventory of existing symptoms and conditions. Evaluators who wish to characterize the health status of a group of children need to take into account past medical events, family history, and current health. In addition, there must be estimates of vulnerability and resiliency, descriptions of health practices and knowledge (nutrition, exercise, and total environment), and accounts of medical service utilization.

Describing Health Change

After defining the limits of health as a subject matter and developing the descriptors to characterize group health status, evaluators must find measures of health change. This can be particularly challenging in the preschool child, as the morbidity itself evolves with age and many of the dysfunctions and disorders are self-limited or transient.

Sometimes changes in health are more apparent than real because different measures are used at different ages. Certain reflexes, for example, can be elicited in children who are three to six months old but not thereafter. Hearing and vision are easier to measure after three years of age than before. Some orthopedic difficulties may not be evident until a child attempts to walk. Children may have immunity to certain diseases at specific ages but not beyond. The descriptors of the health of children thus depend to some extent on which window one looks through at what time.

Just as problematic for evaluators is the high prevalence of self-limited acute or subacute illnesses and the spontaneous health resiliency of young children (Dingle, 1964; Miller et al., 1960). This makes it difficult to study both the occurrence of and recovery from acute disease. It may be particularly hard to attribute symptom abatement to treatment effects.

Behavioral and developmental disorders of early childhood reveal considerable instability over time as well. Although some researchers (Thomas and Chess, 1975; Taft, 1978) have suggested that behavioral characteristics may be maintained from infancy through childhood, others (Bell et al., 1971; Carey et al., 1977) have demonstrated that children who have "behavior problems" at age two or three may not be the same children who have difficulty in school.

It may be impossible to identify precise endpoints of health change. For example, one may not be able to determine whether a child has had one prolonged episode of otitis media that never really healed or multiple ear infections (Giebink and Quie, 1978). This difficulty impedes any precise accounting of numbers of acute illness episodes during a given period.

The measurement of health change is complicated for three reasons: (1) the actual content of health and morbidity evolves with age, (2) many conditions undergo spontaneous remission, and (3) some disorders are closely associated with others and are therefore indistinguishable from one another. Therefore, before looking at the impact of a program on health, evaluators should develop appropriate methods of characterizing change: The health (of a group or individual) may vary depending on the period of time under scrutiny. The measures of health should therefore be dynamic, depending on the age and development of the children in a program. The measurement of health "progression" must somehow be differentiated from normal chronological change. To document enhancement, evaluators must show that a particular child or group of children at the end of two years improved in overall health characteristics. As difficult as this may be, such documentation stands as a critical requisite for the evaluation of health as a progressive phenomenon.

Dealing With Low Prevalence Rates
in Pediatric Morbidity

Pediatric illness differs fundamentally from its adult counterpart. In the latter, a relatively small number of major illnesses (e.g., hypertension, obesity, coronary heart disease, cancer, and diabetes) are likely to be highly prevalent within a population. Evaluators of adult health programs may be able to measure the impact of a program on these distinct entities and thereby generalize about health status and program-induced change. In contrast, there is no single chronic organic condition of childhood common enough to scrutinize in such a fashion without a very large sample. Therefore, in studying chronic medical conditions in a service program for children, it is often necessary to employ aggregate ratings that "lump" children with such disparate conditions as congenital heart disease, juvenile rheumatoid arthritis, nephrotic syndrome, recurrent urinary tract infection, and asthma for purposes of analysis. The alternative is to use samples that are too large for most early childhood projects.

Resiliency in childhood also differentiates child health from adult health. Most child health setbacks are likely to be acute and self-limited, leaving no scars or aftereffects. Cataloging of such events shows that in a single year most children have been "sick" as many as four or five times (Dingle, 1966). For children such morbidity is par for the course, developmentally appropriate, perhaps immunologically necessary, and ultimately inconsequential (Mortimer, 1968). Evaluators thus need to weight acute self-limited disease very differently in children.

Absence of Data on Normalcy

In assaying pediatric health status, we are hampered by a paucity of data on normalcy and normal variation.

While information does exist regarding the prevalence of
specific chronic diseases or congenital anomalies and the
incidence of some acute illnesses, this information tends
to reflect major social class differences (Morris, 1979),
serious problems with reporting (Brewer and Kakalik,
1979; Bureau of Education for the Handicapped, 1979), and
inadequacies in many of the measuring techniques (Balinsky
and Berger, 1975). This distortion makes it especially
difficult to determine if the health status of a particular group of children is below or beyond what ordinarily
might be expected. Normative data are even more deficient
in assessing developmental status, behavior, family
functioning, and health care utilization patterns. Much
of traditional medical research has had the benefit of
normative data. For example, it is possible to study the
effects of a medication on a patient's glucose level,
since norms for blood sugar are available. For many of
the aggregate measures of community child health, however,
no such norms exist (Starfield, 1974). What is "normal"
or "to be expected" for a particular population must
almost always be reestablished in undertaking evaluation
research. In many instances this requires the use of
comparison groups or control populations.

Selecting Outcome Measures

In documenting program effects on health, one critical
issue is the precise outcomes to be measured at designated
outcome points. One might be tempted to consider only
the prevalence of morbidity as an outcome measure. This,
of course, leaves out such issues as parental health
knowledge, patterns of use, and children's health stamina.
Furthermore, it is unlikely that the straightforward
rendering of morbidity statistics constitutes an adequate
reflection of project effectiveness. An early support
project may be beneficial without diminishing the
prevalence of a disorder. For example, one would not
expect a program to lessen the occurrence of myopia, yet
an effective effort might result in a reduction of
previously undetected or untreated nearsightedness. In
fact, an early childhood project may exert its greatest
effects not on prevalence figures but on awareness,
management, coping, and the prevention of complications.
Another issue in selecting outcome measures is the
need for a method of weighting. Health outcomes can be
measured in terms of their severity, their impact (on

function, on families, on society), and their relevance, so that composite morbidity may be subdivided into significance for treatment (prescriptive implications) and potential for impairment of future health or function (predictive weight). Even a low prevalence of disorders that are likely to thwart academic function or behavioral adjustment may be more important than a high occurrence of such disorders as flat feet. Evaluators might also want to select outcome measures that have significant implications for treatment. A project should be judged more harshly if it missed problems that were treatable than if it overlooked those for which no therapy was available.

Outcome measures should not be too global, particularly with regard to developmental and behavioral assessments. A project that uses IQ as an outcome measure will not be pinpointing the prevalence of problems with attention, language, or other isolated information-processing deficits that can seriously impair function (Levine, Brooks, and Shonkoff, 1980). Similarly, the results of a developmental screening test by themselves are unlikely to be sufficient to describe a project's impact on children's development (Meier, 1973; Meissels, 1978). A more comprehensive picture would include parental reports of function, direct observations of behavior, or specific teacher accounts of skills, abilities, and interest.

One challenge for those evaluating early childhood projects is the identification of measures that can be used to provide an in-depth assessment of function to determine whether the program has diminished or minimized the effects of so-called low-severity, high-prevalence dysfunctions of childhood, which include specific learning disabilities, primary attention deficits, and various forms of psychosocial maladaptation during the school years.

In delineating outcome measures, evaluators should consider the objectives of the project under scrutiny. For instance, if health is a high priority of a given project and if assurance of primary care is an explicit goal, then it is appropriate to determine if the project has met that goal by assessing patterns of health care utilization of the enrolled children. This approach may be less relevant in projects that have had only an incidental commitment to health.

Finally, within a given population uniformity of outcome measurement may be unrealistic and inappropriate, especially in programs emphasizing the individualization

of services. To measure gains, evaluators may need to
specify "target subgroups." For a subgroup with hearing
deficits, incremental growth in vocabulary may be a better
measure of program effectiveness than mean developmental
scores at age five. Evaluators can identify areas in
which they would expect or hope to see progress for
particular children. They might also weigh expectations
against accomplishments. For example, a project may not
be able to diminish the prevalence of problems with
short-term memory in children, but it might be able to
achieve a generalized improvement in the reading
proficiency of children with short-term memory problems,
a gain that would surpass what would be expected for
nonparticipating children with this developmental
dysfunction. Thus, although a project may not diminish
the severity or prevalence of short-term memory problems,
it may manage to have "better copers," more competent
readers, and perhaps happier children within this target
subgroup. In some cases a project may want to evaluate
only specific target groups to demonstrate program
effects. When an evaluation becomes this focused,
however, either large numbers or elegant small sample
designs are needed to demonstrate that intervention has
been successful.

Assessing the Cost-Effectiveness
of a Health Program Evaluation

A major challenge exists in the calculation of a
cost-benefit ratio for health program evaluations. There
is constant pressure to balance the expense and difficulty
of acquiring a particular set of data against its ultimate
value for children and its relevance to the objectives of
a project. It may be simple to determine immunization
rates for a particular population, but if the project is
located in a town where most children are well immunized
anyway, despite its economy this will not be a useful way
of measuring program impact. On the other hand, if a
service model is likely to improve a family's ability to
cope with behavior problems, a series of expensive
measures of behavior and parenting may be most relevant
(Haggerty et al., 1975; Roghmann et al., 1973; Haggerty,
1965). There can be no one set of criteria for
evaluating all projects. Those aspects of health chosen
for evaluation will depend largely on the nature of the
community, the objectives of the program, the

availability of evaluation funds, and current public policy questions.

Identifying The Evaluation Consumer

In designing an evaluation of health outcome, it is essential to understand the needs and priorities of those for whom the evaluation is intended. The content of an analysis depends largely on its intended audience. It can be argued, however, that all evaluations should be able to undergo some degree of rigorous scrutiny, even if intended primarily for nonacademics. Purely anecdotal reports and testimonials are inadequate measures of health care provision under any circumstances; highly esoteric statistical analyses, on the other hand, may have little impact on school committee decision making or on the deliberations of legislators. Often evaluations must apply several formats, each designed for a unique constitutuency.

Timing and Staging

A critical issue for evaluation is timing. The health effectiveness of a program can be documented while it is in progress. Alternatively, one could consider assessment of its impact at the end of a project or at a short or long interval following termination. Decisions about timing must consider what is being measured and demon-strated. If a major goal is to minimize morbidity and suffering and to cushion the traumatic impact of daily events and environments, then it is crucial to offer evaluations while the project is in progress. If the goal is to look at the long-range effects of intervention or general service, postintervention analyses are needed. Findings inevitably reflect the timing of an evaluation, and the implications can be great, especially for issues of cost-effectiveness. Because of the instability of health conditions in childhood and the high degree of resiliency, the timing of evaluations significantly influences the attribution of program effects, which can be misleading from a public policy viewpoint. For example, if children in a particular program have less difficulty adjusting to the first weeks of kindergarten than nonparticipants, evaluators may feel that they have documented a measurable effect. It may turn out, however,

that the two groups are virtually indistinguishable if
they are evaluated in mid-February of the kindergarten
year. Allocators of resources would wonder if great
expenditures to promote "educational readiness" were
really worthwhile if their effects were demonstrable only
during the earliest months of kindergarten and thereafter
washed out.

Traditional health issues follow a similar pattern.
If a child's flat feet are detected in an early childhood
project, but the child has no pain or functional limita-
tion and it is documented that the finding would otherwise
not have emerged until the first or second grade, what
has been gained? In any event, by the time the child is
eight or nine, the parents are likely to be aware of the
condition. In that case, what is the value of early
detection? Assuming that the condition is discovered
early and the child given corrective shoes, does it
really make a difference (Bleck, 1971; Cowell, 1977)? In
some cases it may be better not to diagnose a problem
that is going to resolve itself or that may not cause
symptoms or require treatment for several years.

It may be that years after a program ends there is
little difference in the prevalence of previously
undiagnosed findings. One might argue that ultimately
the important problems will be detected. There is a
danger that early detection may obligate programmers to
unnecessary expenditures for interventions, especially
for conditions that are likely to remit spontaneously.
Once again, it is important to review the objectives of a
project. The timing of an evaluation of program effects
should relate to the objectives. In stating objectives
there should be some consideration of the anticipated or
desired duration of effects. Outcome measures can then
be timed to assess these accordingly.

Having delineated these issues for the evaluation of
program effects on health, we now turn to a more detailed
examination of the measurement of health status. The next
section describes this as a necessary step in demonstrating the influence of a specific program on health.

THE SCOPE OF CHILD HEALTH

As early childhood programming expands, the literature
from education (e.g., U.S. General Accounting Office,
1979; Lazar, 1977; Bronfenbrenner, 1975; White, 1975;
Zigler and Valentine, 1979) and pediatrics (e.g.,

Richmond, 1975; Thomas and Chess, 1975; Taft, 1978; Carey
et al., 1977; Roghmann et al., 1973; Klaus and Kennell,
1976; Morris et al., 1976; Badger et al., 1976) makes it
clear that the scope of child health that can be addressed
is very wide. Clearly, evaluators should focus on those
aspects of a health program that are most likely to
reveal efficacy. In our work at the Brookline Early
Education Project (Pierson, 1974) and the school clinics
at Children's Hospital Medical Center in Boston (Levine,
1979), we have found it most helpful to define (1) the
background health characteristics of the children, (2)
the ongoing health and developmental processes at home
and in the program, and (3) the outcomes that the program
intends to achieve. Only with these areas clearly
defined does it become possible to address specific
questions regarding program impact.

Background Variables

From the intrauterine period onward, the experiences
of children vary significantly. Some endure prenatal and
postnatal trauma, some are born into impoverished and
disorganized families, some inherit genetic disorders,
and some fail to receive adequate nurturance. Others,
because of their constitutional makeup, never adjust
optimally to their milieu and continually hunger for
greater satisfaction from it. Still others arrive with
ease, cope readily, and manifest little or no disability
in dealing with the external world.

Programs dealing with young children generally take
these variations into account for staffing and programmatic reasons. To do so for outcome measurement is
equally critical. Children who are more "at risk" will
require greater levels of service; their outcomes may
turn out to be excellent, but they differ from children
not at risk. For instance, the most pertinent outcome
measures for a middle-class deaf child might be ease with
a hearing aid, skill in using a total communication
system, and ability to attend a normal school for at
least some of the day. On the other hand, outcome
measures for a normally hearing child from a socio-
economically depressed and disorganized home might be
assurance of primary health care, money for food, and an
adequate after-school, supervised program.

Because the health needs of children are so varied,
programmers, monitors, and policy makers should keep

sight of "targeted" outcomes. Figure 1 illustrates diagrammatically the idea that individual children require customized health programming. Some entering an early childhood project need little more than routine preventive health care. Others, because of early negative factors, need problem-focused surveillance, while still others demand active intervention. Obviously, those in the preventive or surveillance group may require more active intervention at a subsequent point during the project.

Among the most common risk factors are perinatal stresses, genetic predispositions, low socioeconomic status, and negative critical life events (setbacks). Each of these needs to be assessed separately, since they may have a differential effect on outcome.

Perinatal Influences

Major perinatal complications have been shown to place children at risk for developmental sequelae. However, there is currently considerable debate in the perinatal literature about the ability to predict dysfunction from perinatal catastrophes, especially in the wake of advanced intensive-care technology (Alberman and Goldstein, 1970; Davie et al., 1972). At most, one can say that a child who sustained prenatal or postnatal trauma or illness may be at higher risk of developmental dysfunction in the future. Those most likely to fulfill such predictions are newborns who weigh less than 1,200 grams (Stewart et al., 1977; Kopelman, 1978), those who suffered intra-uterine growth retardation, the so-called small-for-dates babies (Neligan et al., 1976), those born in outlying hospitals who were transported to regional centers for intensive care (Cassady, 1975; Chance et al., 1973), and those identified in the first few days as neurologically impaired (Nelson and Ellenberg, 1979).

While there is still much to be learned about the connections between perinatal problems and later outcomes, early biological events should be recorded so that outcomes can be measured against them. This is most true for children who are in the double jeopardy of early physical stress and socioeconomic hardship or deprivation. A number of studies have shown that these children are at considerable risk (Werner et al., 1971; Institute of Medicine, 1973; Knobloch and Pasamanick, 1966; Sameroff and Chandler, 1975), and their health outcomes definitely

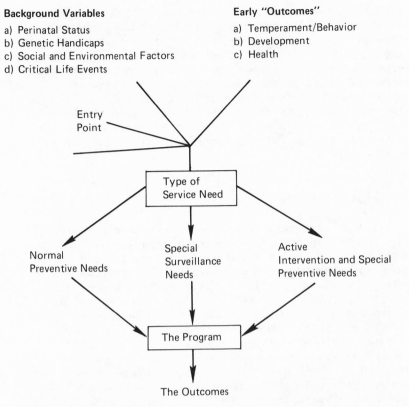

Background Variables

a) Perinatal Status
b) Genetic Handicaps
c) Social and Environmental Factors
d) Critical Life Events

Early "Outcomes"

a) Temperament/Behavior
b) Development
c) Health

Entry
Point

Type of
Service Need

Normal
Preventive Needs

Special
Surveillance
Needs

Active
Intervention and Special
Preventive Needs

The Program

The Outcomes

FIGURE 1 Customized health programming for children in an early childhood project.

can be used as a targeted index of a given program's total performance.

A major problem with the literature on the relationship between perinatal trauma and later life has been the lack of uniform outcome measures. Studies have used different chronological endpoints, including 1 year (Fitzhardinge, 1975; Goldstein et al., 1976), 4 years (Broman et al., 1975), 7 years (Davie et al., 1972), and 10 years (Nelson and Ellenberg, 1979). Most investigations have applied developmental (Tilford, 1976) or intelligence quotients (Fitzhardinge, 1975; Broman et al., 1975); some have inspected functional outcomes, such as school performance (Rubin et al., 1973). Many have accepted neurological disability as the norm for children with perinatal stress

and thus have reported surprise or delight when a
relatively small percentage manifest such problems
(Stewart and Reynolds, 1974). Others have assumed that
any neurological or learning disability, even of the most
subtle degree, is a negative outcome and have therefore
reported large percentages of abnormal consequences (Rubin
et al., 1973; Fitzhardinge and Steven, 1972). It will be
important for program monitors to be aware of these
vagaries of criteria and to be as explicit as possible
when determining which outcomes to follow and where to
draw the lines.

Genetic Disorders

Genetic diseases, such as Down's syndrome, other
chromosomal anomalies, phenylketonuria (PKU), and inborn
errors of carbohydrate and lipid metabolism are known to
predispose children to poor health and developmental
outcome (Milunsky, 1975). Early education projects,
particularly those offering "infant stimulation" are
often designed to help such children (Hayden and
McGuiness, 1977; Bricker and Iacino, 1977). It is
crucial that entry characteristics on genetically
handicapped children be registered and the natural
history of their disorders well understood. For this
group, targeted outcome measures are appropriate
(Tjossem, 1976). As an example, children with treated
PKU have been shown to have significant weaknesses of
perceptual motor function that are disproportionate with
their overall intellectual levels (Koff et al., 1977). A
global cognitive index (such as a standard IQ test) used
as an outcome measure would fail to assess the impact of
a program designed for early intervention for such
children, whereas a specific look at perceptual motor
functioning would do so. Likewise, any assessment of a
Down's syndrome program should gear the outcome standards
for growth and development along a developmentally
appropriate scale (Smith and Wilson, 1973). Those
analyses that have shown the effectiveness of early
intervention have used a targeted approach, and the
evaluators have been familiar with the natural history of
the particular disorders (Horton, 1976).
Finally, in the case of genetic disabilities, outcome
measures should be designed specifically to address the
question: Did this program succeed in preventing
secondary disability in these children? In the words of

Meier (1975:386), who has written extensively on this subject, ". . . the prevention of DD (developmental disability) is also a relative phenomenon, in the sense that the prevention of further disability through early intervention is still prevention of otherwise inevitable further deterioration, although the total disability may not be lessened or fully compensated. The specific genetic inheritance of a DD person may establish certain ceiling limitations for growth and development, but even those lowered ceilings will probably not be reached without appropriate intervention."

Socioeconomic and Environmental Influences

One of the strongest predictors of school performance is socioeconomic status. Furthermore, there is a disproportionate amount of illness among poor children (E. Newberger et al., 1976; National Research Council, 1976). Head Start and other early childhood programs have incorporated health components specifically for this reason (Richmond, 1966).

Documentation of the socioeconomic status of children within a given project is important for service allocation and allows those who are monitoring the program's efficacy to determine how well health goals have been met for the disadvantaged and to identify gaps that remain to be filled by health and welfare agencies.

Knowing that a proportion of children within a program are at a socioeconomic disadvantage, program monitors need to assess sources of primary medical care (Haggerty, 1976; Harvard Child Health Project Task Force, 1977), dental care (Gortmaker, 1979), nutritional adequacy (C. Newberger et al., 1976; Folman, 1977), and home safety (Taylor and Newberger, 1979). While these are outcomes important for all youngsters, they are particularly salient for poor children.

Experience with Head Start and Follow Through has indicated that programmatic gains tend not to be sustained if children cease to receive stimulation. Caldwell's group has pointed to the fact that the extent of home participation can be measured systematically (Elardo et al., 1975). For those programs enrolling children at high socioeconomic risk, outcome measures designed to estimate the extent to which there has been family participation and family growth through the program are increasingly recognized as of major benefit (Zigler and Valentine, 1979; Richmond, 1966).

A goal of the Brookline Early Education Project has
been to teach parents an advocacy role vis-a-vis schools
and other institutions. Mothers and fathers within the
program have indicated to interviewers they feel that
their increased competence in working with and advocating
for their children will promote a healthier environment
(Weiss, 1979). For programs working with high-risk
socioeconomic groups, parental competence and advocacy
could serve as a powerful outcome measure; such
measurement, however, remains elusive.

Other environmental influences, such as family intact-
ness, the quality of housing, patterns of nurturance, and
cultural milieu, are likely to be important to document
and consider in individualizing services. In evaluations,
such data can help document project impacts on specific
subgroups.

Health and Development Over Time

While the entry characteristics mentioned above are
known to be related to some of the negative outcomes
listed in Table 1, community accountability is not
limited to those children whose vulnerability is readily
identified in the first few months or years. Close
community surveillance is justified by the findings of
Smith and Phillips (1978) that 45 percent of a group of
severely developmentally delayed children (excluding
Down's syndrome) were not identified until after they
were 18 months old, and 16 percent of these 131 children
were not diagnosed as handicapped until they were 49 to
60 months old.

Child health and development are characterized by
trends and flux. The fact that a child has pneumonia
once may have almost no significance, but if he or she
has pneumonia multiple times, a serious immunodeficiency,
lung abnormality, or cystic fibrosis may be involved.
Similarly in development, a child may not walk until 18
months of age but then progress normally or may walk
late, talk late, and be cognitively delayed.

In the Brookline Early Education Project, among a
"community" of nearly 300 children, the importance of
trends was underscored by an analysis of risk status
during the first six months of life. Risk groups were
defined on the basis of physical, developmental, neurological, and perinatal findings at three separate time
points: two weeks, three months, and six months.

Considerable instability of membership in the risk groups
was demonstrated, indicating that early childhood projects
that admit only children at risk should have flexible
admission criteria and that project directors must be
aware of the constantly emerging service needs of children
outside the project as well as those enrolled at a
specific time point (Levine, Palfrey, Lamb, et al., 1971).
A parallel analysis of temperamental characteristics from
birth to six months indicates the same instability of
findings, suggesting that enrollment based on temperamental findings should perhaps be flexible as well
(Kronstadt et al., 1979).

One way of using trends is to look at the changes in
children at both ends of the spectrum. This has been the
analysis design of the Educational Testing Service studies
on Head Start. Using this design the group has been able
to isolate factors responsible for the maintenance of the
good effects of Head Start and to begin to make
recommendations for specific program components (Shipman,
no date). Without an analysis of trends, this could not
have been done.

As programs are analyzed, trends must be kept in
mind. The health and developmental factors that should
be followed carefully over time include health status,
sensory abilities, temperament and behavior, and
developmental performance.

In addition to trends, certain individual health events
can have detrimental effects on child outcomes. It is
important, therefore, that these be registered if and
when they occur. Of specific importance because of their
known effects on the central nervous system are meningitis
and encephalitis, major head trauma, and life-threatening
diseases. Furthermore, it is important to document
"critical life events" that can affect a child's development. Such events as parental separation, divorce, or
death may set a child's development off course and help
explain an intermediate or ultimate outcome. Other
critical events, such as a move or birth of a sibling,
may have temporary but significant impact (either positive
or negative). Finally, the documentation of abuse and
neglect is important as one assesses health outcomes.
Those projects that have been family-centered should be
able to document fewer episodes of domestic turmoil and
abuse than would be otherwise predicted.

Acute health and critical life events such as those
listed above pose a problem for those who are documenting
outcomes, since they do not necessarily occur at the

beginning or the end of the project, and they have little
regularity. Despite these issues, major acute events
often carry with them effects on the lives of children,
and careful documentation of them may help sort out
important health outcomes.

"Graduate" Health Profile

Although evaluators should be judicious in their choice
of timing for analysis, an overall perspective can be
obtained at the end of a program, as assessment is made
of the extent to which initial health objectives for
children were met. For example, the goals of the
Brookline Early Education Project (as conceived by the
superintendent of schools) were that no child would
arrive at kindergarten with any undetected health or
developmental problem and that remediation would be in
place prior to school entry for children with problems
(Pierson, 1974). Table 1 is a checklist of such detect-
able problems (a negative outcomes list), which evaluators
of early childhood projects might want to use as a
conceptual "graduate health profile."

In dealing with early diagnosis and intervention, it
is essential that project planners and evaluators be
fully aware of the negative outcomes likely to occur
during the school years and whose effects the early
projects are intended to minimize. In planning service
and evaluation in an early childhood project, it is
therefore helpful to identify those children who appear
to be at risk for such disorders (Oberklaid and Levine,
1980). That is not to say that all such children are in
fact identifiable during the preschool years--some may
be, others may not. Moreover, children who are likely to
have learning disabilities or other kinds of subtle
dysfunctions during the school years may not manifest
them until they are challenged with specific kinds of
academic or cognitive tasks. In addition, although some
children may appear to reveal dysfunction during the
preschool years, they may function normally later on. At
the beginning, during, and after an early education
program, it is helpful to have a good descriptive account
of the developmental health of those in the program. It
is clear that with increasing knowledge of subtle, "low-
severity, high-prevalence" handicaps of childhood,
developmental descriptions of children should go beyond
the simple, traditional milestones.

Listed below are examples of negative health outcomes, some of whose antecedents may be detected, described, and treated in an early childhood project:

1. Poor Growth and/or Nutrition Children suffering from poor growth or nutrition may stand out in a group setting more than they would in the family. Danger signals of growth failure, poor eating habits, or emotional deprivation may be apparent to those involved with the child on a day-to-day basis.

2. Sensory Deficits Hearing and vision defects, which impair function in school, can be readily detected in early childhood (Palfrey et al., 1980; Strangler et al., 1980). Such deficits, however, are often acquired after school entry.

3. Chronic Illness and Symptoms Chronic illness affects childhood performance in multiple ways--not the least of them being the loss of school days. The burden of chronic disease in children is often accompanied by major psychological and social problems (Sultz et al., 1972). Furthermore, children who need to undergo major or recurring hospitalization may suffer functional setbacks as a result. Although there is little a project can offer to prevent most chronic disease, there are a variety of strategies that can be used to help children cope with or control symptoms.

4. Poor Utilization of Health Services Although it is now rare for children not to have access to primary care, there are still demographic pockets where health care provision is inadequate (E. Newberger et al., 1976; Lowe and Alexander, 1974), and it is exactly these children who are at greatest risk on all health and social factors.

5. Recurrent Trauma The child who suffers from multiple accidents may be permanently impaired. Furthermore, the injuries may have been inflicted intentionally and therefore indicative of serious family and social pathology (Smith and Simpson, 1975; Kempe and Helfer, 1972).

6. Neurological Disorder Neurological disorders can be detected and managed, but it would be unreasonable to expect an early education program to have a major impact on basic disease processes.

7. Neurodevelopmental Dysfunctions Children with minor neurologic markers (Wolfe and Hurwitz, 1966; Vukovich, 1968), serious attention deficits (Levine and Oberklaid, 1980), sequencing problems (Rudel and Denckla,

1976), motor delays (Levine, Oberklaid, Ferb, et al.,
1980), language disabilities (Rutter and Martin, 1972;
Wiig and Semel, 1976; Oberklaid et al., 1979; Denckla,
1978), visual spatial dysfunction (Kephart, 1971; Robinson
and Schwartz, 1973), memory problems on "developmental
output failure" (Levine and Meltzer, 1981), or with
combinations of these symptoms are all at serious
disadvantage in school. To the extent possible, early
childhood programs should address these issues.

   8. Psychosocial Morbidity Major negative outcomes
for children in the behavioral or psychosocial sphere are
disorders of personality development, affect, or
self-esteem. These may interfere seriously with learning
and growth and thwart optimal developmental health
(Connolly, 1971; Rutter, 1974; Simmons and Tymchuk, 1973).

   9. Mental Retardation and Multiple Handicapping
Conditions Early childhood programs have the potential
of reducing the serious burdens faced by retarded and
handicapped children by enhancing the normal aspects of
their lives, encouraging those with handicaps to interact
with other children.

   10. Life-Threatening Diseases Specialized programs
for children with life-threatening diseases and their
families may help to ease their suffering and pain.

   With regard to health outcomes then, evaluations of
early childhood programs should involve background
characteristics of the population (e.g., premature versus
term babies, child abuse versus normal environment); the
evaluators should analyze the program variables as well
as health and developmental trends; and finally, they
should consider which of the 10 health outcomes their
program was best suited to address; the evaluators can
then move on to pose specific evaluation questions.

MEASUREMENT OF HEALTH OUTCOMES

   When assessing the impact of an early chldhood program
on children's health, the questions that can be asked
depend to a great extent on the program's stated goals.
For instance, one program may entail only the assurance
that children are obtaining health care "somewhere";
another may strive to achieve a particular level of
health care for its enrolled children; and a third
program may be directly involved in the provision of some
health services. Clearly, the depth and sophistication
of analysis will vary with program characteristics.

To measure a program's health impact, evaluators can choose from a number of questions, including the following:

1. Did the project assume the <u>completion</u> of standard health maintenance (i.e., regular physical examinations, immunizations, and screening)?
2. Did the project assist in the <u>detection</u> of health problems?
3. Did the project <u>prevent</u> health problems?
4. Did the project's <u>intervention</u> help reduce the incidence or the effect of specific health problems?
5. At what cost were these health activities carried out?

Some of the questions are likely to apply universally to early childhood programs, while others would be relevant only in a program that had targeted a specific health outcome. (See Table 2.)

Standard Preventive Measures

Assurance of Adequate Health Care

A major demonstrable health contribution is access to good health care services. For example, there was dramatic, demonstrable change in the provision of health services to children in Berkshire County, Massachusetts, with the initiation of the Berkshire Health Program (Whitfield and Walker, no date). One can document the extent to which programs have facilitated the use of available, comprehensive, and affordable health care for the children enrolled.

Many authors have pointed to the fact that the fragmented system of health care in the United States has significant inequities and gaps (Institute of Medicine, 1973; E. Newberger et al., 1976; National Research Council, 1976). Specifically, many poor and rural areas are underserved medically, and, furthermore, the quality of health care is inconsistent, even in areas where sufficient personnel are available. Poor children are still more likely to receive care in public clinics characterized by unattractive physical surroundings, long waiting times, overburdened and sometimes impersonal staff, and dependence on hospital emergency service for medical treatment, whereas middle-class children are likely to benefit from more personalized private care.

TABLE 2 Measurements Performed to Document the Health Activity of an Early Childhood Project

	Have these been completed at recommended intervals?	What has been detected?	Can prevention be demonstrated?	Can intervention be demonstrated?	What are the costs of monitoring health?	Does the early childhood project have to perform service?
Physical exam	+				Low	No
Immunization	+				Low	No
Screening	+				Mod/High	Possibly
Developmental assessment	+				Mod/High	Possibly
Access to primary care source		+	+	+	Low/Mod	No
Chronic health problems		+		+	Low/Mod	No
Neurological disorders		+		+	Low/Mod	No
Developmental delay		+		+	Mod/High	Possibly
Behavior problems		+		+	Mod/High	Possibly
Environmental stress		+		+/-	Mod/High	Possibly
Child abuse/neglect		+	+/-	+/-	Mod/High	Possibly
Sensory loss		+		+	Mod/High	Possibly
Accidents		+	+/-	+/-	Mod/High	Possibly
Malnutrition		+	+/-	+/-	Mod/High	Possibly

Note: + means that the question is appropriate for this type of measurement; +/- means that the question may or may not be appropriate for this type of measurement.

Monitors of child health programs may not be able to assess the quality of care the children are receiving but they can document two important outcomes relating to comprehensiveness. First, do the children attend a clinic designed to provide continuing (i.e., not episodic) care (Institute of Medicine, 1977)? Do they have a single primary care source as opposed to multiple facilities or the dependence on emergency rooms and outpatient clinics (Levy et al., 1979)? One possible outcome measure entails "documentation of engagement in a primary care source." Our experience at the Brookline Early Education Project (where 97 percent of families have maintained such a source) has been that six-month updates of this measure have been necessary both for service and documentation purposes. Second, it is also helpful to determine if appropriate preventive services are available for children; these issues are addressed below.

Besides documenting the availability and comprehensiveness of health care, one can determine whether there exist barriers to access of care. In some cases these are physical (Harvard Child Health Project Task Force, 1977; Reynolds et al., 1976); in others, financial (Morris, 1979; E. Newberger et al., 1976; Harvard Child Health Project Task Force, 1977). The experience with Medicaid over the past 15 years has dramatically indicated that cost does stand as a major barrier to health care. Studies by the U.S. Public Health Service (1976) have shown that "in 1964, prior to Medicare and Medicaid, the poor of all ages made fewer physician visits per year than the non-poor did, but by 1974, the poor were using physician services at a somewhat higher rate than the rest of the population." Similarly, Gortmaker has recently shown (1979:18) that the rate of dental service use is directly proportional to the availability of Medicaid and other insurance payments for such care. In addition, in California it has been shown that identification of handicapped children is directly proportional to funds for such endeavors (Office of the Auditor General of California, 1979).

With the advent of Medicaid, in those states in which the program is generously funded, cost may stand as less of a barrier to very poor children than it may to lower-middle-class children. Estimates of child health expenditures per year are in the neighborhood of $300 per child. Monitors of early childhood programs may find that this places a particular burden on those families

not covered by insurance and on those families covered by
proprietary insurance companies, such as Blue Cross/Blue
Shield, that do not always pay for preventive services.
In addition, children with serious handicaps may not be
adequately covered by insurance companies because they
are seen as too risky (U.S. Public Health Service,
1976). Financial barriers to care should be recognized
and adjustments made through advocacy for young children.

Enhanced access is a major health outcome for early
childhood programs, particularly in the presence of
geographic, financial, or other barriers. This "spin-off"
is of major interest to a number of audiences concerned
with the provision of services to young children.

Screening

In some cases early childhood programs themselves may
sponsor health screenings. Others may stop at ensuring
that screening has been performed elsewhere for the
children within their programs. In either case the
percentage of participants who have undergone standard
screening procedures may serve as a useful outcome marker.

Frankenburg (1974) points to a number of criteria for
relevant screening measures. These include prevalence,
importance, cost effectiveness, and interventions available. Monitors of health outcomes for children can
assess the extent to which early education programs have
accomplished screening in the following areas:

1. Vision The American Academy of Pediatrics (1972)
has published guidelines for screening the vision of
young children. Prior to age three it is not really
feasible to obtain accurate measures of visual acuity,
but children can be checked for structural anomalies,
squint, and tumors by means of observation and history.
After age three there are a number of procedures that can
be applied to measure acuity (i.e., Allen, 1957; Lippmann,
1974, 1975; Sheridan, 1970). As part of the evaluation
it is certainly reasonable to determine whether this
service has been provided or arranged for in a preschool
program.

2. Hearing A series of international conferences
have recommended periodic screening of children for
hearing loss (Joint Committee on Infant Hearing
Screening, 1971, 1972). Although there is a highly
specialized technology available to detect hearing

impairment in newborn infants, it is not economically
feasible for mass screening nor does it address the issue
of acquired hearing loss. For these reasons there is
consensus that periodic screening supplemented by a
thorough history is the most justifiable approach to the
screening of young children for hearing loss (Palfrey et
al., 1980). Documentation can include the number of
children screened for hearing and the ages at which it
was accomplished.

3. Lead Intoxication Screening Early childhood
demonstration projects are frequently aimed at services
to poor children. A major epidemic among poor children
has been poisoning from the ingestion of peeling lead
paint and plaster (Chisholm, 1971; Center for Disease
Control, 1975). Needleman et al. (1979) have shown that
chronic or repeated ingestion of small amounts of lead
can cause behavioral symptomatology. With current
techniques, screening for lead poisoning is simple and
accurate. One measure of the adequacy of monitoring of
child health, then, might be the provision of an annual
or semiannual screening for lead poisoning, especially in
geographical areas of high prevalence.

4. Anemia Between 2 and 9 percent of preschool
children suffer from anemia almost entirely on the basis
of iron deficiency. Oski and his coworkers (Oski and
Hinig, 1978; Webb and Oski, 1973) have documented the
behavioral consequences of such anemia. In addition,
anemia is a marker of other nutritional needs. In early
childhood programs, screening for anemia can serve as a
possible indicator of poor health status or of family
needs for nutrition education (Folman, 1977). Such
screening could help policy makers determine the extent
to which supplemental food programs, such as those
incorporated within Head Start, have been valuable and to
what extent they should be continued or augmented.

5. Sickle Cell Screening Sickle cell anemia is a
serious disease affecting approximately 1 percent of the
black population. For those programs serving blacks, the
proportion of children who have had sickle cell testing
can be used as one point for evaluation. An additional
measure with regard to sickle cell screening might consist
of an educational survey of parents to determine their
understanding of sickle cell anemia and sickle cell trait.

6. Dental Screening A recent preschool nutrition
survey indicated that throughout the United States the
prevalence of caries is 2.6 to 3.8 per child (Folman,
1977). Other studies have indicated a higher prevalence

of carious teeth among poor children and those attending
Head Start centers than among middle-class children.
Dental screening is a first step in the prevention of
caries, and its provision can be used to assess the
adequacy of overall health services in a project.

As dental screening is undertaken and recorded, a
variety of policy implications emerge. As with anemia,
dental status may be an indirect measure of nutritional
status. Policy makers can determine the extent to which
educational and nutritional services are being provided
to families. In addition, a variety of staffing needs
may be demonstrated, including the necessity for dental
services within a particular program.

Immunizations

In addition to screening, preschool projects can
monitor immunization status, which is one major measure
of a child's health. Recent studies indicate that as
many as 40 percent of the nation's children are not
adequately immunized (Center for Disease Control, 1977).
Reasons for this include poor health care distribution,
family mobility, and noncompliance as well as recent
public apathy about the importance of childhood
immunization.

Clearly, the documentation of immunization levels as a
program outcome measure is of direct benefit to the
individual program. In the larger sense, it is helpful
on the local, state, and federal levels for the documentation of important epidemiological information. In
addition, a recent study by Minear and Guyer (1979) as
well as a study by the Medical Foundation of Massachusetts
(Gottlieb and Wechsler, 1976) have indicated that the
level of immunization within a community can be greatly
enhanced by close and tenacious monitoring at either the
clinic or the school level.

Physical Examination

Completion of periodic physical examinations can serve
as an outcome measure related to child health practices
for a given program. The actual frequency of such
assessments is a matter of continuing controversy. Local
standards should be reviewed, and recommendations should
be made to participants in a project. Compliance could
be a useful health-related outcome.

Developmental Screening

To date, guidelines for developmental screening are at
a more primitive stage than those for vision, hearing,
lead, and anemia screening (Meier, 1973; Meissels, 1978),
in part because developmental screening is particularly
complex and time-consuming. Those involved in the process
have become increasingly convinced that the best approach
is a comprehensive assessment that includes a substantial,
if brief, look at the following areas: (1) gross motor
skill, (2) fine motor function, (3) visual motor integration, (4) receptive language, (5) expressive language,
(6) memory, (7) experiential learning, and (8) behavior
(Levine, Oberklaid, Ferb, et al., 1980).

As an outcome measure, monitors of child preschool
programs can document whether screening procedures have
been carried out over the time period of the program. In
addition, it may be worthwhile to describe what type of
developmental assessment was used and what staff members
carried out the test. The importance of such documentation is that developmental screening on a large scale has
not been performed in this country. However, with the
Early and Periodic Screening, Diagnosis, and Treatment
Program (Frankenburg and North, 1974), the Education for
All Handicapped Children Act (Palfrey et al., 1978), and
state laws recently generated to comply with the federal
regulations, states are being asked to perform developmental assessments of young children. To the extent that
large numbers of data about a variety of assessments can
be gathered, this will help to determine what sorts of
assessment are of most value. The developmental status
of participants can be an important measure for a project.
The demonstration of higher mean performance levels or a
smaller proportion of suboptimal "scores" can be convincing evidence of program efficacy.

Beyond Screening: Detection

Indicating numbers of cases of any disorder detected
in a program can help policy planners in given cities or
rural areas become familiar with the major preschool
health problems in their areas. One would not expect to
find the same prevalence rates for all disorders in all
locations. A project may need to demonstrate a reduction
in the prevalence of one or more conditions in order to
argue convincingly for a significant health impact. This
process may be difficult for several reasons:

(1) existing or expected prevalence rates may not be available or obtainable, (2) a nonparticipant comparison group may be needed, and (3) reporting may be incomplete even within the program.

Prevention

Early childhood programs may be able to demonstrate prevention in a number of important areas, including health care neglect, child abuse and neglect, accidents, and malnutrition. These are primarily areas in which family involvement is needed and in which a clear goal must be set in order to identify effects. To document prevention, evaluators would need data substantiating specific problems in these areas prior to entry into the program (i.e., preprogram prevalence data) or a well-matched contemporaneous control group or large-scale norms for the conditions under study.

Intervention

Many early childhood programs are in effect early intervention programs. The children enter because of handicaps or at-risk status, and attempts are made to alleviate their handicaps or to decrease the special risk. Demonstrating the effects of intervention requires meticulous attention to background variables, program design, and outcomes. The question always in the evaluator's mind is: Would this child have been the same in the absence of the program? This question may not be thoroughly answered, but the compilation of data on similar children inside and outside a program as well as the comparison of youngsters in dissimilar programs will help evaluators judge the likely effect of a program.

Equipped with a number of possible questions, the health evaluator must make decisions regarding the method of evaluation. The next section discusses seven prototypes of health evaluation.

PROTOTYPES OF EVALUATION

The selection of one or more prototypes for evaluation of health services is dependent on multiple factors. First, as noted above, a project is most likely to show

gains in areas that are consistent with its objectives.
Thus, evaluation plans should include systematic scrutiny
of those areas of health that were specifically targeted
for prevention or intervention. Second, the choice of an
evaluation prototype depends on the nature and number of
resources available for the evaluation process. Certainly
some of the evaluation plans discussed below are far more
costly (financially and in terms of human resources) than
others. Third, there may be ethical constraints on a
particular type of evaluation, especially with regard to
the use of comparison groups who receive little or no
intervention. Fourth, the choice is influenced by the
availability of adequate measuring instruments for the
type of evaluation desired. If, for example, it is felt
that the major health impact will be on parenting, then
one may have to decide whether there are good outcome-
measuring instruments for this. If not, another type of
evaluation may be needed that does not require the
documentation of specific outcomes. Fifth, the best type
of evaluation depends to some extent on the numbers of
children involved and more particularly on the kind of
morbidity one wishes to assess. If the latter has a low
prevalence, comparison group studies that will be able to
demonstrate statistically significant differences will be
hard to achieve. In general, the smaller the quantitative
differences in outcome, the larger the numbers of children
that will need to be involved. Six, as noted above, it
is critically important to determine the nature of the
constituency for whom the evaluation is undertaken. That
which will persuade one audience may be ineffective or
irrelevant to the deliberations of another.

The prototypes we describe in this section are by no
means exhaustive. Other forms of evaluation might be
suggested. The seven systems described below are based
on our own experience in planning and implementing an
evaluation for the Brookline Early Education Project.

Comparison Studies

In health-related studies of outcome that use a
comparison group, statistically significant differences
should emerge when one compares a treatment with a
nontreatment group. This methodology carries with it
numerous intellectual and ethical hazards. When it is
effective, a comparative methodology is likely to be the
most convincing, especially to scientific or academic

groups. It is the most amenable to quantitative statistical analysis. In applying this form of evaluative strategy, the following questions need to be considered:

* Should the comparison group be selected and randomized at the same time as the program group?
* Should the comparison group be followed concurrently and evaluated periodically at the same time as the treatment group?
* Is it possible for the comparison group to be evaluated in a truly "blind" fashion? Or is it likely that independent evaluators will still know which children were part of a program?
* Are the outcomes to be measured likely to yield relevant differences between the groups that are great enough to have statistical significance?
* To what extent will the comparison group receive intervention? More specifically, if pathological findings occur during evaluations, will some form of feedback, surveillance, or active intervention be recommended, despite the fact that the children are not in the program?
* Would the design be strengthened by supplementing or replacing ongoing comparison groups with cross-sectional, i.e., "nonlongitudinal," groups? To overcome possible intervention effects for the comparison group, one might want to recruit new subjects for comparison at certain points in the project.
* What is one prepared to do if the comparison group and the treatment group turn out to be ill matched on various extraneous factors (e.g., socioeconomic status, parent educational level, and birth history)? How can this be avoided?

These issues are critical to the design of such evaluations. Once they are dealt with, one can proceed with the selection of the precise outcome measures desired. After selecting the outcome measures, it is helpful to develop mock tables to determine the likelihood of various kinds of outcomes and thus ensure that the numbers in the comparison and experimental groups will be adequate to demonstrate significant differences that may occur.

In many instances, comparison studies need to focus on differential impacts on targeted subgroups. For example, if one wanted to study program effects on children with

chronic diseases or on those with sociodemographic risk
factors, one would need to be certain that there were
comparable and sufficient numbers of such target children
in the experimental and comparison groups. The relatively
low prevalence of most chronic medical problems in childhood can certainly have an impact on the nature of the
outcome study. In the Brookline Early Education Project,
it was necessary to develop clusters of morbidity so that
they could be measurable in sufficient quantity. For
example, among the 300 children studied, there were not
enough premature infants or infants born with jaundice.
However, the use of a composite rating system to characterize a subgroup with high or moderately high levels of
perinatal risk enabled us to amass a large enough group
to evaluate possible program effects. Such a process
does run the risk of "mixing apples and oranges" or
scrutinizing artifical categories.

When comparison groups are not recruited at the same
time as the experimental groups, it is difficult to match
them. If they are noncontemporaneous, it is likely that
the children have undergone changes over time. Even with
contemporaneous comparison groups, there are likely to be
volunteer effects. Parents who agree to have their
children evaluated without benefit of services may be a
very different kind of group from those who agree to
participate in a project. For this reason, whenever
possible it is best to have a random assignment of a
comparison group that is selected at the same time and
from the same pool as the subjects in the regular program.

Comparison group studies are most credible if the
evaluators of the children are not part of the project
itself and are unable to distinguish between participants
and nonparticipants. This can be difficult, because often
times much outcome data need to be obtained through
history taking, during which it is possible, if not
likely, that an evaluator will discover whether a child
has been in the program.

Outcome Studies Without Comparison Groups

In certain instances it may be possible to perform
outcome studies without comparison groups. Such descriptive analyses can be convincing, especially if the
outcomes measured are comparable with those of other
studies or else face valid in general. The following
example might be useful: If in a particular project one

of the major goals is to minimize or prevent the effects of child abuse and neglect, it might be possible to study this without a comparison group. If good data are available about local community prevalence rates for such problems, then the project's documentation of a diminished occurrence may demonstrate effectiveness. One problem for such studies is the likelihood of better reporting within the project than in the community at large, which can tend to diminish the differences. Conditions such as child abuse are likely to be underreported in the nonprogram group.

If the results are dramatic enough, prevalence data may not even be necessary. For example, if a project has not had a single instance of child abuse, that fact has a high level of face validity and does not require the invocation of comparison groups or other studies.

In summary, if good data are available from a comparable population, or if a project is likely to have dramatic face-valid findings, an outcome study without a comparison group can be an effective and economical evaluation system.

Longitudinal Study of Findings

Sometimes it is difficult to draw a clear line between program documentation and evaluation. A careful account of what has occurred in a project can in itself serve as one dimension of evaluation. Early in the history of the Brookline Early Education Project we were asked a key question of interest to public policy makers: "What are you finding, and what are you doing about it?" The need to be responsive to this inquiry led to the development of a method that we have called the Longitudinal Study of Findings (Pierson et al., 1980). It is a project-auditing system with the primary stress on a basic unit called a "finding," defined as a diagnostic observation suggesting service need. The latter might consist of direct intervention or ongoing monitoring and surveillance.

An interdisciplinary team met to discuss each child as he or she passed the age of 42 months. There was an account of all findings for each child, derived from direct classroom experience, physical examinations, neurodevelopmental assessments, psychological tests, and parent reports. Each finding for each child was rated according to a series of relevant measures including severity, certainty (versus the equivocal nature of a

particular finding), predictive significance, prescriptive
significance, prior knowledge of the finding (i.e.,
whether this was the first documentation of the finding),
category of finding (e.g., developmental, health, educational, psychosocial) and modalities of management,
treatment, or observation. Each finding was subject to
longitudinal tracking. After one year there was
accountability for each finding, e.g., whether it had
vanished, diminished, changed in character, remained the
same, or gotten worse. Compliance with the treatment
program also was rated.

Through the Longitudinal Study of Findings a number of
basic questions could be addressed:

- What did you find when you looked at this popula-
tion of children at a particular age?
- What did you decide to do based on what you found?
- What proportion of your findings were predictive
of later problems with health or function?
- What proportion of your findings were in fact
remediable or amenable to some form of treatment?
- What proportion of your findings were both
predictive of later problems and remediable?
- What kinds of treatments did you recommend?
- What proportion of your children required which
kinds of intervention?
- Which forms of intervention were most likely to
engender compliance?
- What 12-month treatment-related outcomes were
seen with regard to the findings?

The Longitudinal Study of Findings as used in the
Brookline Early Education Project was a useful method of
auditing program documentation; it has, however, like
other methods, had some shortcomings. First, the study
was undertaken without a comparison group, making it
difficult to attribute the resolution of findings to
program effects. Second, such an audit system (at least
as it was carried out) is expensive, involving teams of
professionals in prolonged discussions of findings. One
can argue that this activity is also an important dimension of service, since it requires systematic thinking on
the part of the program staff about the needs of participating children. Third, certain aspects of the
Longitudinal Study of Findings are necessarily arbitrary.
For example, the system used to classify findings is
subjective. If one uncovers "hyperactivity" in a child,

for example, is it a medical finding? Is it developmental? Educational? Psychosocial? In our experience
many such dilemmas occurred; the formulation of precise
ground rules was essential, and a detailed scoring manual
was compiled. Fourth, the Longitudinal Study of Findings
is essentially a pathological model. Ideally, findings
should include not only problems but also identified
strengths and their outcomes, although this would, of
course, increase the cost of the process. Finally, to be
useful the Longitudinal Study of Findings must make
distinctions in the effects of findings from child to
child. A particular abnormality in one child may suggest
greater significance and service need than the same
finding in another child. For example, a child with a
language disability who comes from a deprived environment
is likely to have a worse prognosis than a child with
similar language delays in a more enriched milieu.

The Longitudinal Study of Findings prototype can be of
value to public policy makers. For one thing, it enables
one to estimate personnel requirements in an early childhood project. If it turns out that language disabilities
have a high prevalence, then it may follow that the
special educators or early educators in the project should
be trained specifically to deal with these dysfunctions.
The necessity and/or time requirements for a nurse or
physician may depend on the yield of medical findings in
a particular project, although this will vary from site
to site. The Longitudinal Study of Findings can help
answer one question that is particularly germane: What
would have happened to this group of children if the
program did not exist? By looking at an inventory of
findings within the project and by estimating their
prescriptive and predictive effects, one can begin to
assess the toll of neglect. One can develop an argument
about those findings that would go undetected and
untreated were the project not in place. One can then
examine the cost to children and the community of this
degree of neglect. Such data can argue for or against
the value of an early childhood program affecting health.

Case Argument Studies

An economical and often compelling form of evaluation
can be undertaken as "case argument studies." We have
used the word "argument" to differentiate such evaluation
processes from mere testimonials or anecdotal accounts.

In a case argument study one presents a series of clinical examples that include convincing evidence of the impact of the project on a child's or a family's health. The evaluators need to choose successful examples and assemble documented case studies demonstrating program effects. It may be necessary to refer to the literature (i.e., a normative base) on various subjects in order to make a convincing argument that without this project a particular child's health would have been compromised. It is not sufficient to describe programs and changes: Convincing arguments should be made that the changes related causally to program effects and that the particular findings related in the case were unlikely to be self-limited or transient. A case argument study should try to prove the fact that alternative services in the community could not deal as well with this particular child's health issues. One can liken a case argument study to an attorney's brief for use in court. As an argument for the success of a program, it cannot rest its case on circumstantial evidence but must have multiple interlocking substantiations for the efficacy of the program in a particular case.

To summarize, a good case argument study of a child should include the following:

* Full description of the child's conditions and/or vulnerabilities and their severity.
* Argument about the potential negative consequences of relative neglect of these issues.
* Analysis of the cost (financial and human) of neglect or delay.
* Consideration of the cost of detection in the program.
* Presentation of the likelihood of alternative detection or management in the community were the program not in existence.
* Description of the outcome and the likelihood of durable effects of the program on the child.

Such case argument studies can be convincing to public policy makers. Even if quantitative program effects cannot be demonstrated for a project, a selection of well-chosen cases can justify its existence. To cite an extreme example, one might argue that if a project with 300 children in it can prevent 2 of them from becoming juvenile delinquents by age 13, it has more than justified its existence and can be deemed to have a favorable cost-benefit ratio. In all likelihood, it is best for a project to present a number of diverse case argument studies. It is most helpful if these studies can relate directly to some of the primary objectives of the program.

Process Studies of Health

Process studies constitute another important prototype for health evaluation. Documentation of parental satisfaction, attitudinal changes, and sensitivity to health needs are among the relevant dimensions of process evaluation in this area.

Process studies can be undertaken using standardized parent interviews or questionnaires. In several investigations, health diaries have been used to document feelings and behaviors related to health. Such diaries can be useful in both process and outcome studies.

As part of standardized interviews, parents can be asked about their overall levels of satisfaction with the health aspects of an early education project. Listed below are examples of useful questions:

- Did you feel that the doctors (or nurses) in the project were sympathetic and understood your child's needs?
- Were you comfortable or somewhat afraid about asking them questions?
- Did you often have to wait a long time to be seen for a health examination?
- Did the health personnel use words you didn't understand?
- Do you think that the health personnel were good with your child or baby?
- Did you think that the feedback you received from them was adequate?
- Did they often make you afraid?
- Did the personnel in the project communicate well with your own doctor?
- Do you feel that the health part of this project was helpful even though you have your own doctor outside the project?
- Did the health part of this project help you in any way to use your own doctor better?
- Do you feel more knowledgeable about health issues as a result of participating in this project?

• Do you have more confidence in your own ability to make health-related decisions now that you have been in the project?

• Have you switched physicians or sources of medical care while you have been in the project?

• Do you think the project had anything to do with these changes?

• Can you describe anything in the health area that you are doing differently now as a result of having been in the project?

The answers to questions like these can be assembled in such a way as to give a good composite picture of the effect of a program on behavior and attitude. One can also relate, at least qualitatively, a sense of the degree of satisfaction with the health aspects of a project. In interpreting such data, it is of course critical to bear in mind that satisfaction and efficacy may be very different dimensions. There can be a vast discrepancy between what people think they want from a project and what they actually need. A process study may be more effective in getting at "wants" than at needs.

Process studies need not be limited to parents. In the Brookline Early Education Project we undertook a process study of local pediatricians to determine the impact of the project's early-school health services on the practicing community (Hanson and Levine, 1980). The local physicians' satisfaction, awareness, and sensitivity to the project were assayed through a standardized questionnaire. An important advantage of process studies is their ability to evaluate the impact of a project on a broader array of constituents, including those providing existing services, personnel in the schools, professionals within the project itself, trainees, and those responsible for the future care of the children. Another advantage is that process studies can be an ongoing activity, providing relatively immediate feedback and evaluation throughout the life of the program.

Tracer Studies

The use of tracer studies can be economical and effective in evaluating the health impact of a project (Kessner et al., 1974). In these investigations a few key measures, consistent with the objectives of the program, are isolated and sought within the program. The

tracers used should be well documented in the literature,
so that expected prevalence estimates can be obtained.
For example, a good tracer for the efficacy of a health-
related project might be the immunization rate of its
participants. Several other tracers might also be
selected. For example, in an evaluation of pediatric
practices undertaken several years ago, the frequency of
throat cultures was used. This was thought to be a good
index of the thoroughness of a pediatrician. Was he or
she in the habit of prescribing antibiotics without
cultures? Or was a culture usually taken first? In an
early childhood project, three or four tracers might
indicate efficacy, such as the prevalence of accidents or
accidental poisoning, hospitalization rates, alterations
in the use of emergency rooms, the existence of a primary
care source, the ability to name a dentist, or the
existence of certain kinds of safety devices in the home
or automobile.

The assumption underlying the selection of tracers is
that they somehow typify the overall health status of a
child. Sometimes there can be an inherent circularity in
this, particularly when the objectives are too close to
the tracer. For example, if parents in a project were
given safety caps to insert in electric outlets to
prevent shock, and the existence of such devices in the
parents' homes was used as a tracer, the outcome might
not be representative of health status in general.

Tracer studies may or may not entail a comparison
group. They can be descriptive insofar as there exist
data from other studies or face validity for each
specific tracer.

Cost-Benefit Studies

Cost factors can be a part of the prototypes of
evaluation mentioned in this chapter. Often it is
possible to integrate measurements of costs and benefits
into assessments of outcome or process. An analysis of a
series of outcomes might entail a careful examination of
the expenditures that produced these outcomes. In a case
argument study it can be important to document the cost
per child of various evaluations. As projects increasingly merge health and early education activities, it is
essential to document additional costs.

Fundamental questions need to be answered:

• Should a project have its own health education
screening or service component? Or should it use
existing pediatric services in the community? How
extensive should the health component of an early
childhood project be?

• If children are to receive health examinations,
what should they include? Which components of health
evaluation are least likely to be covered by other
programs in the community?

• Are there clear savings to be had by consolidating
health and educational services? For example, if
assessments are to be made of educational readiness in
young children, is there some economy to be derived from
combining these with a preschool physical, neurological,
and sensory examination? Does the combination of such
services yield diagnostic benefits that might not be
present were they fragmented?

The answers to these questions can be derived as part
of project evaluations. However, they will never be
uniformly applicable throughout the United States. The
nature of existing resources, the goals of a particular
project, the nature of a population served, the values of
existing service providers, and public policy makers are
all likely to have strong impacts on the analysis of
costs and benefits.

Choosing a Prototype

While the prototypes listed above are certainly not
the only ones available and combinations are possible,
evaluators must choose among alternative designs. Clearly
the best way to make the choice is to start with the
question for which an answer is desired, since certain
questions dictate certain approaches.

Table 3 matches the types of questions that have been
raised at the Brookline Early Education Project with the
seven suggested evaluation prototypes. As indicated in
the table, a given prototype may be appropriate for one
question or one project but not for another. For
instance, when we wanted to know the prevalence of
hearing defects, an outcome study with or without a
comparison group and a longitudinal study of findings
were both appropriate, while case arguments, process
studies, and tracer studies were not. When our interest
was the prevention of early school dysfunction, clearly

TABLE 3 Evaluation Prototypes Considered in the Brookline Early Education Project

Question	Outcome Studies With Comparison Group			Outcome Studies Without Comparison Group			Longitudinal Study of Findings			Case Study Arguments			Process Studies			Tracer Studies			Cost-Benefit Studies		
	Appropriateness	Cost	Nos. needed	Appropriateness	Cost	Nos. needed	Appropriateness	Cost	Nos. needed	Appropriateness	Cost	Nos. needed	Appropriateness	Cost	Nos. needed	Appropriateness	Cost	Nos. needed	Appropriateness	Cost	Nos. needed
Have planned health activities been completed?	Medium	Medium	Medium	Medium	Low	Low/Medium	Medium	High	Medium	No	--	--	No	--	--	Low/--	Medium	Medium	Low	Low	Any
What has been detected?	Medium	High	High	Medium	Low	Low/Medium	High	High	Medium	No	--	--	No	--	--	No	--	--	Low/--	Low	Any
Can prevention be demonstrated?	Medium	High	High	Low	Medium	Medium/High	Low/--	High	Medium	Low	Low/Medium	Low	No	--	--	Low/--	Medium	Medium	Medium	High	High
Can specific interventions be proved effective?	Medium	High	High	No	--	--	No	--	--	Low	Low/Medium	Low	No	--	--	Low/--	Medium	Medium	Medium	High	Medium/High
Can parent satisfaction be shown?	No	--	--	No	--	--	No	--	--	No	--	--	Medium	Low	Low/Medium	No	--	--	No	--	--

only the outcome studies with comparison groups or cost-benefit studies would suffice. For a question such as parent satisfaction, elaborate comparison group studies were neither necessary nor appropriate, and information obtained from a process study would have limited applicability.

The scope of child health is very wide, and evaluators of early childhood programs should plan carefully before they launch a health evaluation, defining the variables they want to use (particularly background and outcome), the questions they want to answer, and then select the one or two evaluation prototypes that are most likely to yield answers.

CONCLUSION

In surveying the various prototypes for the evaluation of the health impact of a program, it is clear that they are not mutually exclusive. In many instances projects may want to apply more than one prototype to assess a program's efficacy. None of these is foolproof; all need careful application and meticulous interpretation. A large project may need separate evaluations of specific aspects of health care influence. For example, if one can demonstrate that a particular project benefited the health of children in some way, one may then proceed to ask: What aspect(s) of the program had the greatest influence in this regard? It may be that health education made the difference. Or it may be that specific diagnostic examinations or fastidious feedback to the local physician was the major positive influence. Isolating one or more elements of service that were particularly useful obviously has public policy implications. A future project may try to allocate its resources to only those aspects of health services that are likely to have the greatest payoff. Thus, all programs should analyze subcomponents of their health services in order to discern the most beneficial elements.

Measuring the impact of an early childhood project on health has significant implications for medical professionals. It is likely that many of the same methods can be applied to the examination of medical program efficacy. The study of evaluation research can therefore reap benefits for health care research as well as education and public policy determination. If the technology of evaluation is to continue to grow and meet the needs of public policy makers and investigators, cross-fertilization between disciplines is likely to accelerate the process. We will have achieved a great deal if this paper can help foster such collaboration.

REFERENCES

Alberman, E. D., and Goldstein, H.
(1970) The "at risk" register, a statistical evaluation. British Journal of Preventive and Social Medicine 24:129-135.

Allen, H. F.
(1957) Testing visual acuity in preschool children: norms, variables and a new picture test. Pediatrics 19:1093-1100.

American Academy of Pediatrics, Committee on Children with Handicaps
(1972) Vision screening in preschool children. Pediatrics 50:966-967.

Baddeley, A.
(1976) The Psychology of Memory. New York: Basic Books.

Badger, E., Burns, D., and Rhoads, B.
(1976) Education for adolescent mothers in a hospital setting. American Journal of Public Health 66:469-472.

Balinsky, W., and Berger, R.
(1975) A review of the research on general health status indices. Medical Care 13:283-295.

Bell, R. Q., Weller, G. M., and Walding, M. F.
(1971) Newborn and preschoolers: organization of behavior and relations between periods. Monograph of the Society for Research in Child Development 36(1-2).

Bleck, E. E.
(1971) The shoeing of children--sham or science? Developmental Medicine and Child Neurology 13:188-195.

Brewer, G. D., and Kakalik, J. S.
(1979) Handicapped Children. New York: McGraw Hill.

Bricker, D. D., and Iacino, R.
(1977) Early intervention with severely/profoundly handicapped children. In E. Sontag, ed., Educational Programming for the Severely and Profoundly Handicapped. Reston, Va.: Council for Exceptional Children.

Broman, S. H., Nichols, P. L., and Kennedy, W. A.
    (1975) Preschool IQ: Prenatal and Developmental
            Correlates. New York: John Wiley & Sons, Inc.
Bronfenbrenner, U.
    (1975) Is early education effective? In H. J.
            Leichter, ed., The Family as Educator. New
            York: Teachers College Press, Columbia
            University.
Bureau of Education for the Handicapped
    (1979) Progress Toward a Free, Appropriate Public
            Education. A Report to Congress on the
            Implementation of Public Law 94-142: The
            Education for All Handicapped Children Act.
            HEW Publication No. (OE) 79-05003.
            Washington, D.C.: U.S. Department of Health,
            Education, and Welfare.
Carey, W. B., Fox, M., and McDevitt, S. C.
    (1977) Temperament as a factor in early school
            adjustment. Pediatrics 60:621-624.
Cassady, G.
    (1975) Perinatal outcome and referral age.
            Pediatrics 56:160.
Center for Disease Control
    (1975) Increased Lead Absorption and Lead Poisoning
            in Young Children. Atlanta, Ga.: U.S.
            Department of Health, Education, and Welfare.
Center for Disease Control
    (1977) Summary of Immunization Status: Preliminary
            Report: U.S. Immunization Survey, 1976.
            Atlanta, Ga.: U.S. Department of Health,
            Education, and Welfare.
Chance, G. W., O'Brien, M. J., and Swyer, P. R.
    (1973) Transportation of sick neonates, 1972: an
            unsatisfactory aspect of medical care.
            Canadian Medical Association Journal 109:847.
Chisholm, J. J.
    (1971) Lead poisoning. Scientific American 224:15-23.
Connolly, C.
    (1971) Social and emotional factors in learning
            disabilities. In H. R. Myklebust, ed.,
            Progress in Learning Disabilities. Vol. II.
            New York: Grune & Stratton, Inc.
Cowell, H. R.
    (1977) Shoes and shoe corrections. Pediatric Clinic
            of North America 24:791-797.

Davie, R., Butler, N., and Goldstein, H.
  (1972) From Birth to Seven: The Second Report of the
          National Child Development Study. London:
          Longman.
Denckla, M.
  (1978) Naming of object-drawings by dyslexic and
          other learning disabled children. Brain and
          Language 3:231.
Dingle, J. H.
  (1964) Illness in the Home. Cleveland, Ohio: The
          Press of Case Western Reserve University.
Dingle, J. H.
  (1966) The common cold and common cold like
          illnesses. Medical Times 94:186-190.
Elardo, R., Bradley, R., and Caldwell, B. M.
  (1975) The relation of infant's home environments to
          mental test performance from six to thirty-six
          months: a longitudinal analysis. Child
          Development 46:71-76.
Fitzhardinge, P. M.
  (1975) Early growth and development in low
          birthweight infants following treatment in an
          intensive care nursery. Pediatrics 56:162-172.
Fitzhardinge, P. M., and Steven, E. M.
  (1972) The small for date infant. II. Neurological
          and intellectual sequelae. Pediatrics
          50:50-57.
Folman, S. J.
  (1977) Nutritional Disorders of Children:
          Prevention, Screening and Follow-up. HEW
          Publication No. (HSA) 77-5104 Washington,
          D.C.: U.S. Department of Health, Education,
          and Welfare.
Frankenburg, W. K.
  (1974) Selection of diseases and tests in pediatric
          screening. Pediatrics 54:612-616.
Frankenburg, W. K., and North, A. F.
  (1974) A Guide to Screening for the Early and
          Periodic Screening, Diagnosis and Treatment
          Program (EPSDT) Under Medicaid. HEW
          Publication No. (SRS) 74-24516. Washington,
          D.C.: U.S. Department of Health, Education,
          and Welfare.
Giebink, G. S., and Quie, P. G.
  (1978) Otitis media: the spectrum of middle ear
          inflammation. Annual Review of Medicine
          29:285-306.

Goldstein, K. M., Caputo, D. V., and Taub, H. B.
(1976)   The effects of prenatal and perinatal
         complications on development at one year of
         age. Child Development 47:613-621.
Gortmaker, S. L.
(1979)   Access to and Utilization of Ambulatory
         Medical and Dental Services Among Children in
         Genesee County, Michigan. Community Child
         Health Studies, Harvard School of Public
         Health, Cambridge.
Gottlieb, N. H., and Wechsler, H.
(1976)   Immunization levels in Boston schools--a
         second look. New England Journal of Medicine
         294:1459.
Haggerty, R. J.
(1965)   Family diagnosis: research methods and their
         reliability for studies of the medical-social
         unit, the family. American Journal of Public
         Health 55:1521-1533.
Haggerty, R. J.
(1976)   Who will monitor access? Pediatrics
         57:169-170.
Haggerty, R. J., Roghmann, K. J., and Pless, I. B.
(1975)   Child Health and the Community. New York:
         John Wiley & Sons, Inc.
Hanson, M. A., and Levine, M. D.
(1980)   Early school health: an analysis of its
         impact on primary care. Journal of School
         Health 50:577-580.
Harvard Child Health Project Task Force
(1977)   Toward a Primary Medical Care System
         Responsive to Children's Needs. Cambridge,
         Mass.: Ballinger Publishing Co.
Hayden, A. H., and McGuiness, G. D.
(1977)   Bases for early intervention. In E. Sontag,
         ed., Educational Programming for the Severely
         and Profoundly Handicapped. Reston, Va.:
         Council for Exceptional Children.
Horton, K. B.
(1976)   Early intervention for hearing-impaired
         infants and young children. In T. Tjossem,
         ed., Intervention Strategies for High Risk
         Infants and Young Children. Baltimore, Md.:
         University Park Press.
Institute of Medicine
(1973)   Infant Death: An Analysis by Maternal Risk
         and Health Care. Washington, D.C.: National
         Academy of Sciences.

102

Institute of Medicine
  (1977) <u>Primary Care in Medicine. A Definition</u>.
          Washington, D.C.: National Academy of
          Sciences.
Joint Committee on Infant Hearing Screening
  (1971) Joint committee statement on infant hearing
          screening. <u>Journal of the American Speech and
          Hearing Association</u> 13:79.
Joint Committee on Infant Hearing Screening
  (1972) Joint committee statement on infant hearing
          screening. <u>Journal of the American Speech and
          Hearing Association</u> 16:160.
Kempe, C. H., and Helfer, R. E., eds.
  (1972) <u>Helping the Battered Child and His Family</u>.
          Philadelphia, Pa.: J. B. Lippincott Co.
Kephart, N. C.
  (1971) <u>The Slow Learner in the Classroom</u>. Columbus,
          Ohio: Charles E. Merrill.
Kessner, D. M., Snow, C. K., and Singer, J.
  (1974) <u>The Assessment of Medical Care for Children</u>.
          Volume 3. Washington, D.C.: Institute of
          Medicine.
Klaus, M. H., and Kennell, J. H.
  (1976) <u>Maternal-Infant Bonding</u>. St. Louis, Mo.:
          C. V. Mosby Co.
Knobloch, H., and Pasamanick, B.
  (1966) Prospective studies on the epidemiology of
          reproductive causalty: methods, findings and
          some implications. <u>Merrill-Palmer Quarterly
          of Behavior and Development</u> 12:27-43.
Koff, E., Boyle, P., and Pueschel, S. M.
  (1977) Perceptual-motor functioning in children with
          phenylketonuria. <u>American Journal of Diseases
          of Children</u> 131:1084-1087.
Kopelman, A. E.
  (1978) The smallest preterm infant. <u>American Journal
          of Diseases of Children</u> 132:461-462.
Kronstadt, D., Oberklaid, F., Ferb, T., and Swartz, J.
  (1979) Infant behavior and maternal adaptation in the
          first six months of life. <u>American Journal of
          Orthopsychiatry</u> 49(3):454-464.
Lazar, I.
  (1977) The Persistence of Preschool Effects: A
          Long-Term Follow-up of 14 Infant and Preschool
          Experiments. Report prepared for the Adminis-
          tration for Children, Youth, and Families,
          U.S. Department of Health, Education, and

Welfare by the Education Commission of the States.

Levine, M. D.
(1979) The School Function Program: Profile of a General Pediatrics Consultative Service Model. Report prepared for the Robert Wood Johnson Foundation under Grant No. 4293.

Levine, M. D., and Oberklaid, F.
(1980) Hyperactivity--symptom complex or complex symptom. American Journal of Diseases of Children 134:409-414.

Levine, M. D., Brooks, R., and Shonkoff, J. P.
(1980) A Pediatric Approach to Learning Disorders. New York: Wiley Medical.

Levine, M. D., and Meltzer, L.
(1981) Developmental output failure: impaired productivity in the school aged child. Pediatrics 67:18-25.

Levine, M. D., Oberklaid, F., Ferb, T. E., Hanson, M. A., Palfrey, J. S., and Aufseeser, C. L.
(1980) The pediatric examination of educational readiness: validation of an extended observation procedure. Pediatrics 66:341-349.

Levine, M. D., Palfrey, J. S., Lamb, G. A., et al.
(1977) Infants in a public school system: the indicators of early health and educational need. Pediatrics 60:579-587.

Levy, J. D., Bonanno, R. A., Schwartz, C. G., and Sanofsky, P. A.
(1979) Primary care: patterns of use of pediatric medical facilities. Medical Care 17:881-893.

Lippmann, O.
(1974) Directions for Use of the H.O.T.V. Test. The Good-Lite Company, Forest Park, Ill.

Lippmann, O., Illiterate, E., Frankenburg, W. K., and Camp, B. W., eds.
(1975) Pediatric Screening Tests. Springfield, Ill.: Charles C Thomas.

Lowe, C. U., and Alexander, D. F.
(1974) Health care of poor children. In A. Schorr, ed., Children and Decent People. New York: Basic Books.

Meier, J.
(1973) Screening and Assessment of Young Children at Developmental Risk. President's Committee on Mental Retardation. HEW Publication No. OS-73-90. Washington, D.C.: U.S. Department of Health, Education, and Welfare.

Meier, J.
   (1975)   Early intervention in the prevention of mental
            retardation. Pp. 385-409 in A. Milunsky, ed.,
            Prevention of Genetic Disease and Mental
            Retardation. Philadelphia, Pa.: W. B.
            Saunders Company.
Meissels, S. J.
   (1978)   A Guide to Early Childhood Developmental
            Screening. Massachusetts State Department of
            Education.
Miller, F. J. W., Court, S. D. M., Walton, W. S., and
Knox, E. G.
   (1960)   Growing Up in Newcastle Upon Tyne. London:
            Oxford University Press.
Milunsky, A.
   (1975)   Prevention of Genetic Disease and Mental
            Retardation. Philadelphia, Pa.: W. B.
            Saunders Company.
Minear, R. E., and Guyer, B.
   (1979)   Assessing immunization services at a
            neighborhood health center. Pediatrics
            63:416-419.
Morris, A. G., London, R., and Glick, J.
   (1976)   Educational intervention for preschool
            children in a pediatric clinic. Pediatrics
            57:765-768.
Morris, J. N.
   (1979)   Social inequalities undiminished. Lancet
            1(8107):87-90.
Mortimer, E. A.
   (1968)   Frequent colds. Pp. 211-215 in M. Green and
            R. J. Haggerty, eds., Ambulatory Pediatrics.
            Philadelphia, Pa.: W. B. Saunders Company.
National Research Council
   (1976)   Toward a National Policy for Children and
            Families. Advisory Committee on Child
            Development. Washington, D.C.: National
            Academy of Sciences.
Needleman, H. L., Gunnoe, C., Levitan, A., et al.
   (1979)   Deficits in psychologic and classroom
            performance of children with elevated dentine
            lead levels. New England Journal of Medicine
            300:659-665.
Neligan, G. A., Kolvin, I., Scott, N. M., et al., eds.
   (1976)   Born too soon or born too small. Clin. Dev.
            Med. 61. Philadelphia, Pa.: Spastics
            International Medical Publications, J. B.
            Lippincott Co.

Nelson, K. B., and Ellenberg, J. H.
    (1979) Neonatal signs as predictors of cerebral
            palsy. Pediatrics 64:225-232.
Newberger, C. M., Newberger, E. H., and Harper, G. P.
    (1976) The social ecology of malnutrition in
            childhood. In J. Lloyd-Still, ed.,
            Malnutrition and Intelligence. Lancaster,
            Pa.: Medical and Technical Publishing Co.
Newberger, E. H., Newberger, C. M., and Richmond, J. B.
    (1976) Child health in America: toward a rational
            public policy. Milbank Memorial Fund
            Quarterly (Summer):249-298.
Oberklaid, F., and Levine, M. D.
    (1980) Precursors of school failure. Pediatrics in
            Review 2:1 (July).
Oberklaid, F., Dworkin, P., and Levine, M. D.
    (1979) Developmental behavioral dysfunction in
            preschool children. American Journal of
            Diseases of Children 133:1126-1131.
Office of the Auditor General of California
    (1979) Special Education Financing Warrants Review
            Report, No. 843. Sacramento, Calif.
Oski, F. A., and Hinig, A. S.
    (1978) The effects of therapy on the developmental
            scores of iron-deficient infants. Journal of
            Pediatrics 92:21-25.
Palfrey, J. S., Mervis, R. C., and Butler, J. A.
    (1978) New directions in the evaluation and education
            of handicapped children. New England Journal
            of Medicine 298:819-824.
Palfrey, J. S., Hanson, M. A., Norton, S., et al.
    (1980) Selective hearing screening for very young
            children. Clinical Pediatrics 19:473-477.
Pierson, D.
    (1974) The Brooklyn Early Education Project: model
            for a new education priority. Childhood
            Education 50:132-136.
Pierson, D. E., Levine, M. D., Ferb, T. E., and Wolman, R.
    (1980) Auditing Multidisciplinary Assessment
            Procedures: A System Developed for the
            Brooklyn Early Education Project. Paper
            presented at the Third International
            Conference on Early Identification of Children
            Who Are Developmentally "At Risk," Teton
            Village, Wyo., September 22-26.

Public Health Service
    (1976) Forward Plan for Health FY 1978-1982.
             Washington, D.C.: U.S. Department of Health,
             Education, and Welfare.

Reynolds, R. C., Banks, S. A., and Murphee, A. H.
    (1976) The Health of a Rural Community. Gainesville,
             Fla.: University of Florida Press.

Richmond, J. B.
    (1966) Communities in action: a report on Project
             Head Start. Reading Teacher 19:323-331.

Richmond, J. B.
    (1975) An idea whose time has arrived. Pediatric
             Clinics of North America 22:517-523.

Robinson, M. E., and Schwartz, L. B.
    (1973) Visuo-motor skills and reading ability: a
             longitudinal study. Developmental Medicine
             and Child Neurology 15:281.

Roghmann, K. J., Hecht, P. K., and Haggerty, R. J.
    (1973) Family coping with everyday stress: self
             reports from a household survey. Journal of
             Comparative Family Studies 4(1):49-62.

Rubin, R. A., Rosenblatt, C., and Balow, B.
    (1973) Psychological and educational sequelae of
             prematurity. Pediatrics 52:352-363.

Rudel, R., and Denckla, M.
    (1976) Relationship of IQ score and reading score to
             visual, spatial and temporal matching tasks.
             Journal of Learning Disabilities 9:169.

Rutter, M.
    (1974) Emotional disorder and educational
             underachievement. Archives of Disease in
             Childhood 49:249.

Rutter, M., and Martin, J. A. M., eds.
    (1972) The child with delayed speech. Clinics in
             Developmental Medicine, No. 43. London:
             Spastics International Medical Publications.

Rutter, M., Tizard, J., and Whitmore, K.
    (1970) Education, Health and Behaviour. London:
             John Wiley & Sons, Inc.

Sameroff, A., and Chandler, M.
    (1975) Reproductive risk and the continuum of
             caretaking casualty. In F. Horowitz, ed.,
             Review of Child Development Research, Vol. 4.
             Chicago, Ill.: University of Chicago Press.

Sheridan, M.
    (1970) Stycar Vision Test Manual. 2nd rev. ed.
             Windsor, Berks, England: NFER Publishing Co.

107

Shipman, V.C.
(no   Maintaining and Enhancing Early Intervention
date)   Gains. Abridged version of Project Report
          76-21 prepared for the Office of Child Develop-
          ment, U.S. Department of Health, Education, and
          Welfare, under Grant No. H-8256.
Simmons, J. Q., and Tymchuk, A.
(1973)   The learning deficits in childhood psychosis.
          Pediatric Clinics of North America 20:665-680.
Smith, B., and Phillips, C. J.
(1978)   Identification of severe mental handicap.
          Child: Care, Health and Development 4:195-203.
Smith, D. W., and Wilson, A. A.
(1973)   The Child with Down's Syndrome. Philadelphia,
          Pa.: W. B. Saunders Company.
Smith, S., and Simpson, K.
(1975)   The Battered Child Syndrome. London:
          Butterworth.
Starfield, B.
(1974)   Measurement of outcome: a proposed scheme.
          Milbank Memorial Fund Quarterly (Winter):39-50.
Stewart, A., and Reynolds, E. O. R.
(1974)   Improved prognosis for infants of very low
          birth-weight. Pediatrics 54:724-735.
Stewart, A. L., Turcan, D. M., Rawlings, G., et al.
(1977)   Prognosis for infants weighing 100 grams or
          less at birth. Archives of Disease in
          Childhood 52:97-104.
Strangler, S. R., Huber, C. J., and Routh, D. K.
(1980)   Screening Growth and Development of Preschool
          Children. New York: McGraw-Hill Book Company.
Sultz, H. A., Schlesinger, E. R., Mosher, W. E., and
Feldman, J. G.
(1972)   Long Term Childhood Illness. Pittsburgh,
          Pa.: University of Pittsburgh Press.
Taft, L. T.
(1978)   Child development: prenatal to early
          childhood. Journal of School Health
          (May):281-287.
Taylor, L., and Newberger, E. H.
(1979)   Child abuse in the international year of the
          child. New England Journal of Medicine
          301:1205-1212.
Thomas, A., and Chess, S.
(1975)   Temperament and Development. New York:
          Brunner/Mazel.

Tilford, J. A.
 (1976) The relationship between gestational age and
 adaptive behavior. Merrill-Palmer Quarterly
 22:319-326.
Tjossem, T.
 (1976) Early intervention: issues and approaches.
 In T. Tjossem, ed., Intervention Strategies
 for High Risk Infants and Young Children.
 Baltimore, Md.: University Park Press.
U.S. General Accounting Office
 (1979) Early Childhood and Family Development
 Programs Improve the Quality of Life for Low
 Income Families. HRD-79-40. February 6.
Vukovich, D. M.
 (1968) Pediatric neurology and learning
 disabilities. In H. R. Myklebust, ed.,
 Progress in Learning Disabilities. Vol. I.
 New York: Grune & Stratton, Inc.
Webb, T. E., and Oski, F. A.
 (1973) Iron deficiency anemia and scholastic
 achievement in young adolescents. Journal of
 Pediatrics 82:827.
Weiss, H. B.
 (1979) Parent Support and Education: An Analysis of
 the Brookline Early Education Project. Thesis
 presented to the faculty of the Graduate
 School of Education, Harvard University.
Werner, E. E., Beirman, J. M., and French, F. E.
 (1971) The Children of Kauai: A Longitudinal Study
 from the Perinatal Period to Age Ten.
 Honolulu: University of Hawaii Press.
White, B. L.
 (1975) Critical influences in the origins of
 competence. Merrill-Palmer Quarter 21:243-266.
Whitfield, T., and Walker, D.
 (no Personal communications regarding ongoing
 date) studies of the Community Child Health Studies
 Group at Harvard School of Public Health.
Wiig, E., and Semel, E.
 (1976) Language Disabilities in Children and
 Adolescents. Columbus, Ohio: Charles E.
 Merrill.
Wolff, P. H., and Hurwitz, I.
 (1966) The choreiform syndrome. Developmental
 Medicine and Child Neurology 8:160-165.
Zigler, E., and Valentine, J., eds.
 (1979) Project Head Start: A Legacy of the War on
 Poverty. New York: The Free Press.

Measuring the Outcomes of Day Care

Jeffrey R. Travers, Rochelle Beck, and Joan Bissell

Day care in the United States comprises a very heterogeneous collection of "programs"--some of them public,
some private, some institutional, some informal. It can
be a large, smoothly run, full-day nursery school in a
splendid facility with highly professional staff; it can
also be Mrs. Jones taking care of Mrs. Smith's kids in
the Jones' family playroom. Its goals and functions are
as varied as its sponsors and practitioners, and its
clients range from infants to school-age children, from
the poorest to the wealthiest families. This heterogene-
ity poses major challenges for outcome measurement. It
requires an arsenal of measures appropriate to different
goals, different settings, and different client
populations.

Problems of measurement are exacerbated by the fact
that day care is highly politicized, in the broadest
sense of the term. Day care has many "constituencies";
many groups with divergent interests have different
perceptions of its proper goals and functions. A few
examples illustrate the range: Day care can be seen as a
service to children, intended to equip them with "school
readiness" skills or to support the development of their
social skills and emotional strengths. It can be seen as
a service to parents, designed to free them for work or
other pursuits. It can be seen as a family support
service, intended to strengthen families by allowing them
to increase earnings while still meeting their childrearing responsibilities. It can be seen as a societal
tool, designed to increase employment and upward mobility,
augment the tax base, and reduce the welfare rolls. It
can be seen as a vehicle for delivering services such as

health care, nutrition, parent education, family counseling, and the like to low-income families. While these views are not necessarily incompatible, each points to a different kind of emphasis in outcome research. Day care also has organized opponents, who see it as undermining the family and who see government support for day care as unwarranted intrusion into family rights and responsibilities. This negative view, too, has implications regarding unintended outcomes, which should be considered in evaluating day care programs.

Issues of measurement for day care demonstrations are rendered even more complex by the fact that demonstrations can address two distinct types of questions, which might be termed "program" questions and "policy" questions. Program questions have to with the best ways of operating day care programs, e.g., the most effective methods of recruiting and training staff, the most effective "curricula" or activities to use with children, or the most effective means of eliciting parent involvement. Policy questions have to do with the proper roles of the various levels of government and with the most effective means of achieving governmental goals. Examples include: Should the federal government encourage out-of-home care for young children, through subsidies or other incentives, or should it subsidize parents who stay home and care for their own children? Which day care subsidy mechanisms (e.g., vouchers, direct purchase of care, income disregard[1]) maximize parental choice? Which maximize quality of care? Which maximize cost-effectiveness? What is the most appropriate and/or effective division of labor among the federal government, states, and localities in regulating and monitoring the quality of care? Should health and social services be delivered through "client-oriented" day care or through more

---

[1] Income disregard is a system under which mothers receiving Aid to Families with Dependent Children (AFDC) under Title IV-A of the Social Security Act are allowed to earn income above the maximum levels normally permitted for those receiving such aid, provided that the surplus is spent for child care. The system is designed to prevent the cost of child care from becoming a barrier to prevent welfare mothers from entering the labor force.

specialized service agencies, such as health clinics?
Clearly, demonstrations addressed to these different
levels of question require different outcome measures.
For example, different measures are needed to assess an
exemplary day care program designed to demonstrate
innovative techniques for educating children and a model
information and referral system or a voucher experiment
designed to demonstrate ways to stimulate private
initiative and maximize parental choice.

Given the multiplicity of goals of day care programs,
of day care constituencies, and of demonstrations in day
care, it seems obvious that outcome research must itself
be multifaceted. No single study could address all of
the (quite legitimate) concerns sketched above. Thus day
care confronts researchers with the need to stake out
their turf clearly--to start with an explicit framework
of values, goals, concepts, and questions and to recognize
that alternative frameworks exist and to take that broader
context into account. While any one study must be limited
in focus, it is important for researchers, and those who
interpret research, not to draw erroneous policy conclusions from data that address only one domain of concern.
For example, it might be the case, as some have argued,
that the most cost-effective way to enhance children's
cognitive development is through the education of parents
and/or in-home intervention with very young children.
But such a claim (if true) would not necessarily argue
against support of developmental day care, since the
latter potentially provides other benefits to families.
(Other examples are cited below, particularly in connection with our discussion of the effects of day care on
employment and family income.)

The admittedly ambitious aim of this paper is to map
the broad terrain of outcome measurement for day care
from a bird's-eye view. We begin with a brief overview
of day care in the United States and a discussion of the
concerns of the many constituencies of day care--children,
parents, providers, researchers, and policy makers. The
body of the paper provides a taxonomy of potential outcomes addressed to these multiple concerns, surveys the
current status of measurement with respect to each class
of outcomes, and suggests needed additions and improvements. The final section summarizes the paper's main
conclusions about the state of outcome measurement for
day care and its recommendations for the future.

BACKGROUND

Day Care in the United States: An Overview

The use of day care in the United States, although not
entirely work related, is intimately linked to the labor
force participation of women, which has increased dramatically in recent decades. In 1950 only one fifth of all
mothers with children under 18 were employed; by 1978 the
proportion had increased to more than one half. The
largest percentage increase occurred among women with
children under six, whose labor force participation
nearly tripled (from 14 percent to 40 percent) during
this period (Congressional Budget Office, 1978:44).
Labor force participation of mothers is highest among
women who head single-parent families. Among two-parent
families, the labor force participation of mothers is
greatest when the father's income is low (Johnson and
Hayghe, 1977).

The above data can be and have been interpreted as
evidence for an abiding and increasing demand for child
care. There is, however, heated controversy over the
proper public response to this apparent increase in
need. Some commentators, often remarking on the activist
family policies of the governments of other industrial-
ized nations, have argued for increased public subsidy of
child care. Others have argued that the increase in
demand has been exaggerated and that private market
mechanisms are adequate to cope with it. Still others
have decried the labor force trends as indicators of the
decline of the family, construing the demand for increased
subsidy as an invitation to increased government encroachment on family rights. It is not our purpose to take
sides on these issues but to describe the day care
"market" as it currently exists, the role of the government within that market, and certain new developments
that seem likely to raise salient program and policy
issues in the 1980s. Subsequent sections of the paper
outline concomitant issues of outcome measurement.

We use the term "day care" broadly to mean care
provided on a regular basis by persons other than
immediate family members (parents, live-in grandparents,
older siblings). However, our primary focus is on paid
care by nonrelatives, provided in the child's home or
elsewhere.

Full- or part-time day care is an experience shared by
large numbers of American children. According to a

national consumer survey published in 1975 (UNCO, Inc., 1975, Vol. II:6-8 to 6-11), more than 5 million children age 13 or younger were at that time cared for essentially full time by someone other than a parent, i.e., for 30 or more hours per week. Another 6 million children receiving care from persons other than their parents for periods between 10 and 30 hours per week. Somewhat more than half the children in full-time care were supervised by someone other than a relative, and about two thirds were in care outside their own homes--statistics that also imply, of course, that in-home care and care by relatives accounted for a large portion of full-time nonparental care.

Most out-of-home care is "family day care," provided in the care giver's home to small numbers of children (six or fewer, including the care giver's own children, by federal regulatory definition.) According to the consumer survey, approximately 1.3 million family day care homes serve 2.4 million children full time, 2.8 million children from 10 to 29 hours per week, and much larger numbers on an occasional basis. Only about 900,000 children received care in centers during 1976-1977, according to a national telephone survey of more than 3,000 centers, roughly one of every six in the country (Coelen et al., 1978). (This survey employed a relatively strict definition of the term "day care center" and excluded mixed care arrangements, in which children are in nursery school for part of the day and in family day care for the rest of the day.)

Children of different ages are distributed unequally across types of care. Preschoolers (ages three through five) are the predominant age group among children in full-time care by nonrelatives. School-age children predominate among those in part-time care. Among children who receive care in their own homes, more than half are of school age, and almost 30 percent are children under three (infants and toddlers); only 20 percent are in the preschool age range. Conversely, as suggested by the consumer survey and confirmed in the recent national telephone survey of day care centers (Coelen et al., 1978), most of the children served in centers (70 percent) are preschoolers; the remainder is divided equally between younger and older children. In family day care, children under three are the largest group served.

There is some controversy over the proper interpretation of those distributional facts. Surveys of parental preferences (e.g., Hill, 1977, 1978; Steinberg and Green, 1979; Rowe et. al., 1972; Fosburg and Hawkins, 1981) indicate that parents are relatively reluctant to place very young children in day care and, when they do so, prefer to use in-home care or home-like, family day care, often within close proximity to the home. As children approach preschool age, parents are more willing to use out-of-home care and are more likely to turn to day care centers as sources of group educational and social experiences that may help prepare children for school. When children reach school age, the school itself provides group experiences; parents again turn to informal in-home or family day care arrangements to provide supervision during after-school hours. On one hand, the existing pattern of care can be seen as a reflection of parental preferences, thereby reflecting--for those who believe that parents know what is best for their children--the interests of children. On the other hand, parents cannot choose forms of care that are unavailable or beyond their means, and they are unlikely to state preferences for forms of care about which they know little. Thus the widespread preference for and use of informal, small-scale arrangements may in part reflect a lack of awareness and/or access to other forms of care, particularly formal, enter-based care, especially for children of school age and those under three.

Whatever the reasons for the distributional facts, the facts themselves represent important realities with which demonstration projects and outcome measurement must reckon. Outcome measurement in the domain of child development has, for valid historical and theoretical reasons, focused on the effects of center care; particular attention has been given to its effects on infants and toddlers. Though this research has yielded relatively clear and valuable insights, it has concentrated on the least-used form of care and on an age group that is underrepresented in that form of care. (Fewer than 40,000 children under two are in center care, most of them in the Southwest, as reported by Ruopp et al., 1979.) Until recently, research has neglected the informal care arrangements that affect most children under three and many older children as well.

Although the role of government in child care is a bitterly debated topic, massive involvement of government at all levels, especially the federal level, is already a reality--with which outcome measurement must deal if it is to be relevant to policy. In fiscal 1977 estimated

federal and state expenditures for day care and other
early childhood programs exceeded $2.7 billion. This sum
includes expenditures on services other than day care as
conventionally defined, e.g., Head Start and the
Department of Agriculture's Child Care Food Program,
which provides food subsidies to child care facilities
serving children from low-income families. However, its
largest component is the $809 million spent on day care
through grants to states under Title XX of the Social
Security Act, followed by $500 million in tax revenues
foregone under the child care tax credit. It also
includes an estimated $500 million in state and local
matching funds (Congressional Budget Office, 1978).

Although federal funds are used to purchase care in
all types of facilities, those monies targeted for the
poor are disproportionately allocated to centers. About
70 percent of Title XX funds are spent in centers, 17
percent in family day care homes, and 14 percent on
in-home care (U.S. Department of Health, Education, and
Welfare, 1978). Approximately 200,000 children from
low-income families receive center care that is wholly or
partially subsidized. However, low-income parents who
receive subsidies through the AFDC income-disregard
mechanism disproportionally choose family day care over
center care.

Closely linked to governmental funding of child care
is governmental regulation. States and a few localities
maintain licensing codes, which set standards that child
care facilities must meet in order to be allowed to
operate. These codes affect virtually all centers and,
in some areas, family day care homes as well. Most
family day care, however, is unlicensed--90 percent,
according to one survey (Westinghouse Learning Corp. and
Westat Research, Inc., 1971)--and licensing requirements
for family day care, where they exist, tend to be enforced
erratically if at all. In-home nonparental care is not
subject to licensing. In addition, the federal government
maintains purchasing standards, which specify the types of
facilities in which federal dollars may be spent. These
standards, the Federal Interagency Day Care Requirements,
established in 1968 and currently being revised (see the
Federal Register, March 19, 1980) are stricter than the
licensing standards of most states, especially with
respect to required ratios of numbers of staff to children
and have therefore been controversial because of their
potential cost implications. In practice, federal
purchasing standards, like state licensing requirements,

have affected centers more than family day care homes and
are likely to continue to do so. Also, the federal
standards primarily affect the care purchased by the
states and their local delegate agencies using Title XX
money; care purchased by the poor under the income-
disregard mechanism and care purchased by middle- and
upper-class families using the tax credit are effectively
unregulated by the federal government. Thus, whether one
views federal and state regulations as necessary and
benevolent attempts to set a floor under the quality of
care or an unwarranted intrusion of government in the
child care market, some form of regulation is a reality
for most centers but for only a fraction of family day
care homes.

In sum, government at all levels is heavily involved
in child care. Government purchases or underwrites care
for large numbers of children, primarily for the poor but
also for the more advantaged classes (through tax
credits). The principal policy tools used by government
for influencing the type and quality of care received by
children have been funding strategies and regulations.
This public presence in the day care market has not been
guided by a coherent national child care policy. It has
arisen in part as a by-product of other policies designed
to support low-income families or to induce low-income
single parents to work, thus reducing welfare expenditures, and in part as an effort to provide tax relief to
the middle class. Federal support for child care to
low-income families coexists with other federal policies,
such as Aid to Families with Dependent Children, which
subsidizes parents to care for their children at home.
In this regard, American day care policy stands in sharp
contrast to the policies of other industrial nations in
Europe. The European countries make a much larger
relative investment in children and families, and they
have relatively clear-cut policies designed to encourage
either parental care or parental employment, depending on
their respective labor markets (Kamerman and Kahn, 1978).
There have been repeated calls by prestigious groups in
the United States for a national child care policy
(Keniston and the Carnegie Council on Children, 1977;
National Research Council, 1976). It is impossible to
say whether the 1980s will see a serious attempt to
establish such a policy. However, with or without such
an attempt, it is clear that debates about funding and
regulation will continue, and that policy researchers
will be called on to produce data relevant to those
debates.

An overview of the American day care scene would not
be complete without some discussion of relatively new
developments that may pose new policy questions for the
1980s. Some states, such as California, have begun to
experiment with funding mechanisms such as vouchers,
designed to increase parental discretion in the purchase
of care and to capitalize on the responsiveness of private
providers. A related development is the growth of information and referral services, some of them publicly subsidized; these services are designed to facilitate the match
between parental needs and existing child care resources.
The increased labor force participation of women also has
led to the beginnings of new demands on unions and employ-
ers to include child care in employee benefit packages.
New experiments with union- or industry-supported child
care may be in the offing. The financing of day care is
likely to become an increasingly salient issue, as the
field becomes increasingly professionalized and as day
care workers--among the nation's lowest paid--seek
recognition and increased compensation for their services.
Informal, low-cost care by friends and relatives may
absorb less of the latent demand than it has in the past
as women who heretofore provided such services enter the
labor force. These developments, and others as yet
unforeseen, are sure to create needs for new forms of
evaluation design and new outcome measures.

Who Cares About Day Care--
and What Do They Care About?

As suggested earlier, day care has many constitu-
encies--groups sharing common interests and perceptions
of the aims and functions of day care. Some of these
groups, such as children and parents, are beneficiaries
of day care; others, such as researchers and policy
makers, are gatekeepers, who control public information
and decision making. Some are providers and the persons
who train them. The interests and perceptions of the
various groups are not mutually exclusive; they overlap
and intersect at many points. Moreover, the views of the
various groups need not necessarily receive equal weight
in the choice or the development of outcome measures; a
case could be made, for example, that the needs of children and families are paramount. Nevertheless it is
useful to enumerate the constituencies and identify the
outcome measures most salient for each, to provide a

comprehensive framework within which existing measures can be located and evaluated.

First among the constituencies are children. They are not a political constituency in the usual sense; they do not speak for themselves, individually or collectively, but rely on adult advocates to express their needs and defend their rights. Yet they nonetheless have needs and interests that may differ from those of every other group, perhaps even their parents. They need physical activities and educational experiences to stimulate their development. They need to interact with adults and other children in order to begin to learn about themselves--what they enjoy, what they do well, what they want to be--and about how to form relationships with others. Some adult advocates feel that they need to begin to develop a sense of their cultural as well as personal identities. Moreover, given that many children spend 8 to 10 hours of their 12-hour waking day in care, the quality of life available to them while in care is a prime concern in itself, regardless of its developmental effects. Children need a safe and pleasant physical environment, appealing and nutritious food, and, in some cases, special services such as diagnostic screening and health care, which may be available only through day care. The need to measure development comprehensively--not to rely on traditional measures of cognitive skill or ability that have been used in evaluating other programs for children--has been widely recognized but only partially met by day care researchers. The need to measure immediate quality of life has barely been acknowledged as such, although relevant aspects of the environment have been studied.

Second are parents, who may have several purposes for using day care in addition to providing the child with a pleasant and stimulating environment: to enable a second or single parent to enter the labor market, to learn about child rearing, to feel less isolated, to help get through temporary crises. Availability of day care might permit some mothers to participate in vocational education, thus improving their marketable skills. Availability of day care might permit single mothers to work, and fewer might apply for welfare as a result. Parents might feel more confident about their abilities to raise their families, as a consequence both of their improved economic situation and of the help and advice given by the day care providers. The consequent reductions in stress might even result in fewer single parents being

institutionalized or referred for psychiatric care.
Obviously, a wide range of measures is needed to address
these questions and to capture the equally wide range of
outcomes that parents might expect from day care.

Third are families. As a unit the family has somewhat
different needs from its individual members. For example,
a family may need a day care program to help it maintain
a viable income, to help it stay intact during a troubled
time, to help its members interact more positively, or to
prevent negative interactions such as spouse or child
abuse. Does the availability of day care decrease the
need for foster care or institutional placements? Would
fewer families disintegrate under economic pressures or
in times of illness or crisis if they had day care
arrangements to relieve some of the daily burdens of childrearing? Are families more nurturing if they have outside
sources of respite or advice? Is the incidence of spouse
or child abuse reduced as a result? Again, a range of
measures that goes beyond that normally associated with
day care is indicated.

Fourth are communities. While we do not usually think
of communities per se as having an interest in day care,
there may be legitimate outcomes worth measuring from the
perspective of the community. For example, a community
with insufficient or low-quality day care programs may
have higher welfare expenditures or it may discourage
families with two wage earners from living in it. A
community offering high-quality care, by contrast, may be
able to attract businesses and families and thereby
increase the tax base. Aside from the various economic
implications, the availability of day care services may
in part characterize a community as hospitable or not,
intimate or not, accessible or not, a good place for
families or not--a characterization that may itself
affect families living in that community, their
interactions, and their expectations for their children.

Fifth are care givers. Employees in the growing day
care industry comprise a wide variety of people: from
neighbors with no training or professional experience,
who baby-sit for several children, to highly trained
professionals in large day care centers, with theories,
equipment, and routines for handling groups of children.
What is measured, how it is measured, and the interpretation of the results directly affect livelihood, reputa-
tion, self-image, and future income. While the employees
often share with the children and parents a concern for
many of the outcomes deemed important in child care (such

as the quality of daily interaction and the happiness of the child), their stake as providers of this service colors their outlook and their need for information. Their working conditions, wages, job stability, professional recognition, and professional growth are concerns that others may not share. And evaluation, especially if it involves direct observation of their interactions with children, may be threatening to them and may therefore require extensive consultation, explanation, and justification.

Sixth is the research community, particularly (1) experts on child development and the family and (2) policy researchers and program evaluators. Though these two groups may overlap in membership and outlook, they are distinct in objective: The first seeks basic and applied knowledge about children's psychological growth and family functioning, and the second studies the effects of programs and public policies. Often the research conducted by both groups focuses on the concerns of parents, providers, and communities, but this is not always the case. Because researchers view day care from particular theoretical perspectives, through the lenses of particular research techniques, the measures they choose sometimes communicate important information to other researchers but are incomprehensible or irrelevant to parents and care givers. For example, many parents and community advocates were genuinely surprised when the most widely publicized early evaluations of Head Start looked primarily at intellectual development and used measures narrowly applicable to school success. Many had never seen that outcome as the overriding purpose of the program, and they wondered why reports concerning such important outcomes such as the delivery of health, social, and nutrition services did not receive equal attention or why some of the dynamics of introducing a community-controlled program into poor and minority neighborhoods could not be measured. Day care research has suffered from a similar narrowness of focus.

Finally, there are policy makers and government program managers at the local, state, and federal levels. Responsible for decisions about the allocation of resources and the administration of programs, for the creation and implementation of laws and regulations, for assessing the needs of children and families, and for setting priorities and creating programs to address those needs, policy makers often are interested in outcomes that have to do with the functioning of the service delivery system.

While the effects of programs on individual children and
families are important, in many cases the outcomes most
relevant to policy makers address issues of access,
equity, and efficiency that transcend the concerns of
individual children, parents, or providers: How many
children have been served? At what unit cost? From what
revenues? Is the delivery system working efficiently?
Is it freeing or draining local funds for other needed
public services? Have families increased their earnings
and hence contributed additional federal, state, and
local taxes? What is the total day care capacity in the
community? What ways are there to measure unmet needs
reliably? What is the nature of the day care market? Is
it mixed enough (i.e., public vs. private, school vs.
nonschool, family vs. center, subsidized vs. fee) to
allow for real choice? Is parents' knowledge about day
care options sufficient or increasing, so they can make
informed choices among services? Do different types of
care (e.g., family day care homes, small group homes,
larger day care centers) work together in an integrated
manner, by sharing resources, making referrals, and so
on? Have parents who are active in the decision making
of their day care facilities become more active in other
community institutions or political processes? Have
licensing or other regulatory mechanisms improved the
quality of care? Limited its availability? Changed the
nature of the people or organizations that enter the
field? Is day care an efficient vehicle for the delivery
of other services to children, such as health care? What
agency or agencies, at what level or levels of government,
should be responsible for day care policy? The answers
to many of these and other important questions may involve
simple accounting procedures and may not fit into any
theoretical framework. Yet these atheoretical indicators
may have as much value in assessing day care programs as
research findings arising from traditional experimental
designs and measures.

Questions such as the ones above apply in different
ways and to different degrees at the different levels of
government; hence, different "systemic" outcome measures
are salient for different policy audiences. Local policy
makers operate within a framework of laws and regulations
established at higher levels. They tend to be concerned
with issues of compliance and with the detailed fit of
available services to local needs. State policy makers
and program managers tend to be concerned with issues of
equity, access, and cost of services across localities

within the state as well as with trade-offs among human
services within constraints of the state budget and of
discretionary federal programs, such as Title XX. They
are also concerned with issues of accountability and
monitoring and with the administrative machinery needed
to carry out these functions.

Federal policy makers are concerned with issues of
uniformity of basic levels of service across states,
leadership, fostering research and innovation, other goals
important to the nation as a whole (such as a literate
citizenry, a productive work force, and low unemployment
and tax rates), and equality of opportunity for women and
minorities. Thus, policy makers at the national level
often frame the purposes of programs and outcomes to be
measured in terms that are somewhat removed from the
concerns of individual children, parents, or local
communities. Sometimes they formulate outcomes in terms
of the rhetoric that led to successful legislation of the
program or that pertains to other salient political
goals. For example, day care often "sells" as a device
for reducing welfare rolls because many middle-class
voters view the reduction of welfare expenditures as a
legitimate goal but are reluctant to support underwriting
additional social services. From this perspective, the
reduction of welfare rolls or overall taxpayer cost
savings (the cost of welfare compared with the cost of
child care, training, and job placement) become salient
outcomes; direct measures of services received do not
suffice. Existing research has made only sporadic use of
atheoretical indicators of the functioning of the child
day care system as a whole and has not systematically
addressed the concerns of policy makers and program
managers at the various levels of government.

A TAXONOMY OF DAY CARE OUTCOMES

As the foregoing discussion suggests, the researcher
who sets out to evaluate a demonstration program in day
care is confronted with a confusing welter of potential
program and policy objectives. Maximizing achievement of
some objectives may not be fully compatible with maximizing the achievement of others. Inevitably the researcher
must choose to stress certain outcomes, or trade-offs
among outcomes, while downplaying or ignoring others.
What is crucial is that this choice be informed and
deliberate--that it be based on an appreciation of the

goals of a particular demonstration and or the information
needs of the intended audiences of the evaluation and not
on expediency, convention, or failure to consider important outcome domains.

To facilitate informed choice, this section sets forth
a taxonomy of potential outcomes, based on consideration
of the interests of the many constituencies of day care.
The taxonomy is intended to be systematic and complete in
identifying broad categories of outcomes to be considered.
Within these broad categories, numerous specific outcomes
are listed; however, at this more specific level the
taxonomy is intended to be suggestive rather than exhaustive. Many of the outcomes discussed are not usually
thought of as such; they include, for example, measures
of service delivery and of the quality of the physical
and social environment provided to children. In most
existing research, such variables, if considered at all,
are treated as "independent"; dependent measures
(outcomes) in most studies are measures of developmental
change in children. We argue, however, that traditional
conceptions of outcomes, derived primarily from developmental psychology, must be broadened to take account of
the diverse purposes of day care demonstrations and the
concerns of its constituencies.

The section also surveys some of the major types of
measures used in existing studies and comments on their
adequacy; gaps in measurement are identified wherever
they exist. Again, the intent is not to review every
measure ever used in day care research but rather to
identify broad areas of strength and weakness in current
measurement. Although substantive findings are mentioned,
the discussion is not a comprehensive review of the
literature nor does it comment systematically on the
quality of research designs or the soundness of
substantive conclusions.

The taxonomy of measures represents a widening circle,
beginning with children and the effects of day care on
their daily experiences and development, then spiraling
outward to encompass providers, parents and families, the
community, and ultimately the entire child care and
social service delivery systems.

Children's Experiences in Day Care

Day care is a physical and social environment in which
children spend a substantial portion of their waking

hours. Therefore, it does not seem unreasonable to begin
thinking about the effects of day care on children by
asking what kinds of experiences various day care settings
provide and whether these experiences are intrinsically
good or bad. Curiously, this approach has been little
used in day care studies in developmental psychology and
evaluation research (with exceptions to be described
shortly), although it is used routinely by parents in
deciding whether and where to place their children in
care. Researchers have tended to view the experiences of
children as means, not ends--the ends being various forms
of developmental change, such as enhanced cognitive or
social skills. This view is also implicit in many
discussions of day care policy. For example, part of the
justification for federal support of care for children
from low-income families lies in the presumed educational
and socializing effects of the preschool group experience.

Individual developmental change is perfectly appropriate to use as one standard in assessing the benefits of
day care for children; however, there are serious
technical and philosophical reasons for objecting to
exclusive use of this standard. Such a narrow focus of
evaluation places the burden of proof of merit on measures
and modes of analysis that, given the current state of
the art, inherently limit the ability of a program to
demonstrate its worth. Moreover, exclusive focus on
individual change ignores the goals and practices of many
day care programs and providers, and it implies value
judgments that are open to question, particularly with
respect to the justification for public subsidy for the
care of the children of the poor.

The emphasis on developmental outcome measures reflects
an assumption, ubiquitous but often tacit in debates among
policy makers and researchers, that early childhood programs are justified primarily by future gains to the child
and/or to society, such as enhanced educational achievement, enhanced employability and income, and reduced
delinquency and dependence on welfare. Rarely in such
discussions are programs justified by immediate benefits
to the child--the child's opportunity to spend several
years of his or her life in a good environment, both in
day care itself and in the family. Public expenditures
on children are viewed as investments in the future, not
as purchases of goods and services to be consumed in the
present. This sort of thinking seems so natural that it
is hardly ever questioned in some circles, but it is by
no means the only way to think about programs for
children.

Historically, such single-minded preoccupation with individual development would have seemed aberrant. In the early 1900s child care programs, such as the day nurseries of settlement houses in low-income areas in cities serving minority populations (considered then, too, to be "culturally deprived"), did not measure success in terms of psychological growth. Instead, the number of baths and delousings per child per week, the number of shoes cleaned, the number of garments disinfected, and the number of slum babies saved from filth and degradation were the outcomes valued by administrators, philanthropists, and policy makers. The measures were accounts of these direct services in columns in ledgers capturing the theme of the Progressive Era's discovery of the management and professionalization of human services. To cite a more contemporary contrast, no one would dream of justifying public programs for the elderly primarily in terms of their future contribution to society. Advocates for such programs base their claims on the humanitarian premise that society has an obligation to provide a decent life for those for whom it has assumed some degree of financial responsibility. Surely, similar reasoning could be applied to children, particularly the children of the poor.

We do not wish to overstate the case or pose a false dichotomy. Obviously, parents and providers care about children's futures, and money spent on young children may well be a wise long-term social investment. Moreover, there is evidence that various indices of the quality of the day care environment are linked to indices of individual growth. For example, in the New York Infant Day Care Study (Golden et al., 1978), two-year-olds who experienced a high degree of cognitive stimulation in the day care environment performed better than other children on measures of language comprehension and social competence at age three. In the National Day Care Study (Ruopp et al., 1979), preschool children in classrooms with high levels of cooperation and engagement in activities involving reflection and innovation on the part of the child also performed well on standardized tests of cognitive development. Nevertheless, potential future gains do not obviate the need for evaluations to give equal weight to the present—to the child's immediate needs and experience.

To address issues of the "quality of life" within day care itself requires at least three classes of measures: (1) measures of the quality of the physical environment;

(2) measures of the quantity and quality of "supplementary" services to children, such as nutrition and health
care (including screening and diagnostic services); and,
most importantly, (3) measures of the quality of interaction among children and between adults and children in
the day care setting. (Measures of the quality of life
in the family are discussed later.)

The Physical Environment

Evaluations of child care facilities often include
descriptions of the physical environment. Objective
descriptors abound: square footage of indoor and outdoor
space, inventories of equipment and materials, counts and
checklists of health- and safety-related features such as
numbers of toilets and fire exits, protection around
electrical outlets, sanitary features of kitchen facilities, etc. Many of these physical characteristics are
covered in state and local licensing codes and health,
fire, and safety regulations. Thus, minimal characteristics necessary for safety and sanitation are fairly
well established (by common sense and the practical
experience of providers and relevant monitoring agencies).
To go beyond the basics to subtler descriptors of
environmental quality is more difficult. Crowding or its
absence, lighting, color, noise level, the accessibility
of materials as opposed to their sheer physical presence,
the layout of space as opposed to its sheer size, the
presence or absence of private places, and countless
other physical characteristics of child care settings can
potentially affect children's behavior within those
settings. Two recent review papers on the effects of the
physical environment in day care (Prescott and David,
1976; Kruvant et al., 1976) cite a number of relevant
studies on the behavioral effects of square footage
available per child and a few studies of acoustics, play
equipment, and other features of the environment.
However, both papers are striking in the contrast they
present between the poverty of systematic empirical
knowledge and the wealth of opinion about the impact of
the environment on children.
A few studies attempt to define global features of the
environment, such as "softness" or "inclusion-seclusion
potential," or to examine the physical environment as
part of a broader "closed vs. open" atmosphere (e.g.,
Prescott et al., 1967, 1972, 1975; Prescott and Milich,

1974). However, most studies focus on one objective
feature of the environment--usually square footage per
child--and attempt to relate it to one or more behavioral
variables, especially the amount of social interaction
(positive and negative) and the frequency of aggressive
or destructive acts (see Prescott and David, 1976, for
references). Existing research thus provides little or
no basis for understanding how features of the environment
(e.g., the amount of space and its arrangement) interact.

In short, the physical environment is the subject of
detailed prescriptions by regulatory agencies and advocacy
groups, but these prescriptions are based at best on the
practical experience of providers and at worst on specula-
tion. There is a lack, not of potential measures, but of
well-founded knowledge about which measures to use and how
to combine specific indicators so as to form more general
and meaningful variables characterizing the physical
environment.

Supplementary Services

Day care facilities, especially centers serving
children from low-income families, often provide
"supplementary" services such as nutrition, health, and
dental care. Such services are supplementary only in the
sense that they go beyond supervision of children during
the working day. For children who may not receive them
elsewhere, these services may be fundamental to the
child's well-being. (Day care facilities also frequently
offer services such as parent counseling, which can
potentially affect parent-child relations and family
functioning; these services are discussed later.)

Health and related services pose problems of measurement that are analogous to those posed by the physical
environment. For example, it is a fairly straightforward
(though perhaps burdensome) matter to keep records of
screenings and immunizations. It is not at all straightforward, however, to determine whether these services
actually improve children's health. (See Levine and
Palfrey in this volume for a thorough discussion of the
difficulties involved.)

In addition, because these services are not universal
in day care and because different facilities arrange for
them in different ways (some by direct provision and some
by referrals), service delivery measures themselves can
be ambiguous and difficult to standardize. For example,

it is obviously inappropriate to equate "referrals" that
require working parents to take the initiative in securing
services for their children with referrals in which the
day care facility center makes contact with the providing
agency, arranges transportation, and does any necessary
follow-up. Without careful attention to the differences
in the ways in which services are made "available" to
children, measures are likely to be perfunctory and
unrevealing.

Interaction with Care Givers and Peers

The study of children's behavior in group settings,
including but not limited to day care, has an extensive
history in developmental psychology. Until recently, most
studies were theoretically motivated, designed to identify
consistent dimensions of behavior and sometimes to relate
them to characteristics of the setting or the supervising
adult (for example, see Baumrind and Black, 1967, Becker
and Krug, 1964, Kohn and Rosman, 1972, Peterson, 1961,
Schaefer, 1961). More recent studies of children's
behavior in natural settings have examined the effects of
day care, usually in comparison to home rearing--although
comparisons of different day care settings have gained
increasing attention in the past few years. Useful
reviews that cover these studies, among others, are
provided by Belsky and Steinberg (1978), Belsky et al.
(1981), Etaugh (1980), Hoffman (1974), Meyer (1976), and
Riccicuti (1976). Many of the day-care-related studies
have used frequency counts or ratings of behavior to draw
inferences about traits of individual children, which
might potentially be influenced by the day care environment; thus, the proper place to consider the outcome
measures used in these studies is the section below that
deals with measures of developmental change. Other
observation studies, however, have provided data that can
be interpreted as characterizing the social climate of
the environment to which the child is exposed; measures
used in the latter studies are discussed below. (We
recognize that the distinction between studies of the
social environment and studies of social development is
often difficult to draw and that many studies of the
environment are motivated by its personal effects on
development. Nevertheless, we maintain the distinction
because we believe it is important philosophically.)

A number of studies have examined the behavior of care givers and children of various ages in different settings--centers, family day care, and the child's own home. There also exist comparative studies of day care centers with different configurations of staff and children (e.g., staff-child ratios, age mixes, group sizes, levels of staff training) and different physical resources (e.g., space and equipment). One recent study has compared different types of family day care-- unlicensed, licensed, and "sponsored" (the latter term referring to homes that are part of larger child care systems). In almost all of these studies, measures are ratings or frequency counts based on natural observations. A partial list of variables examined in these studies includes the following:

1. Care giver nurturance, responsiveness, and care giver-child contact (see Cochran, 1977; Heinicke et al., 1973; Rubenstein et al., 1977; Ruopp et al., 1979).
2. Care giver restrictiveness, "management" and behavior, and emphasis on rules and routines (see Cochran, 1977; Fosburg and Hawkins, 1981; Prescott et al., 1967; Ruopp et al., 1979; Stallings and Porter, 1980).
3. Cognitive and verbal stimulation and teaching on the part of the care giver (see Carew, 1979; Cochran, 1977; Fiene, 1973; Fosburg and Hawkins, 1981; Hawkins et al., 1979).
4. Provision of opportunities for children to initiate activities (see Heinicke et al., 1973).
5. Involvement in activities on the part of children (see Golden et al., 1978; Prescott, 1973; Ruopp et al., 1979).
6. Conflict, aggressiveness, and destructiveness on the part of children (see Carew, 1979; Hutt and Vaizey, 1966; Loo, 1972; Shapiro, 1975).
7. Isolation, inactivity, and aimless wandering by children (see Carew, 1979; Fosburg and Hawkins, 1981; Rubenstein and Howes, 1979; Ruopp et al., 1979; Shapiro, 1975).
8. Overt distress (crying) among infants (e.g., Rubenstein and Howes, 1979; Ruopp et al., 1979).

These studies, varying widely in scope and emphasis, suggest that naturalistic observations of children and care givers can potentially be used to capture important elements of quality in child care and to discriminate among different types of day care environments. However,

observational studies raise important practical and
methodological issues that have received insufficient
attention from many researchers using observational
techniques in day care settings. Some studies have used
time-sampled counts of relatively fine-grained, objec-
tively defined behaviors. This approach provides a
record that is both detailed and faithful to the temporal
prevalence of events. However, it requires well-trained
observers and is expensive and time-consuming. And it is
subject to the criticism that there is no necessary
relationship between the psychological significance of an
event and its frequency or duration. Studies based on
global ratings of the classroom environment by observers
in effect filter the flow of events through the eye--that
is, the value system and the implicit or explicit psychological theory--of the beholder. This approach thus has
the potential advantage of weighting events according to
their significance and the potential disadvantage of
greater observer bias than the event-record approach.
There has been little or no comparative study of pictures
of the same day care settings painted by the two different
methods. (In one case, in which the same children were
studied by different researchers using the two different
methods, rather different pictures, especially of the
children's "aggressiveness," emerged (compare Lay and
Meyer, 1973, with Schwarz et al., 1974). Moreover, while
observer bias and interobserver agreement have received
attention from researchers, other serious sources of bias
have received much less attention. It has long been
known that instability of behavior is a threat to the
reliability of behavioral measures (Medley and Mitzel,
1963). Mathematical techniques exist for assessing the
distortions introduced by observers, fluctuation of
behavior over time, and other sources (Cronbach et al.,
1972). However, only a few recent studies have put them
to use. Thus, if observational measures are to fulfill
their promise, a great deal must be learned about the
properties of alternative recording strategies and
possible trade-offs between expense and objectivity.

Developmental Change

As indicated earlier, most research on the effects of
day care arising within the disciplines of developmental
psychology and early childhood education has focused on
changes in children's social and cognitive development.

For expository convenience we will distinguish between
developmental and educational lines of research on day
care, although the boundary between the two is fuzzy.
The former is concerned primarily with children's socioemotional development and interpersonal skills. The
latter is concerned primarily with cognitive ability and
achievement and, to a lesser extent, with practical,
self-care skills. The two lines of research correspond
to two different views of day care: as a socializing
environment and as a mini-school. Though most contemporary day care, at least in centers, incorporates elements
of both views and though some research projects attempt
to assess outcomes in both domains, the distinction is
worth maintaining because the two emphases have different
implications for the choice of outcome measures.

Until recently, research on developmental change in
day care focused on comparisons between children reared
for substantial periods in group care environments and
children reared at home or children reared in group
environments for considerably shorter periods. This
research was intended to measure the outcomes of group
care per se, not of particular kinds of group care,
although it in fact concentrates on a relatively narrow
and not particularly typical range of group care environments, as several reviewers (Belsky and Steinberg, 1978;
Etaugh, 1980) have noted. In the past few years,
researchers have begun to compare different types of day
care, such as in-home care, center care, and family day
care (e.g., Golden et al., 1978; Clarke-Stewart, 1979,
1980). Others have examined variations within particular
types of care; for example, Ruopp et al. (1979) examined
variations within center care that were associated with
different staffing and grouping patterns.

Research on children in group settings began as early
as the 1930s, when the first studies of the effects of
nursery school entered the literature of child development. Some of these studies provided our earliest
demonstrations that preschool education can boost the
scores of disadvantaged children on standardized tests of
ability and achievement. For example, one study (Barrett
and Koch, 1930) found that orphanage children gained 20
points on the Merrill-Palmer Test after six months'
exposure to nursery school. However, most of the early
nursery schools were not hothouses for cognitive development. Primarily serving middle- and upper-class children,
they were devoted to developing the "whole child." Play,
arts and crafts, and a general emphasis on human relations

were prominent in their curricula. Correspondingly, early
studies generally looked for social benefits in the form
of increased participation, cooperation, impulse control,
and communicative skills on the part of preschool children
(e.g., Parten, 1932). While these studies succeeded in
documenting interesting aspects of children's growth and
behavior in group settings, they were on the whole method-
ologically naive by modern standards and were inconclusive
in their attempts to demonstrate that nursery school
conveys special benefits in contrast to home rearing.

Another line of research, beginning a decade or so
after the nursery school studies and extending into the
1960s, sheds much-needed light on the dark underside of
child care: the care of infants and young children in
institutions. Rene Spitz's influential essays documented
appalling rates of apathy and morbidity among infants in
institutions where care was inadequate and inconsistent
(Spitz, 1945). Subsequent studies found retardation of
the onset of vocalization, motor skills such as crawling
and creeping, visually guided reaching and grasping,
smiling, and other forms of responsiveness to the physical
and social environment (e.g., Provence and Lipton, 1962;
White, 1969, Dennis, 1941; Dennis and Najarian, 1957;
Paraskevopoulos and Hunt, 1971). (That these early
deficits would have enduring consequences was often
implicitly assumed and therefore rarely investigated
directly). These observations were interpreted as
evidence of the devastating effects of early maternal
deprivation (Bowlby, 1969), though later work called this
interpretation into question, suggesting that general
physical and social stimulation--not specifically maternal
interaction--is what the worst institutional settings
lack (e.g., Gouin-Decarie, 1965).

Modern day care in the United States may bear considerable resemblance to nursery school (in fact the two may
be indistinguishable, save for the length of the session),
but only in a minority of cases does it bear much resemblance to the bleak, underfunded, understaffed institutions observed by Spitz and others. Nevertheless, studies
of institutionalized children, like studies of nursery
school, continue to exert an influence on our thinking
(e.g., Fraiberg, 1977). Public debate about the merits
and perils of day care as an environment for children
continues to center on issues raised by these studies.
Critics allege that day care weakens the bond between
mother and child, robbing the child of the security and
emotional attachment necessary for healthy development.

Such criticisms mean that demonstrations in day care, more than demonstration programs in other child-related areas (e.g., in early education or health care), must not only prove their positive benefits but must also prove that they do not actually harm children. Consequently, the outcomes measured in early studies of nursery schools and of institutional care remain relevant today, as do some of the actual measures used in those early studies.

Many contemporary studies of the impact of day care can trace their intellectual descent from the early studies of institutionalization through the theoretical formulations of Bowlby (1969), with a link by marriage to experimental techniques for assessing the degree and quality of mother-child bonding. Most prominent among these are variants on the Ainsworth "strange situation" techniques (Ainsworth and Wittig, 1969), in which the child is separated from its mother and introduced to a strange adult. The amount of exploratory behavior shown in the mother's presence; the amount of distress, approach, and avoidance shown in response to the stranger; and the amount of proximity-seeking shown on the mother's return are used as indices of the security of the child's attachment to the mother. By comparing the behavior of home-reared children with that of children who have spent a substantial proportion of their early years in day care, studies using the "strange situation" and adaptations thereof have directly addressed the issue of whether exposure to day care weakens the mother-child bond.

Thoughtful, comprehensive discussions of these studies appear in Belsky and Steinberg (1978) and Belsky et al. (1981). These reviewers point out that the "strange situation" is designed for use with children between 12 and 18 months of age and that it entails a complex coding system (Ainsworth et al. 1978). Used appropriately it is reliable, valid, and predictive of later social development (Sroufe, 1979). However, many day care researchers have used unvalidated variants of the "strange situation," often with children two years old or older. For example, several studies have examined the child's reactions to separation and reunion with the mother during dropoff and pickup at day care, recording frequencies of distress, clinging, avoidance of the mother, exploratory behavior, and the like. While separation and reunion may be important to study, they cannot be assumed to measure attachment in the same way as does the "strange situation"--particularly when children are considerably older than one year, when overt attachment is most salient.

Subject to the above caveat, Belsky and his colleagues report that most studies find no deleterious effects of day care on attachment. Reports of such effects (e.g., Blehar, 1974; Ricciuti, 1974; Cochran, 1977) are difficult to replicate or open to alternative explanations. However, one recent study using the "strange situation" in the manner prescribed by Ainsworth (Vaughn et al., 1980) suggests that there may be damage to the attachment relationship for certain highly vulnerable infants placed in day care before one year of age.

The nursery school studies also have descendants, though the line of descent is less clear and direct than is the case for studies of attachment. Research on child care turned toward heavy emphasis on cognitive skills during the 1960s. Influential basic research studies and syntheses pointed to the malleability of intelligence (Hunt, 1961; Bloom, 1964). Numerous preschool education programs sprang up, many of them affiliated with universities, most directed at compensating for presumed environmental deficits experienced by the children of the poor. Positive results from many of these programs, based primarily on improvements in children's scores on standardized tests of ability and achievement, soon appeared in the literature of developmental psychology and early childhood education (see Weikart, in this volume.) And, of course, Head Start was established, soon to be followed by the widely publicized Westinghouse-Ohio evaluation, based almost exclusively on standardized tests (Westinghouse Learning Corporation and Ohio University, 1969). Research on day care, as opposed to compensatory education, began to appear somewhat later, as new policy issues came to the fore under pressure from the women's movement, advocacy groups, and labor market trends. What is striking is that many studies on the impact of group care continued to include standardized measures of cognitive ability and achievement, such as the Bayley Scales, the Stanford-Binet Test, the Preschool Inventory Test, and the Peabody tests, in their outcome measurement batteries. The general finding of this large body of work is that day care has no effect, positive or negative, on the scores of children from relatively advantaged backgrounds, and for children from low-income families day care seems to forestall the decline in test scores that usually occurs with age (Belsky and Steinberg, 1978).

Fewer studies have examined indices of cognitive and linguistic development other than general scores on standardized tests. The list of more specific abilities

studied, however, is long and rather impressive--
problem-solving, abstraction, and planfulness, measured
through ratings of natural behavior (Macrae and
Herbert-Jackson, 1976; Schwarz et al. 1974); concept
formation, memory and recognition vocabulary, measured
with standardized tests (Kagan et al., 1976); age of onset
of speech and complexity and maturity of speech patterns
(Fiene, 1973; Cochran, 1977); and for infants a variety
of motor skills. The various studies do not lend themselves to easy summary; no overwhelming positive or
negative effects of day care have emerged. What is more
important here is the sheer variety of outcomes and
outcome measures, and the fact that no consensus has
emerged as to what should be measured and how.

In the domain of social development, the picture is
even more complex. A wide variety of individual traits
and social skills have been assessed by means of global
ratings or systematic frequency counts based on naturally
occurring behaviors and by means of tests, administered
both verbally and as structured problem situations to
which the child must respond. Variables assessed on the
basis of natural observations include dependency,
nurturance, sociability toward peers, attitudes toward
the care giver, cooperation with peers and adults,
hostility, aggressiveness, general activity level,
assertiveness, conformity, and exploratory behavior;
tests and structured situations have been used to assess
curiosity, the capacity to adopt the perspective of others
(social role-taking), the capacity to give assistance,
relationship to parents, sex typing, impulse control, and
cooperation. Examples of studies employing natural
and/or structured measures of social development include
Clarke-Stewart (1979, 1980), Caldwell et al. (1970),
Schwarz et al. (1974), Lay and Meyer (1973), Macrae and
Herbert-Jackson (1976), Moore (1975), Doyle (1975), and
Lippman and Grote (1974). Again, no simple summary of
findings is possible; what is important for our purposes
is the wide range of outcomes for which measurement has
been attempted and the lack of convergence on a particular
set of outcomes or measures.

How good are the various development and educational
measures that have been discussed, and how useful for
evaluating programs and shaping policy? To answer these
questions measure by measure would require a long
dissertation indeed, but a number of general comments can
be made.

Contrary to what one occasionally hears, there is no
lack of candidate outcome measures for a wide variety of
cognitive and social skills. However, as a reader of an
early draft of this paper put it, there is good reason to
question whether any of the candidates merit election.
It is striking that a relatively small set of (inter-
correlated) measures of general cognitive skills are used
in study after study, while anarchy reigns in the measurement of social development and more differentiated
cognitive skills.

The attraction of standardized cognitive measures such
as IQ appears to derive from their relatively high
reliabilities (in the traditional psychometric sense) and
their predictive validity against a criterion of success
in school as well as from the historical influences of
Head Start and its precursors. However, despite their
widespread use, there is equally widespread dissatisfaction with those measures, even among many who use them.
There are many reasons for dissatisfaction: Poor and
minority children score less well on the tests than other
children, leading to charges of cultural bias. The tests
are generally designed to be insensitive to specific
learning experiences, making them questionable as outcome
measures for intervention programs of any kind. The most
widely used tests do not attempt to measure creativity,
persistence, flexibility, and resourcefulness in attacking
problems or a host of other aspects of cognitive skill
and style that may ultimately indicate much about a
child's potential as a learner or future ability to use
what is learned. Unfortunately, instruments designed to
measure the latter aspects of cognitive development,
though influential in basic research, have on the whole
not demonstrated the reliabilities and predictive
validities of the general ability measures, nor have they
achieved public acceptance and widespread use in evaluation as measures of intellectual potential. There is a
serious question in the psychometric literature as to how
measurable these traits are and how separable from general
intellectual ability.

Similarly in the area of social skills, a bewildering
variety of potential measures exists (see compendia by
Johnson and Bommarito, 1971; Walker, 1973). Used
primarily by highly trained researchers in academic
settings, these measures have nevertheless not been
impressive on psychometric grounds, especially when used
by researchers other than their developers and especially
when used in field settings. Although a few brave souls

have stepped forward to suggest a definitive instrument
battery for measuring "social competence" as an outcome
of early childhood programs (Zigler and Trickett, 1978),
no single instrument, let alone battery, has commanded
widespread acceptance.

It is not for lack of effort in the basic research
community that measures of cognitive style and socioemotional development lag behind standardized tests of
general cognitive and linguistic skill on psychometric
grounds. When years of effort fail to produce a desired
result, it is worth asking whether the enterprise is
misconceived. Trait measures are inherently individualistic. They focus on characteristics of the child, not
on the social matrix within which those characteristics
are nurtured. However, there is massive evidence throughout the literature of child development (summarized most
pointedly by Bronfenbrenner, 1979) that situational and
cultural contexts profoundly affect young children's
behavior. Thus, while the search for better trait
measures should and will continue, perhaps researchers
should also begin to devote equal effort to finding
better ways of characterizing child/environment systems.
Many day care programs have begun to try to produce and
sustain change in children by changing their home environments through services to families. The individualistic
focus of trait measures diverts attention from the impact
of day care on family functioning and family-community
relations. Such impacts are not only "goods" in themselves but may redound to the benefit of the child. For
example, if day care relieves economic pressure and
consequent interpersonal stress within the family, the
child can potentially benefit from the improved home
environment. Similarly, when day care acts as a vehicle
for connecting families with community services (e.g.,
health care or food programs), the child is again likely
to be a beneficiary.

In the same vein, while there is evidence for
longitudinal stability of some social traits, such as
aggressiveness and dependency, from the elementary school
years on, evidence for stability of all but a few traits
from the infant, toddler, and preschool years is slight
(Kagan and Moss, 1962). There is evidence for stability
of certain broad features of temperament from infancy on,
chiefly in the work of Chess, Thomas, and their colleagues
(e.g., Thomas et al., 1969). However, it is questionable
whether temperamental differences are very susceptible to
environment and whether temperament, as distinguished

from social behavior and social skills, is what day care
providers try to influence. It is also difficult to know
how to search for longitudinal stability in social traits.
We cannot simply assume that a given pattern of behavior
in adults or older children derives developmentally from
a superficially similar pattern in younger children. We
need a theoretical framework to tell us which behavior
patterns should be associated over time. Thus, to demand
that any program for young children prove its worth by
demonstrating that it produces enduring change in social
behavior is to demand a great deal.

We have much to learn about the time course of effects
of early childhood programs. The typical finding for
measures of cognitive gain is an appreciable effect by
the end of the program, gradually diminishing as the
child progresses in school. On the other hand, there is
exciting recent evidence of long-term "sleeper" effects,
which manifest themselves in the late elementary school
years or beyond. Recent work suggests that these long-
term effects may be due partly to socialization--to
changes in work habits, motivation, and the like (see
Weikart, in this volume.) There is also some evidence
for sleeper effects in social development, though not for
effects specifically attributable to intervention programs
(Kagan and Moss, 1962). Until we understand the temporal
structure of intervention effects in the social domain,
evaluations of the effects of day care and intervention
programs in this domain will remain hit-or-miss.

Finally, almost without exception the variables,
measures, and study designs arising from developmental
and educational research reflect scant attention to the
information needs of policy makers. Much of the research
is, properly, motivated by theoretical concerns. Even
where the concerns are practical, they tend to be narrow.
Virtually all of the measures used within developmental
psychology and early childhood education address pieces
of a single concern of policy makers, i.e., the quality
of programs, in particular their benefits for children.
This focus is obviously appropriate to the fields in
question--but if the policy maker's broad concerns for
access, equity, and efficiency as well as quality are to
be addressed, disciplinary boundaries will have to be
broken and new, integrative efforts at measurement must
be undertaken. Some tentative steps already taken in
this direction are discussed in the later section on the
effects of alternative day care policies on the child
care delivery system.

Outcomes for Care Givers

We do not often think of outcomes for providers of a
service--and outcomes for care givers are, admittedly,
secondary relative to outcomes for children and families.
However, day care is somewhat unusual in this regard.
Such outcomes are of interest to federal policy makers,
as evidenced by the facts that (1) a provision for employment of low-income mothers was formerly included in
federal day care purchasing standards and (2) the government has supported a credentialing organization, the
Child Development Associate (CDA) consortium, which sets
standards and implements procedures by which day care
workers can receive a formal, transferable certificate of
competence for on-the-job experience and training.
Potential outcomes for care givers thus include changes
in income, working conditions, job satisfaction, and
professional growth as a consequence of experience and
training. To our knowledge the effects of the CDA
program (on care givers or on children) have not been
evaluated. More generally, while the low wages of care
givers have been documented and their behavior has been
studied insofar as it affects children, attitudes and
behaviors have not been assessed from the perspective of
care givers themselves to any significant extent. A great
deal remains to be learned about what care givers like and
do not like about their jobs, what kinds of training and
other assistance they find useful, what causes "burnout,"
and what kinds of care-giving arrangements are best for
them.

Outcomes for Families and Communities

An earlier section suggested several ways in which day
care programs might benefit parents and families, with
concomitant benefits for the child. This section takes
up the theme of effects on parents, families, and the
wider community directly. In this domain, unlike that of
developmental effects, there is not a wide range of
measures from previous research to consider. Basically
there have been four types of relevant research: (1)
studies of effects of day care on parent-child interaction
and family functioning; (2) studies of parental preferences and satisfaction; (3) studies of parent-provider
relationships; and, at a different level, (4) studies of
the effects of the availability of child care on parental

employment and income. Only the fourth type of research, on economic impact, has been at all extensive.

Parent-Child Interaction and Family Functioning

A few studies have examined effects of day care on mother-child interaction in laboratory settings (Ramey and Mills, 1975; Falender and Heber, 1976). Some results suggest that low-income mothers of children in day care interact more and give more positive and less negative feedback in a training task than mothers of home-reared children, but these results are subject to various interpretations, and later work has found no differences in parent-child interaction (Ramey et al., 1979; Farran and Ramey, 1980). Several studies have used Caldwell's Index of Home Stimulation (a set of descriptors of the home that have been shown to correlate with intellectual achievement) with mixed results as to whether day care produces any differences, positive or negative (Fowler and Khan, 1974, 1975; Ramey and Mills, 1975). Other measures used in studies of family impact have been Schaeffer and Aaronson's Maternal Inventory, designed to measure the mother's attitude toward and interest in her child (Fowler and Kahn, 1974, 1975); parents' self-reports of knowledge about childrearing (Steinberg and Green, 1979); parents' attitudes toward children's rights (Ramey et al., 1981); mothers' self-reports of marital satisfaction (Meyers, 1973; Steinberg and Green, 1978); and family structure and functioning as measured by the St. Paul's Profile (Golden et al., 1978).

Several comments can be made about those studies as a group. First, and most important, there are few such studies (and several of these cited are either unpublished or still in progress). The potential effects of day care on the child's experience in the family and on the climate, cohesiveness, and strength of the family itself are neglected areas of research that deserve much greater attention. We lack a systematic theoretical treatment of the aspects of family functioning that might be affected by day care.

Second, the above listing does not differentiate day care programs that have active parent counseling or education components from those that do not. Presumably, effects on mother-child interaction ought to be greatest in programs that teach mothers how to care for their children; similarly, marital satisfaction and family

functioning ought to profit most from programs with
family counseling components. There is a clear need to
tailor outcome measures to the goals and practices of
programs. Also, there is a substantial literature on the
effects of parent education and counseling (e.g., Brim,
1959; Goodson and Hess, 1978). Obviously, studies of day
care programs with such components would do well to borrow
from that literature; the few existing studies have begun
to do so. Again, lacking systematic thought on day care
as it affects the family, we are in need of more work to
determine under what circumstances such supplementary
services are useful and supportive to families and under
what circumstances they are superfluous or intrusive.

Third, despite evidence of a growing concern with day
care's effects on the family, a potential larger step has
not been taken. There do not yet appear to be studies
that relate the availability of child care at the
community level to social indicators bearing on the
health of families within communities--e.g., rates of
divorce and desertion, child abuse, out-of-home
placements of children, etc.

Parent Preferences and Parent Satisfaction

A number of studies have used interviews and questionnaires to assess parent preferences for different types
of day care arrangements as well as parents' satisfaction
with the child care facilities they use (e.g., Hill,
1977, 1978; Steinberg and Green, 1979; Rowe et al., 1972;
Fosburg and Hawkins, 1981). In general, these studies
show that parents are reasonably well satisfied with the
care they use and that they prefer care close to home,
usually family day care or in-home care for infants and
toddlers and center care for preschoolers, because of its
presumed educational benefits. However, their options in
choosing particular day care facilities are set largely
on the basis of cost, location, and schedule.

Some ambiguities of interpretation surrounding the
preference data were alluded to earlier. Concerning
satisfaction data, existing results are largely tainted
by the fact that most such information has been collected
from parents whose children are currently in day care;
presumably those who were seriously dissatisfied would
have withdrawn their children from day care and themselves
from the researchers' samples. In general, this is an
area of investigation that seems ripe for imaginative

instrumentation and research design, aimed at providing
qualitative insight into the reasons for parental
preferences and satisfaction or dissatisfaction.
Existing preference data tell us little more than the
facts the market itself reveals.

Parent-Care Giver Relations

Relations between parents and the people that serve
their children are a topic of intense political interest.
Federal day care purchasing standards require that parents
be represented on the boards of centers serving large
numbers of subsidized children and that parent participation in general be encouraged. However, as a reviewer of
the literature on parent involvement—and a strong
advocate for it—notes, "the assumption that some form of
parent participation would increase parental proximity to
surrogate child care establishments, and that increased
proximity would improve the quality of child care or ease
the child's transition from home to institution, has
never been directly assessed" (Fein, 1976).
In the years since that review, several projects have
examined parent-care giver relations. One study focused
on the frequency and nature of contacts and on center
policies that facilitate or discourage contact (Powell,
1977, 1978). Measures were based on self-reports in
interviews and questionnaires. Another study focused on
the conflicting expectations of both black and white
parents and staff in educationally oriented day care
centers operated by the California public schools (Joffe,
1977). A third study examined parents' preferences for
different kinds of participation and found that they
preferred active roles in the classroom (e.g., as
volunteer aides) as well as participation in educational
programs and social events (Travers et al., 1977; Layzer,
1980). Parents in federally funded centers were far more
likely than those in parent-fee centers to want to
participate in center governance through membership on
governing boards. A great deal remains to be learned
about relations between parents and providers, especially
about how these relations affect children. Continuities
and discontinuities related to social class and ethnic
culture are important to investigate in this regard.

Effects on Employment and Income

The impact of the availability and/or subsidy of day care on families' employment patterns and wages is an outcome important to policy makers, because federal and state day care policies have often been determined in relation to broader economic policies and, more specifically, in relation to welfare-reform objectives.

Several studies have examined the effect of child care on women's labor force participation (Conly, 1975; Ditmore and Prosser, 1973; Jusenius and Shortlidge, 1975; Kurz et al., 1975; Shaw, 1974). The principal conclusion drawn from these studies and related data has been that the provision of day care does not significantly affect the labor force participation of women. The principal determinants are rather the availability of suitable jobs and the existence of other barriers to employment of low-income women. The studies suggest that readily accessible child care services induce no more than 10 percent of nonworking, low-income mothers to enter the work force; the figure is higher if families having children under three are excluded.

Although the availability of day care may not induce many women to enter the labor force, there is some evidence that those mothers who are enabled to work by the availability of day care enjoy economic benefits, such as higher income (Peters, 1973), more education (Lally, 1973), Ramey et al., 1981), and enhanced work skills (Ramey et al., 1981). Not all studies find such benefits, however. The New York Infant Care Study (Golden et al., 1978) found few effects on income. Perhaps more important for policy purposes, the cost-effectiveness of day care seems particularly questionable for parents at the low end of the income scale. Several studies have shown that it would be less costly for the government to provide income maintenance than to provide day care in "developmental," center-based programs while requiring low-income mothers to work (Rivlin, 1973; Woolsey, 1977).

In our view the studies cited above highlight the needs, cited at the beginning of this paper, to frame the goals and value assumptions of outcome measurement clearly and to draw policy conclusions with great care, considering not only findings in a single outcome domain but taking account of other domains as well. Consider first the finding concerning the relatively modest impact of day care on women's labor force participation. It is not at all clear that increasing such participation is a generally agreed upon policy goal. (From the point of view of those who fear ill effects of day care on children, it is clearly to be avoided.) If the goal of day care policy is to ensure that children will be adequately cared for when their mothers choose to work and are able to find employment, it is irrelevant whether the availability of day care affects women's propensity to enter the labor force. Only if day care is seen primarily as a device for reducing the welfare rolls is its modest effect on labor force participation important. And even then, the 10 percent increase need not be viewed as small; in the absence of prior data, it merely establishes an empirical benchmark--a realistic expectation-- against which alternative policies can be evaluated.

Consider next the studies that suggest that income maintenance may be more cost-effective than day care. Such studies weigh immediate economic benefits (employment, income, reductions in public expenditure, tax contributions) against the costs of care. However, consideration of nonmonetary costs and benefits and/or long-term benefits--psychological effects on the child and parent, possible effects on family conflict and dissolution, possible long-term improvements in the mother's earning power, and possible increases in the likeliood that the child will become economically self-sufficient--might shift the balance of interpretation. Also, cost-benefit studies of subsidized day care have for the most part been based on the assumption that developmental day care centers will be the principal delivery mechanism. However, utilization studies demonstrate that informal day care arrangements such as neighborhood family day care are currently used by working mothers with far greater frequency than are formal centers. The fundamental question regarding what kind of day care should be eligible for subsidy must be examined as a policy issue in connection with any thorough assessment of the cost and benefits of providing day care to low-income families as a concomitant to employment.

The above remarks relate to a broader issue: the need to improve the theoretical framework for linking day care policies to family economic functioning. While some research exists attempting to model the complex interrelationships involved in these areas, further development is necessary. Without such development, predictions and interpretations of the effects of day care on employment behavior and economic outcomes are frequently based on

assumptions that do not reflect the range of alternative
policies available to decision makers or the complexities
of actual relationships in these areas.

Conclusion

In conclusion it is important to stress that whole
areas of investigation are missing from the list of four
topics considered above. To the degree that day care
provides parents with counseling and advocacy, intended
to make them more effective in dealing with social service
agencies, schools, and other community institutions,
potential effects on relations between parents and such
institutions are critical outcomes to examine. These
outcomes have not been investigated in connection with
day care, though they have been examined in connection
with comprehensive family service programs attached to
Head Start. The difficult issues that arise in assessing
these programs are discussed by Hewett and Deloria, in
this volume.

Even more broadly, the effects of a healthy day care
market on the economic and social well-being of a
community have, to our knowledge, never been studied. To
do so would require careful selection of communities and
ingenious use of a wide range of social indicators, not
only the labor force participation of mothers but also
the influx of industry, in-migration and out-migration of
families, perhaps even real estate values. This kind of
investigation would clearly bear little resemblance to a
laboratory study; it would attempt to explicate complex
community dynamics, blending qualitative and quantitative
information with the ultimate aim of logical coherence
and empirical plausibility, rather than statistical
generalizability in the strict sense.

Effects of Alternative Day Care Policies on
the Child Care Service Delivery System

This section returns to the issue with which our
taxonomy of day care outcomes began: service delivery.
We began by considering the services received by the
individual child and argued that they could legitimately
be considered outcomes of care for some purposes. We end
by considering the effects that alternative governmental
policies might have on the aggregate profile of day care
services in a community, state, or the nation.

Policy makers have a number of broad concerns with respect to any social service program: (a) access to services on the part of the target population; (b) equity of service delivery across ethnic groups, residents of different geographic regions, and any other subgroups of the population with a legitimate claim to services; (c) quality and effectiveness of programs in achieving service objectives; and (d) efficiency of delivery--cost effectiveness and administrative burden relative to other means of delivering the same service or to alternative uses of funds. Most of this paper has addressed issues of quality and effectiveness, as has most research on day care. However, issues of access, equity, and efficiency will loom large in the 1980s as increased demands are made on both public and private systems for providing child care. In fact, as argued by Kennedy and McDaniels in this volume, policy makers, particularly at the federal level, often leave determinations of quality and effectiveness to consumers, providers, professionals, and local administrators, on the theory that these issues are best addressed in the context of local needs and interests.

As indicated in our introduction, policy makers have but a few primary tools for influencing the profile of care--funding mechanisms, regulations, and administrative guidelines and practices. They need to know how the profile of services and associated costs will be affected by policy choices between emphasis on categorical block-grant funding, as under Title XX, and mechanisms such as income disregard, the tax credit, and vouchers, which give greater scope to parental initiative, or between strict and lenient regulatory policies. They also need to know how public services interact with preexisting private mechanisms of service delivery. For example, does public subsidy of day care reduce dependence on the extended family as a source of child care? (Answering this basic service delivery question is a prerequisite to answering questions about whether day care strengthens or weakens families, destroys or extends natural support mechanisms.) Policy makers also have secondary tools such as the ability to provide training and information and referral services, which can potentially enhance the operation of the system as a whole. They need to know how these services affect the supply of qualified care givers and the supply and demand for different types of care. As suggested earlier, many of the policy maker's concerns are systemic, in that he or she cares not about

a program in isolation but about a program in the context
of other programs or service delivery mechanisms—both
those that actually exist and those that might be funded.

These systemic service delivery questions can be
addressed through a wide variety of atheoretical
indicators—quantitative measures deriving from no
particular conceptual framework. Examples include the
numbers of clients served, types of services provided,
costs of services, capacity and utilization rates,
licensure rates for different types of facilities, cost
variations across types of facilities, employment
characteristics of the day care industry, etc.
Researchers have not in general made much use of such
measures, and as a consequence research has been less
informative to policy than it might be. Precisely
because these measures are atheoretical, they tend to
fall outside the concerns of the specific disciplines and
to seem intellectually uninteresting. What has been
missed is the potential intellectual excitement of
constructing a picture of an extremely complex
phenomenon—the day care market—within which these
measures would take on meaning.

CONCLUSIONS AND RECOMMENDATIONS

First, the outcomes of day care are difficult to
measure because different constituencies have different,
often conflicting views about what day care is intended
to accomplish, what is important to know, and what
measures are appropriate to use. This multiplicity of
views can lead to confusion, distortion, misuse, and
unfulfilled expectations between the public and the policy
makers regarding the results of research; hence, it may
undermine the credibility of research itself. Furthermore, to the extent that the concerns of some constituencies are excluded from research altogether, important
questions may go unanswered, and the utility of research
may be further reduced.

Second, day care research in developmental psychology
has for the most part sought to compare the long-term
developmental effects resulting from group care as
opposed to home rearing. Much attention has focused on
attachment to the mother and on cognitive skills as
measured by standardized tests. While many other aspects
of social behavior and development have been examined in
individual studies, no consensus on critical variables or

measures has emerged. Moreover, little is actually known about the duration of effects, their generality across situations and other important properties. Measures of the child's immediate experience--his or her interactions with care givers and peers--have received insufficient attention as indices of the quality of care. Measures of impact of enhanced nutrition, health care, and other "supplementary" services have been neglected to an even greater degree. Only limited attempts have been made to differentiate the effects of center care from those of family day care; in-home care by persons other than the parent--relatives or paid helpers--has hardly been studied at all.

Third, except in the areas of income and employment, effects of day care on parents, families, and communities have received insufficient attention. Little is known about effects on family functioning, family-community relations, or the social climate of the community as a whole. For example, virtually nothing is known about the impact of day care on child abuse, marital stability, out-of-home placements, etc.

Fourth, perhaps because day care research has focused more on program than on policy issues, aggregate atheoretical indicators of service delivery have rarely been treated as outcomes. Matters of great concern to policy makers--numbers of children served, availability of services to members of ethnic minority groups, the handicapped, residents of rural as well as urban areas, etc.--have not aroused the intellectual interest of researchers. In only a few studies have questions of cost been juxtaposed with questions of quality. Thus the policy maker's legitimate concerns with access, equity, cost-effectiveness, and efficient management have largely been bypassed in favor of researchers' preoccupation with selected aspects of the quality of care, thwarting the application of simple, useful measures to larger questions and widening the gulf between research and policy. Systemic effects, such as the impact of alternative funding mechanisms and regulations on the availability of different types of care, or the impact of publicly subsidized care on informal service delivery systems, such as the extended family, have not been adequately studied.

Finally, a fundamental conclusion not stressed earlier that underlies many of the more specific conclusions documented in the foregoing pages is that existing day care research lacks an overarching theoretical framework.

Day care has been studied in the absence of an integrative theory that deals with it as a developmental environment, part of an interlocking web of social institutions, and a social service regulated by government policies.

Until these issues are confronted, basic research and technical tinkering to improve outcome measures will probably have limited payoffs. Future efforts in science and technology are more likely to lead to fundamental improvements in outcome measurement if systematic efforts are made to address the enumerated shortcomings of existing approaches, which we enumerate below.

Processes must be established to ensure that the views of all relevant constituencies are reflected in choosing outcomes. While not every constituency has a stake in every evaluation, those who do must be represented if a particular evaluation is to be credible. Researchers must learn to ask, systematically and routinely: What outcomes are important? For whom? What measures will communicate most meaningfully? To whom? What actions or decisions will be based on the resulting information? A process for ensuring that these questions are asked and that the answers generated inform the measurement process may avert or reduce the inappropriateness, misuse, lack of credibility, and limited usefulness that have afflicted many past studies of day care.

In the domain of developmental effects, dependence on a handful of standardized measures of cognitive skills and an unstandardized grab bag of measures of social behavior must be reduced. To do so will ultimately require nothing less than a broader, deeper, and more systematic concept of development. To fully understand the developmental effects of day care, we need an empirical taxonomy of skills and dispositions and a clear understanding of how cognitive and socioemotional characteristics interrelate. We need to understand which aspects of behavior are situationally controlled and which can be expected to generalize across situations. We need to understand the time course of development of various characteristics, so that we know when to expect short-term but transient effects, when to expect longitudinal stability, and when to expect sleeper effects. All this, of course, is a tall order, tantamount to saying that we need a more mature science of developmental psychology. But until we begin to achieve these goals, we must be extremely cautious about evaluating programs in terms of their developmental effects as currently measurable. Thus this recommendation is only

in part a predictable plea of the researcher for more
research; it is also an exhortation to modesty and,
implicitly, a suggestion that basic researchers may
profit from attention to applied problems. A serious
attempt to understand how different day care environments
foster or impede development can only lead to a more
thorough understanding of development itself.

The immediate experiences of children in day care must
be seen as ends in themselves, not merely means--as
immediate outcomes, which may also be processes through
which long-term developmental outcomes are achieved.
Quality of care from the point of view of the child
depends not only on long-term developmental effects but,
in the first instance, on the physical and human environment in which the child spends a substantial portion of
his or her time. To treat children's experiences as
outcomes requires that we develop descriptors of the
physical environment that capture what is important for
children--elusive qualities such as privacy, accessibility, stimulation, and, of course, safety. More
importantly, we need richer yet more practical ways to
describe human interaction in the day care setting
through refinements and extensions of existing
observation systems and rating scales. Once again, an
interplay of basic and applied research is indicated.

Specific effort must be devoted to inventing measures
of children's experiences and development that capture
the distinctive advantages and disadvantages of the
different environments in which they receive nonparental
care, i.e., centers, family day care homes, the homes of
relatives, and their own homes. Very different claims
are made by proponents of the various types of care; for
example, centers are said to provide group experiences
that prepare the child for school, while family day care
is said to provide a home-like environment and in-home
care the security of the home itself. Efforts at
measurement have begun to address those claims, but until
this work comes to fruition, the claims will remain in
the realm of rhetoric, and parental choices will be made
and policy debates conducted on essentially ideological
grounds.

Attention must be paid to the host of existing
atheoretical indicators, such as counts of children
served and descriptors of services delivered. Such
measures have immediate practical utility as management
devices and tools of accountability. In addition, they
have enormous potential value in assessing the systemic

outcomes of day care and (intended and unintended)
systemic effects of day care policies, e.g., shifts in
the distribution of types of care in response to funding
and regulatory policies. What is needed is not so much
development of new measures, but development of a better
conceptual framework for interpreting existing measures.
Many atheoretical indicators have little meaning in
themselves; most are influenced by many factors and
therefore are ambiguous when viewed in isolation. Yet
when interpreted in contexts provided by well-chosen
questions, well-conceived studies, and other measures,
they can yield invaluable insights.

Finally, several of the above recommendations imply
what is perhaps the most fundamental recommendation of
all: We must somehow grope our way toward an approach to
day care that is less fragmented than that afforded by
existing disciplines, that will allow us to comprehend
day care as a whole rather than as a collection of
disconnected elements or relationships. Perhaps the most
promising conceptual framework currently available for
integrating the disparate levels of description that have
so far been applied to day care is the "ecological"
framework proposed by Bronfenbrenner (1979). That
framework has already been applied to day care by
Bronfenbrenner and others (Belsky et al., 1981). We are
aware that pleas for holistic social science can become
hollow cliches and that science often proceeds by
analysis and dissection. Yet ultimately science puts its
intellectual pieces back together in a new and more
meaningful way. Perhaps through interdisciplinary
borrowing and sustained attention to day care itself, as
a developmental environment, an adjunct support for
families, a social service, and a policy tool, we can
begin to reassemble the jigsaw-puzzle picture left us by
existing studies in psychology, sociology, economics, and
policy research.

REFERENCES

Ainsworth, M. D. S., Blehar, M., Waters, E., and Wall, S.
    (1978) Patterns of Attachment. Hillsdale, N.J.:
        Lawrence Erlbaum.
Ainsworth, M. D. S., and Wittig, B. A.
    (1969) Attachment and exploratory behavior of
        one-year-olds in a strange situation. In B.
        M. Foss, ed., Determinants of Infant
        Behavior. Volume 4. London: Methuen.

Barrett, H. S., and Koch, H. C.
(1930) The effect of nursery school training upon the mental test performance of a group of orphanage children. The Pedagogical Seminary and Journal of Genetic Psychology 37:102-122.

Baumrind, D., and Black, A. E.
(1967) Socialization practices associated with dimensions of competence in preschool boys and girls. Child Development 38:291-327.

Becker, W. C., and Krug, R. S.
(1964) A circumplex model for social behavior in children. Child Development 35:371-396.

Belsky, J., and Steinberg, L. D.
(1978) The effects of day care: a critical review. Child Development 49:929-949.

Belsky, J., Steinberg, L. D., and Walker, A.
(1981) The ecology of day care. In M. Lamb, ed., Childrearing in Non-Traditional Families. Hillsdale, N.J.: Lawrence Erlbaum.

Blehar, M.
(1974) Anxious attachment and defensive reactions associated with day care. Child Development 45:683-692.

Bloom, B.
(1964) Stability and Change in Human Characteristics. New York: John Wiley & Sons, Inc.

Bowlby, J.
(1969) Attachment and Loss. Volume I: Attachment. New York: Basic Books.

Brim, O. G.
(1959) Education for Child Rearing. New York: Russell Sage Foundation.

Bronfenbrenner, U.
(1979) The Ecology of Human Development. Cambridge, Mass.: Harvard University Press.

Caldwell, B. M., Wright, C. M., Honig, A. S., and Tannenbaum, J.
(1970) Infant care and attachment. American Journal of Orthopsychiatry 40:397-412.

Carew, J.
(1979) Observation Study of Care Givers and Children in Day Care Homes: Preliminary Results from Home Observations. Paper presented at the biennial meeting of the Society for Research in Child Development, San Francisco, April.

Clarke-Stewart, K. A.
    (1979) Assessing Social Development. Paper presented
           at the biennial meeting of the Society for
           Research in Child Development, San Francisco,
           March.
Clarke-Stewart, K. A.
    (1980) Complementary strategies for studying day care
           and social development. In S. Kilmer, ed.,
           Advances in Early Education and Day Care.
           Greenwich, Conn.: JAI Press Inc.
Cochran, M.
    (1977) A comparison of group day and family
           child-rearing patterns in Sweden. Child
           Development 48:702-707.
Coelen, C., Glantz, F., and Calore, D.
    (1978) Day Care Centers in the U.S.: A National
           Profile 1976-1977. Volume III of the final
           report of the National Day Care Study.
           Cambridge, Mass.: Abt Books.
Congressional Budget Office
    (1978) Children and Preschool: Options for Federal
           Support. Washington, D.C.: U.S. Government
           Printing Office.
Conly, S. R.
    (1975) Subsidized Day Care and the Employment of
           Lower Income Mothers: A Case Study. Ph.D.
           dissertation, Department of Economics,
           University of South Carolina.
Cronbach, L. H., Gleser, G. C., Nanda, H., and
Rajaratnam, N.
    (1972) The Dependability of Behavioral Measures:
           Theory of Generalizability for Scores and
           Profiles. New York: John Wiley & Sons, Inc.
Dennis, W.
    (1941) Infant development under conditions of
           restricted practice and of minimum social
           stimulation. Genetic Psychological Monographs
           23:143-184.
Dennis, W., and Najarian, P.
    (1957) Infant development under environmental
           handicap. Psychological Monographs 71:(Whole
           No. 436).
Ditmore, J., and Prosser, W. R.
    (1973) A Study of Day Care's Effect on the Labor
           Force Participation of Low-Income Mothers.
           Washington, D.C.: Office of Economic
           Opportunity.

Doyle, A. B.
  (1975) Infant development in day care. Developmental
          Psychology 11:655-656.
Etaugh, C.
  (1980) Effects of nonmaternal care on children.
          American Psychologist 35:309-319.
Falender, C., and Heber, R.
  (1976) Mother-Child Interaction and Participation in
          a Longitudinal Program. Unpublished paper.
          Rehabilitation Research and Training Center,
          Madison, Wisconsin.
Farran, D., and Ramey, C.
  (1980) Social class differences in dyadic involvement
          during infancy. Child Development 51:254-257.
Fein, G.
  (1976) Infant day care and the family: regulatory
          strategies to ensure parent participation.
          Unpublished paper prepared for the Assistant
          Secretary for Planning and Evaluation, U.S.
          Department of Health, Education, and Welfare.
Fiene, R. J.
  (1973) The differential structural characteristics of
          sentences formed by preschool children in
          family and group care centers. Unpublished
          paper. Department of Psychology, State
          University of New York at Stony Brook, August.
Fosburg, S., and Hawkins, P.
  (1981) Final Report of the National Family Day Care
          Home Study. Volume I: Summary. Cambridge,
          Mass.: Abt Books.
Fowler, W., and Khan, N.
  (1974) The Development of a Prototype Infant and
          Child Day Care Center in Metropolitan
          Toronto. Ontario Institute for Studies in
          Education. Year III Progress Report.
          Unpublished.
Fowler, W., and Kahn, N.
  (1975) The Development of a Prototype Infant and
          Child Day Care Center in Metropolitan
          Toronto. Ontario Institute for Studies in
          Education. Year IV Progress Report.
          Unpublished.
Fraiberg, S.
  (1977) Every Child's Birthright: In Defense of
          Mothering. New York: Basic Books.

Golden, M., Rosenbluth, L., Grossi, M., Policare, H., Freeman, H., and Brownlee, E.
    (1978) The New York City Infant Day Care Study. New York: Medical and Health Research Association of New York City.

Goodson, B. D., and Hess, R. D.
    (1978) The effects of parent training programs on child performance and parent behavior. In B. Brown, ed., Found: Long-Term Gains from Early Education. Boulder, Colo.: Westview Press.

Gouin-Decarie, T.
    (1965) Intelligence and Affectivity in Early Childhood. New York: International Universities Press.

Hawkins, P., Wilcox, M., Gillis, G., Porter, A., and Carew, J.
    (1979) Observation Study of Care Givers and Children in Day Care Programs. Paper presented at the biennial meeting of the Society for Research in Child Development, San Francisco, Spring.

Heinicke, C., Friedman, D., Prescott, E., Puncel, C., and Sale, J.
    (1973) The organization of day care: considerations relating to the mental health of child and family. American Journal of Orthopsychiatry 43:8-22.

Hill, C. R.
    (1977) The child care market: a review of the evidence and implications for federal policy. Unpublished paper prepared for the Assistant Secretary for Planning and Evaluation, U.S. Department of Health, Education, and Welfare.

Hill, C. R.
    (1978) Private demand for child care: implications forpublic policy. Evaluation Quarterly 2:523-545.

Hoffman, L. W.
    (1974) Effects of maternal employment on the child. Developmental Psychology 10:204-208.

Hunt, J. McV.
    (1961) Intelligence and Experience. New York: Ronald Press.

Hutt, C., and Vaizey, M. J.
    (1966) Differential effects of group density on social behavior. Nature 209:1371-1372.

Joffe, C. E.
  (1977) Friendly Intruders: Childcare Professionals
          and Family Life. Berkeley, Calif.:
          University of California Press.
Johnson, B. L., and Hayghe, H.
  (1977) Labor force participation of married women,
          March 1976. Monthly Labor Review 100:32-36.
Johnson, O. G., and Bommarito, J. W.
  (1971) Tests and Measurements in Child Development: A
          Handbook. San Francisco, Calif.:
          Jossey-Bass, Inc., Publishers.
Jusenius, C. L., and Shortlidge, R. L.
  (1975) Dual Careers: A Longitudinal Study of Labor
          Market Experience of Women, Columbus, Ohio:
          Ohio State University, Center for Human
          Resource Research.
Kamerman, S., and Kahn, A.
  (1978) Family Policy: Government and Families in
          Fourteen Countries. New York: Columbia
          University Press.
Kagan, J., and Moss, H.
  (1962) Birth to Maturity. New York: John Wiley &
          Sons, Inc.
Kagan, J., Kearsley, R. B., and Zelazo, P. R.
  (1976) The Effects of Infant Day-Care on Psychological
          Development. In The Effects of Early
          Experience on Child Development. Symposium
          presented at the meeting of the American
          Association for the Advancement of Science,
          Boston, February.
Keniston, K., and the Carnegie Council on Children.
  (1977) All Our Children: The American Family Under
          Pressure. New York: Harcourt Brace
          Jovanovich, Inc.
Kohn, M. L., and Rosman, B. L.
  (1972) A social competence scale and symptom checklist
          for the preschool child: factor dimensions.
          Their cross-instrument generality and
          longitudinal persistence. Developmental
          Psychology 6:430-444.
Kruvant, C., Redish, G., Dodge, D. T., Hurt, N. J.,
Passantino, R. J., and Sheehan, R.
  (1976) The effects on children of the organization
          and the design of the day care physical
          environment--appropriateness of the federal
          interagency day care requirements. Unpublished
          paper prepared for the Assistant Secretary for

Planning and Evaluation, U.S. Department of
Health, Education, and Welfare.

Kurz, M., Robins, R., and Spiegelman, R.
(1975)   A Study of the Demand for Child Care by
Working Mothers.   Menlo Park, Calif.:
Stanford Research Institute.

Lally, R.
(1973)   The Family Development Research Program.
Progress Report. Unpublished paper. Syracuse
University.

Lay, M., and Meyer, W.
(1973)   Teacher/child behaviors in an open environment
day care program. Unpublished paper.
Syracuse University Children's Center.

Layzer, J.
(1980)   Interviews with parents. In Technical
Appendices to the National Day Care Study.
Volume IV-B:185-216 of the final report of the
National Day Care Study. Cambridge, Mass.:
Abt Associates, Inc.

Lippman, M. A., and Grote, B. H.
(1974)   Socioemotional Effects of Day Care. Final
project report. Grant No. OCD-CB-219, Office
of Child Development.

Loo, C.
(1972)   The effects of spatial density on the social
behavior of children. Journal of Applied
Social Psychology 2:372-382.

Macrae, J. W., and Herbert-Jackson, E.
(1976)   Are behavioral effects of infant day care
programs specific? Developmental Psychology
12:269-270.

Medley, D. M., and Mitzel, H. E.
(1963)   Measuring classroom behavior by systematic
observation. In N. L. Gage, ed., Handbook of
Research on Teaching. Chicago, Ill.: Rand
McNally.

Meyer, W.
(1976)   Staffing Characteristics and Child Outcomes.
Unpublished paper prepared for the Assistant
Secretary for Planning and Evaluation, U.S.
Department of Health, Education, and Welfare.

Meyers, L.
(1973)   The relationship between substitute child
care, maternal employment and female marital
satisfaction. In D. Peters, ed., A Summary of
the Pennsylvania Day Care Study. University
Park, Pa.: The Pennsylvania State University.

Moore, T.
   (1975) Exclusive early mothering and its
           alternatives: the outcome to adolescence.
           Scandinavian Journal of Psychology 16:255-272.
National Research Council
   (1976) Toward A National Policy for Children and
           Families. Advisory Committee on Child
           Development. Washington, D.C.: National
           Academy of Sciences.
Paraskevopoulos, J., and Hunt, J. McV.
   (1971) Object construction and imitation under
           differing conditions of rearing. Journal of
           Genetic Psychology 119:301-321.
Parten, M. B.
   (1932) Social participation among preschool
           children. Journal of Abnormal and Social
           Psychology 27:243-269.
Peters, D.
   (1973) A Summary of the Pennsylvania Day Care Study.
           University Park, Pa.: The Pennsylvania State
           University.
Peterson, D. R.
   (1961) Behavior problems in middle childhood.
           Journal of Consulting Psychology 25:205-209.
Powell, D. R.
   (1977) The Interface Between Families and Child Care
           Programs: A Study of Parent-Caregiver
           Relationships. Detroit, Mich.:
           Merrill-Palmer Institute.
Powell, D. R.
   (1978) The interpersonal relationship between parents
           and care givers in day care settings. American
           Journal of Orthopsychiatry 48:680-689.
Prescott, E.
   (1973) A Comparison of Three Types of Day Care and
           Nursery School/Home Care. Paper presented at
           the biennial meeting of the Society for
           Research in Child Development, Philadelphia,
           Pa., March.
Prescott, E., and David, T. G.
   (1976) Concept Paper on the Effects of the Physical
           Environment on Day Care. Unpublished paper
           prepared for the Assistant Secretary for
           Planning and Evaluation, U.S. Department of
           Health, Education, and Welfare.

159

Prescott, E., Jones, E., and Kritchevsky, S.
   (1967) Group Day Care as a Child-Rearing Environment.
           Report prepared for the Children's Bureau,
           U.S. Department of Health, Education, and
           Welfare. Pacific Oaks College, Pasadena,
           Calif.
Prescott, E., Jones, E., Kritchevsky, S., Milich, C., and
Haselhoef, E.
   (1975) Assessment of child-rearing environments.
           Part II. An Environmental Inventory. Pacific
           Oaks College, Pasadena, Calif.
Prescott, E., Kritchevsky, S., and Jones, E.
   (1972) The Day Care Environmental Inventory. Pacific
           Oaks College, Pasadena, Calif.
Prescott, E., and Milich, C.
   (1974) School's Out: Group Day Care for the School-
           Age Child. Pacific Oaks College, Pasadena,
           Calif.
Provence, S., and Lipton, R.
   (1962) Infants in Institutions. New York:
           International Universities Press.
Ramey, C., Dorval, B., and Baker-Ward, L.
   (1981) Group day care and socially disadvantaged
           families: effects on the child and the
           family. In S. Kilmer, ed., Advances in Early
           Education and Day Care. Greenwich, Conn.:
           JAI Press, Inc.
Ramey, C., Farran, D., and Campbell, F.
   (1979) Predicting IQ from mother-infant
           interactions. Child Development 50:804-814.
Ramey, C., and Mills, J.
   (1975) Mother-Infant Interaction Patterns as a
           Function of Rearing Conditions. Paper
           presented at the biennial meeting of the
           Society for Research in Child Development,
           Denver, Colo., April.
Ricciuti, H. N.
   (1974) Fear and development of social attachments in
           the first year of life. In M. Lewis and L. A.
           Rosenblum, eds., The Origins of Human
           Behavior: Fear. New York: John Wiley & Sons,
           Inc.
Ricciuti, H. N.
   (1976) Effects of Infant Day Care Experience on
           Behavior and Development: Implications for
           Social Policy. Unpublished paper prepared for
           the Assistant Secretary for Planning and

Evaluation, U.S. Department of Health,
Education, and Welfare.

Rivlin, A.
  (1973) Child care. In C. L. Schultz et al., eds.,
          Setting National Priorities: The 1973
          Budget. Washington, D.C.: The Brookings
          Institution.

Rowe, R., et al.
  (1972) Child Care in Massachusetts: The Public
          Responsibility. Report prepared for the
          Massachusetts Advisory Council on Education.
          Cambridge, Mass.: Harvard University Press.

Rubenstein, J. L., and Howes, C.
  (1979) Caregiving and infant behavior in day care and
          in homes. Developmental Psychology 15:1-24.

Rubenstein, J. L., Pedersen, F. A., and Yarrow, L. J.
  (1977) What happens when mother is away: a
          comparison of mothers and substitute care
          givers. Developmental Psychology 13:143-154.

Ruopp, R., Travers, J., Coelen, C., and Glantz, F.
  (1979) Children at the Center. Volume I of the final
          report of the National Day Care Study.
          Cambridge, Mass.: Abt Books.

Schaefer, E. S.
  (1961) Converging conceptual models for maternal
          behavior and for child behavior. In J .C.
          Glidewell, ed., Parental Attitudes and Child
          Behavior. Springfield, Ill.: Charles C
          Thomas.

Schwarz, J. C., Strickland, R. G., and Krolick, G.
  (1974) Infant Day Care: Behavioral Effects at
          Preschool Age. Developmental Psychology
          10:502-506.

Shapiro, S.
  (1975) Preschool ecology: a study of three environ-
          mental variables. Reading Improvement
          12:236-241.

Shaw, L. B.
  (1974) The Utilization of Subsidized Child Care in
          the Gary Income Maintenance Experiment: A
          Preliminary Report. Washington, D.C.: Office
          of Economic Opportunity.

Spitz, R. A.
  (1945) Hospitalism: an inquiry into the genesis of
          psychiatric conditions in early childhood.
          Psychoanalytic Study of the Child 1:53-74.

161

Sroufe, L. A.
 (1979) The coherence of individual development:
early care, attachment and subsequent
developmental issues. American Psychologist
34:834-841.
Stallings, J., and Porter, A.
 (1980) National Day Care Home Study Observation
Component. Final report to the Day Care
Division, Administration for Children, Youth,
and Families, U.S. Department of Health,
Education, and Welfare. Menlo Park, Calif.:
SRI International.
Steinberg, L., and Green, C.
 (1978) Three types of day care: causes, concerns and
consequences. Unpublished paper, Program in
Social Ecology, University of California,
Irvine.
Steinberg, L., and Green, C.
 (1979) How Parents May Mediate the Effects of Day
Care. Paper presented at the biennial meeting
of the Society for Research in Child
Development, San Francisco, Calif., March.
Thomas, A., Chess, S., Birch, H. G., Hertzog, M. E., and
Korn, S.
 (1969) Behavioral Individuality in Early Childhood.
New York: New York University Press.
Travers, J., Coelen, C., and Ruopp, R.
 (1977) National Day Care Study Second Annual Report
1975-1976. Cambridge, Mass.: Abt Associates,
Inc..
UNCO, Inc.
 (1975) National Child Care Consumer Study: 1975.
Report prepared for the Office of Child
Development, U.S. Department of Health,
Education, and Welfare.
U.S. Department of Health, Education, and Welfare
 (1978) Social Services U.S.A.: July-September 1976.
Administration for Public Services.
Washington, D.C.: U.S. Government Printing
Office.
Vaughn, B. E., Gove, F. L., and Egeland, B.
 (1980) The relationship between out-of-home care and
the quality of infant-mother attachment in an
economically disadvantaged population. Child
Development 51:1203-1214.

Walker, D. K.
    (1973)   Socioemotional Measures for Preschool and
               Kindergarten Children San Francisco, Calif.:
               Jossey-Bass, Inc., Publishers.

Westinghouse Learning Corporation and Ohio University
    (1969)   The Impact of Head Start: An Evaluation of
               the Effects of Head Start Experience on
               Children's Cognitive and Affective
               Development. Westinghouse Learning
               Corporation and Ohio University.

Westinghouse Learning Corporation and Westat Research,
Inc.
    (1971)   Day Care Survey--1970; Summary Report and
               Basic Analysis. Report prepared for the
               Office of Economic Opportunity, Washington,
               D.C.

White, B. L.
    (1969)   Child development reseach: an edifice without
               a foundation. Merrill-Palmer Quarterly
               1:47-78.

Woolsey, S.
    (1977)   Pied piper politics and the child-care
               debate. Daedalus (Spring):127-145.

Zigler, E., and Trickett, P. K.
    (1978)   IQ, social competence and evaluation of early
               childhood intervention programs. American
               Psychologist 33:789-798.

Informing Policy Makers About Programs for Handicapped Children

Mary M. Kennedy and Garry L. McDaniels

When it comes to federal education legislation, the
saying "last but not least" applies well to handicapped
children. They have been last to receive the attention
of Congress, receiving federal educational assistance
only after services have been authorized for disadvantaged
and bilingual children. The services that have been
authorized, however, have by no means been trivial. Over
the past 15 years Congress has sponsored a number of
different programs for handicapped children, including
research and demonstration, teacher training, and the
production of media and materials for handicapped
learners. In 1975 congressional assistance for handicapped children culminated in a major piece of civil
rights legislation: the Education for All Handicapped
Children Act of 1975.

This chapter describes two particular federal programs
established for handicapped children. Through these
examples we hope to illustrate the kinds of information
federal policy makers need to improve their policies
regarding handicapped children as well as the kinds of
evaluation studies that would provide such information.
The two programs differ in funding mechanisms, requirements, and intent, thus offering a valuable contrast for
exploring questions regarding the types of evaluations
and outcome measures that are useful to federal policy
makers. The Handicapped Children's Early Education
Program is a discretionary grant program, offering federal
funds to public or private agencies that plan to develop
new strategies for serving young handicapped children.
The Education for All Handicapped Children Act of 1975 is
a formula grant program, providing funds to all school
districts serving handicapped children and stipulating a
variety of standards that must be met. The 1981

appropriations for these two programs were $20 million and $940 million, respectively.

Congress has rarely questioned the effectiveness of either of these programs during its authorization or appropriations hearings. Still missing from the history of federal legislation for the handicapped is the large national impact study and the ensuing debate over the interpretation of the data. These twin events, the yin and yang of educational evaluation, have been a tradition in other areas of federal education legislation, but have not been involved in programs for handicapped children. This paper aims to discover why that is and to determine what kinds of outcome measures are of interest to federal policy makers.

This paper has five sections. The first two describe the two programs. The third discusses the federal role that has apparently been adopted for the education of handicapped children. The fourth section describes outcomes of interest to federal policy makers, and the fifth section describes contributions evaluators can make.

THE HANDICAPPED CHILDREN'S EARLY EDUCATION PROGRAM: DISCRETIONARY GRANTS FOR EARLY EDUCATION

The Handicapped Children's Early Education Program was initiated during a period of high expectations for early intervention. The rationale for the program was put forth by the chairman of the Select Committee on Education when he opened the 1968 House hearings on the proposed program (U.S. Congress, House, 1968:2):

> Studies of child development have shown that early education can accelerate the development of handicapped children; yet most parents find that, while their children may be diagnosed as handicapped at birth or shortly thereafter, they must keep those children at home from school until they are at least five or six years of age. This is a waste of the critical years of a child's life.

The chairman's conviction was reiterated by the first witness, who said, "There is no sounder proposition in education than that the earlier the child is educated, the greater the return for the energy spent."

The program began with $1 million in 1968 and continues today with $20 million annually. It followed on the heels

of such federal programs as Head Start and Follow Through.
The projects supported by the program were labeled as both
"experimental" and "demonstrations"; that is, the program
offered a situation in which theoretical concepts could
be transformed into real activities and tested under real
circumstances. By supporting demonstration projects
Congress showed its faith in the general concept of early
childhood intervention and provided a forum in which
specific ideas might be tested, elaborated, and refined.
The Handicapped Children's Early Education Program aimed
not only to serve young handicapped children but also to
stimulate a new pattern of interactions among professionals, one in which ideas could readily pass from one
researcher to another and from researchers to
practitioners.

The implication is that the goal of Congress was not
to provide a particular type of early education to young
handicapped children but to stimulate interest in and
explorations into the possibilities of early education
for handicapped children. From the point of view of
Congress, then, the effectiveness of particular program
variations was an issue for the research community to
address, whereas the "outcome" of interest to Congress
was whether these explorations were occurring.[1]

How one measures the success of a program in expediting
exploration or in stimulating the production of new ideas
is not clear. The program does emphasize the dissemination of new program strategies, and funds are used to
support a number of mechanisms for communicating ideas.
Roughly a fourth of the projects are funded specifically
for outreach activities, and many of the remaining
demonstration projects are associated with colleges and
universities, whose faculty disseminate research findings
through professional journals. In addition, two centers
for technical assistance foster cross-fertilization of
ideas among projects by brokering assistance and by
holding conferences (U.S. Office of Education, 1979).
These activities are often designed not only to stimulate
the research community and agencies that provide services

_____

[1]This is not to say that they do not care whether the
projects would benefit young handicapped children; they
seemed to assume that benefits would accrue and therefore
to concentrate their efforts on stimulating program
development.

to handicapped children but also to stimulate the general
public as well. Concomitant with the activities
supported by the program has been a growing public
concern about the needs and rights of handicapped
children.

The Education for All Handicapped Children Act:
Financial Assistance to Schools

Since 1968 Congress's interest in education has
evolved in such a way that civil rights and equitable
educational treatment have superseded targeted compensation as a national priority. The Education for All
Handicapped Children Act of 1975 is a good example of
this newly evolving federal concern. It came into being
in the company of such federal initiatives as the Family
Education Rights and Privacy Act and the Emergency School
Aid Act. The need for the act was justified by such
statements as, "More than half of the handicapped children
in the United States do not receive appropriate educational services which would enable them to have full
equality of opportunity," and "[It is] in the national
interest that the federal government . . . provide
programs that meet the educational needs of handicapped
children in order to assure equal protection of the law"
(P.L. 94-142, Section 3). The act was designed to ensure
each handicapped child a free, appropriate public education commensurate with his or her unique needs. It
contains the following four requirements:

1. The program and placement for any given handicapped child must be determined on the basis of his or
her individual needs rather than on the basis of any
category or label that might be assigned to the child.
2. The child's individual needs are to be determined
by a group of individuals that includes the child's
teacher and parents (and, where appropriate, the child).
3. If the parents and school personnel disagree as to
what constitutes an appropriate educational program, the
dispute should be resolved by a neutral third party.
Either the parents or the school can request a court
ruling or an impartial hearing.
4. To the extent possible, the child's needs should
be met in a setting in which the child will be able to
interact with nonhandicapped children.

The first three requirements are built on a different set of assumptions from those held by most members of the research and development community. Researchers tend to assume that the ultimate criterion for the appropriateness of educational programs is an empirical one; this assumption leads to the inference that one of the "outcomes" that should be measured for the Education for All Handicapped Children Act is the empirical validity of the individual educational programs. Yet these three requirements imply not only that what is appropriate for a child must be determined individually, but also that the child (or, more often, the parents) has a right to contribute to the final decision, even to take it to federal court if necessary. This means that the people deemed best qualified by Congress to judge the appropriateness of individual educational programs are not necessarily those who apply empirical criteria.

The first requirement disallows reliance on knowledge of a child's labeled handicapping condition to prescribe an educational program. By contrast, most research related to the education of handicapped children has been conducted using categories of handicapping conditions as independent variables. Such data allow researchers to define trends and establish predictable patterns regarding the relative benefits of different programs to different kinds of children. Since this requirement restricts the use of such labels for prescribing educational programs, in principle it curtails the use of a significant body of educational research.

While the first requirement involves the type of information that can be used to make educational decisions, the second states who is to be involved in developing programs for children. The child's educational program needs are to be determined by both parents and the school staff-- people who know the child well. The empirical information that can be used is not restricted by this requirement, but encouraging the contributions of personal and professional judgments, in principle at least, effectively reduces the relative contribution of empirical information.[2]

---

[2]We are emphasizing here the apparent intent of the legislation rather than its actual effects. There is evidence, for example, that school personnel may actually use more data when interacting with parents in order to justify their proposed programs.

The third requirement suggests that negotiators who disagree should turn to impartial third parties to resolve their disputes regarding the appropriate educational program for a child. At these impartial hearings, testimony from a number of witnesses, some of whom may present empirical evidence and some of whom may not, is considered. Once again, the contribution of empirical information to decision making is tempered by an emphasis on the personal values of individuals who may use whatever criteria they choose.

The fourth requirement appears to differ from the first three. Whereas the first three requirements establish a decision-making process and indicate no preference about the outcome, the fourth requirement actually lays down a criterion for what kind of educational programs are appropriate. Congress has taken the position that for handicapped children integrated education is, in general, more appropriate than segregated education. The main reason integration has not been left completely to the discretion of parents and teachers is that Congress anticipated resistance from both these groups. Teachers of non-handicapped children often feel burdened by the presence of handicapped children in their classrooms, and parents of handicapped children may worry about the effects of exposing their children to the mainstream, preferring for them the more protective environment of separate classes or schools. In addition, many handicapped adults--the deaf population, for example--enjoy the security and familiarity of a separate culture in many communities. Parents of deaf children often argue that the most appropriate education for their sons and daughters is one in which they are exposed primarily to other deaf children.

The requirement for placing children in the least restrictive environment is particularly interesting from a researcher's perspective--one cannot help but wonder whether Congress was privy to any empirical evidence to the effect that such placements are more educationally effective. In fact, some testimony to the contrary was introduced to Congress in 1963 (U.S. Congress, House, 1963:20):

A recurring question is that of special classes for educable mentally retarded children. Are such classes really helpful or do they tend to keep these youngsters out of contact with other children? The results of a four-year research project concerned with the efficacy of special

classes for educable mentally retarded children,
completed at the University of Illinois, show that
with a well-designed curriculum and trained
teachers certain clear differences are emerging
between those groups of identified educable
mentally handicapped youngsters who have had
special classes and those who have not. A group
of children attending special classes since school
entrance appeared to be more advanced academically
and socially than those who entered and remained
with a group attending regular classes. Moreover,
intelligence quotients as measured by standard
tests showed improvement, in many instances to the
degree where an individual who at 6 years of age
was judged to be mentally retarded was now
considered to have advanced to the slow learner
level and possibly even within the slow average
range. Implications based on the final results of
this research emphasize the need for early
identification and placement into special classes.

If this is the case, then why should education in a normal
classroom be part of the entitlement? The answer is
closely related to the reason for establishing a right to
education in the first place. Those who value access to
education often defend their position by pointing to
long-range results, stating, for instance, that education
provides children with the "basic minimum skills necessary
for the employment of the rights of speech and the full
participation in the political process" (San Antonio
Independent School District v. Rodriguez, 36 L.Ed. 2d 45,
1973); or, in the case of the Education for All
Handicapped Children Act, by stating that education can
"enable them to have full equality of opportunity" (P.L.
94-142, Section 3, emphasis added). Those who hold that
education is a means to other opportunities also tend to
believe that integration involves more than simply not
denying opportunities, that it is an important mechanism
for social change because it exposes the minority and
majority groups (handicapped and nonhandicapped, in this
case) to one another, presumably increasing each group's
tolerance and understanding of the other. By forcing
interactions between these groups, integration tends to
blend them so that the "different" children lose many of
their distinguishing characteristics. This effect, known
as "normalization," is often used to justify integrated
education for handicapped children. The effects of

normalization are evident in this mother's statement
(Brightman and Sullivan, 1979:14):

> I used to hide behind a tree outside the playground
> and just watch. It was painful to see him with
> regular kids, this retarded kid of mine. Then one
> day, I went up to get him after school and for a
> few moments I couldn't find him. He looked like
> all the other kids. His posture, the way he
> walked, everything. . . . I think separate schools
> where every kid has the same disability is the
> worst thing you can do for a kid. It just serves
> to reinforce the disability.

The children affected by this law are those who have
traditionally received special education in separate
classrooms, often in the school basement or in Quonset
huts in the school yard. In small districts, special
education children of all ages and handicapping conditions
were often pooled in a single classroom; in larger
districts, a variety of classrooms were usually used--one
for the mentally retarded, one for the learning disabled,
one for the emotionally disturbed, and so on. Once
children were labeled with a particular handicapping
condition, the program assignment followed automatically.
These practices persist in part because teachers are
certified to teach categories of children, and they
persist despite evidence that neither tests nor professional judgments can discriminate among relatively mild
forms of retardation, learning disabilities, and emotional
disturbances (Craig and McEachron, 1975). Many of the
classroom activities designed for children with mild
handicapping conditions look much like classes for
disadvantaged youngsters (Goldstein et al., 1976).
Rather than raising questions about the appropriateness
of services relative to issues of child development and
curriculum, these practices led to questions regarding
the administration of special education and the extent to
which children's rights to an appropriate education were
being met.

Federal Role in the
Education of the Handicapped

In neither the Handicapped Children's Early Education
Program nor the Education for All Handicapped Act has
Congress actually made any educational stipulations.

Rather than defining the quantity, location, or type of
preschool education to be offered to young handicapped
children, the Handicapped Children's Early Education
Program is designed to stimulate the development and
dissemination of preschool program innovations and to
heighten awareness among a variety of different groups
regarding the nature of handicapping conditions and the
benefits of early childhood services to handicapped
children. To ensure that ideas extend beyond researchers,
the legislation also requires that individual projects
acquaint the community to be served with the problems and
potentialities of such children. And, just as the
Education for All Handicapped Children Act requires
parent involvement in the development of individualized
educational programs, the Handicapped Children's Early
Education Program requires parent involvement in the
development and operation of early childhood projects.
For both enactments, then, the primary influence on
practice has not been to define it, but to define the
decision-making processes that affect practice and to
expand the number and types of participants involved in
these decisions. There are several reasons why Congress
chose this particular strategy.

First, education has traditionally and constitu-
tionally been viewed as a state and local enterprise, and
as such it has been considered an activity for which local
control should be paramount. Because of the pervasive
influence of education on society and on the lives of
individuals, however, both the quality of education and
the distribution of educational services are of concern
to federal policy makers, who see education as an
attractive means for promoting social changes. Thus,
although Congress wants to improve both the quality of
education and the distribution of educational services,
it does not want to take major decision-making powers
away from state or local education agencies. Hence,
Congress encourages educational improvements without
mandating what the improvements ought to be.

Second, even when Congress is interested in providing
an entitlement for educational services (as with the
Education for All Handicapped Children Act), a definition
of that entitlement is elusive. Education is not a
tangible product that can be exchanged between individuals, nor can one determine what quantity of it is
sufficient. Moreover, the diversity of the handicapped
population further complicates the problem of defining a
blanket entitlement or a "best" program. The population

of handicapped children varies from children with mild
speech impairments, to blind children who have adapted to
their blindness and can function in regular classrooms,
to children who are so severely retarded or physically
disabled that they continue to need training in feeding
themselves when they are teenagers. All of these children
are expected to benefit from programs for the handicapped.
The sheer diversity of the population of handicapped
children precludes a narrowly focused mandate; it leads
instead to the sort of mandates written into the
Handicapped Children's Early Education Program and the
Education for All Handicapped Children Act, in which the
kind of education given to handicapped children is under
the scrutiny of a variety of groups who have a stake in
the matter.

Third, the Congress of the United States is an elected
body that makes its own decisions by group processes.
New policies are formed through a complex sequence of
committee meetings, hearings, negotiations, and votes.
It is a group that is accustomed to participatory decision
making, and one that assumes that these processes lead to
reasonable conclusions. The Handicapped Children's Early
Education Program and the Education for All Handicapped
Children Act reflect a belief that if the right people
are involved in a decision, it will, for the most part,
be a reasonable decision. No empirical tests of
correctness are necessary.

Fourth, Congress is constrained in a very practical
way by the extent to which its policies or laws can be
enforced. Some laws are easily enforceable; others are
not. Those that regulate material quantities or mechanical performances (such as automobile mileage) are
relatively easy to monitor. Other laws, such as those
defining public broadcasting, are enforceable in large
part simply because the activities are public. Citizens
who are aware of and in agreement with these policies
serve as volunteer overseers of compliance. Without
their aid the government would not be able to monitor
compliance. Many educational policies, which fall into
yet another category, relate to behaviors that are not
necessarily public: the behavior of individual teachers
toward children in their classrooms or the decisions
school staffs make about their students. In the case of
the Education for All Handicapped Children Act, Congress,
fearing that some school staffs might make unfair or
uninformed decisions about services for handicapped
children, created the opportunity for parents to partici-

pate in the process. This essentially converted the
decision-making process from a private one to a public
one, thereby enlisting the aid of sympathetic citizens to
help oversee compliance. Such a requirement does more
than simply provide parents with a right to participate:
It also opens the process to the scrutiny of local
advocacy groups. These groups, being more familiar with
educational jargon and often more knowledgeable about
parents' rights than are parents themselves, may be
invited by the parents to accompany them to the school
when decisions are being made concerning their
handicapped children.

Outcomes of Interest to Congress

Although education per se is essentially a state and
local issue, many educational problems are widely
distributed across the country--so much so that they come
to be recognized as national issues. If Congress
perceives a particular educational issue as nationally
distributed, it may respond by providing financial
assistance to state and local agencies to help them
address the issue. Such a response creates issues that
are uniquely federal, having to do with federal funding
mechanisms; federal, state, and local agency relationships; eligibility rules; and so forth. These federal
issues involve areas that are controllable by the federal
administration--management and funding, for example--and
are separate from the educational issues that may have
stimulated the original legislation.

Many researchers are unaware of the difference between
the federal goals for such programs (which involve the
interrelationships among agencies and other groups) and
educational problems (which are more likely to involve
the cognitive or social development of handicapped
children). These researchers assume that since local
programs are designed to affect children's development,
the outcome of most interest to Congress is the program's
national educational impact; that is, an aggregation of
local effects or a kind of "gross national product" of
cognitive changes in children. And while it is true that
Congress hopes to influence these outcomes, it is also
true that its primary concerns relate to those issues
that it can control. In the case of the Handicapped
Children's Early Education Program and the Education for
All Handicapped Children Act, the most salient federal

issues involve federal-state relationships; school-parent relationships; and relationships among researchers, local program developers, parents, and the federal government.

The initial hearings held when H.R. 17829, a bill proposing the Handicapped Children's Early Education Program, was being considered illustrate this difference. Although the congressional members referred to the new projects as "experimental," they demonstrated little interest in evaluations of whether the programs were beneficial to handicapped children. In fact, in 89 pages of testimony, only one series of questions touched on evaluation (U.S. Congress, House, 1968:11-12):

> Congressman John Erlenborn: I think it is understood in any demonstration project or experimental project that some projects will be worthwhile and some will be failures. Will you be prepared, after the first year of operations, to make this judgment and say that those programs that have not proven themselves will no longer be funded? Or will they continue because they have gotten in on the ground floor?

James Gallagher, representative of the administration, responded to what appeared to be a request for assurance of effectiveness by describing the uses of both formative and summative evaluations of programs. Erlenborn was not interested in evaluation, however, in the way Gallagher thought he was, as Erlenborn's next questions demonstrate; Gallagher's replies are omitted (U.S. Congress, House, 1968:11-12):

> With an appropriation of $10 million for fiscal year 1970, with 50 states no doubt wanting to participate, and with 435 members of Congress and a hundred Senators as proponents of their States, how are you going to determine where you are going to establish these demonstration projects?

> Maybe I could get at the question another way. How many programs do you believe will be funded with the $10 million, 50, or more or less?

> You may have two or more programs in a single state?

> Do you think you might have any state that would not have a program?

Erlenborn's questions suggest two things. First, he was more interested in the possibility of political influences in the placement of grants than in the effectiveness of projects per se. For him, the importance of evidence of program effectiveness lay in its potential to mitigate these political influences. Second, although Erlenborn expressed an oblique interest in the effectiveness of individual projects, he demanded no assurances that the overall program would be effective.

In fact, the kinds of assurances that these policy makers wanted were primarily related to the distribution of funds. Congressman Augustus Hawkins (Calif.) said (U.S. Congress, House, 1968:13), "I assume there are already some models . . . to be built upon. I was wondering whether or not the approach would be to go to those areas which have pioneered, such as California, for example, and concentrate on the experience and background of the experimentation that has already gone on?" Congressman John Dent (Pa.), describing the experiences of his home state, said, (U.S. Congress, House, 1968:10):

You can measure the neglect of our handicapped children by the miles that the handicapped child lives away from a metropolitan center. I have the kind of State that has city and rural areas. . . . I am hoping . . . you will not worry too much about large classes but, more important, to get classes out into the rural areas so that rural school systems can get some kind of impetus to their programs.

Congressman William Scherle introduced yet another consideration into the funding decision (U.S. Congress, House, 1968:11): "I think top priority should be given to these institutions already established for physically disabled preschool children." These people were clearly worried about how the small appropriation for the program would be distributed among several, and in their view worthwhile, priorities. They asked whether priorities would be set according to political pressures, the experience or expertise of the requesting agencies, the distribution of children between urban and rural areas, or the type of handicapping condition served by an agency. How could they develop funding criteria that would be both valid and fair? This problem was obviously a difficult one, one that Congress must frequently

grapple with. It is also uniquely federal--that is,
although issues of whether and how to serve young
handicapped children are raised throughout the nation,
questions about how to distribute federal funds are
raised only in Washington.

Contributions Evaluators Can Make

Enactments like the Handicapped Children's Early
Education Program and the Education for All Handicapped
Children Act affect more than just handicapped children.
They affect parents, teachers, researchers, and local and
state educational administrative agencies. Both enactments initiate far-reaching changes in the patterns of
relationships among individuals and in so doing they alter
the demand for, as well as the supply of, educational
services. The nature of Congress's efforts suggests that
the authors of these bills may have had a somewhat
complex (if not always explicit) idea of what a better
society might be like, a vision that includes notions
about the relationship between the individual and government, the relationship between education and government,
and the relationship between education and other aspects
of social life. Included in this vision are a number of
assumptions about who should be involved in educational
decision making and how the several parts of society--
parents, educational agencies and researchers--should
interact to affect educational practices.

If these interactions represent the "outcomes" of
interest, then traditional investigative methods using
two-variable models, i.e., models with one cause and one
effect, will be inappropriate for measuring them. And it
may not even be possible to test two-variable subsystems
within the total system. A variable identified as
independent may not be amenable to manipulation or
control by a researcher because it is continually being
influenced by other components of the social-educational
system. And investigations of naturally occurring events
may also be inadequate if they are limited to discrete
pieces of the system. If investigations are to be of
interest to Congress, then the outcomes investigated must
be based on models of the social-educational system that
approximate the complexity of the interactions these
programs might produce--models that could take into
account mutual influences, chain reactions, and other
tangled networks of causes and effects. For example, the

Handicapped Children's Early Education Program was based
on the explicit premise that early childhood programs
provide an important contribution to handicapped
children's development, and its design implies a number
of congressional assumptions regarding the relationship
between early childhood educational programs and other
early childhood services; the role of federal, state, and
local agencies in offering these services; and the
contributions research and development can make toward
improving services. Similarly, the Education for All
Handicapped Children Act was based on the explicit idea
that an individual has the right to participate in
decisions that will affect him or her. That premise is
associated by Congress with a number of implicit
assumptions regarding parent-school relationships, the
role of education in enabling children to enjoy equal
opportunities, the social and personal effects of
integration, and so on. It is these implicit assumptions
that researchers must discover, test, and incorporate
into their research models if they are to be useful to
policy makers.

Suppose, for example, one wished to evaluate the
effectiveness of the due process system involved in the
Education for All Handicapped Children Act. Since there
are several stages in the process of dispute resolution,
he or she might want to describe its effects at each
step. Keeping in mind that while the dispute is being
settled, the child is still being educated somewhere, the
researcher must ask how different the current educational
program is from the program eventually determined to be
appropriate and what the consequences of temporary placement are for the child pending resolution of the dispute.
If the researcher were to expand the study in order to
measure the program characteristics well enough to
describe the difference between the original program and
the one eventually determined to be appropriate, there
would still be no way of determining whether the original
program's "degree of appropriateness" was acceptable
relative to the appropriateness of the parents' right to
due process. Measures of these two effects of the act
could not be equated, nor could they be summed to provide
a net outcome of the policy. To add yet another layer of
complexity to the problem, it is possible for either party
to terminate the dispute at any time on the grounds that
the proceedings themselves are having an adverse effect
on the child, for which the child would not be compensated
if that party won the dispute. An appropriate model for

investigating dispute resolution, then, is one that can
enlighten policy makers about how all these facets of the
system interact or fail to interact.

For purposes of informing policy makers, however, the
model would not have the elegance and precision that two-
variable models tend to have. Although the enactments may
imply that their creators had a clearly focused picture
of the social processes involved, the picture is no doubt
impressionistic. The first contours were probably
sketched in by political scientists, and over the years
the testimony of many witnesses has added more brush-
strokes, so that what researchers are given to study
blurs in some places, has overlays of paint in others,
and multiple images in still others. Even if researchers
were to refine a model of the social-educational system
so that it was focused more precisely, it might not be
more useful to Congress, which, as it is, can affect the
system in only general ways.

A reasonable model for describing the special educational system, then, is one that is developed by using
the language and the degree of precision appropriate to
the policy-making process. Such models, however, should
not be considered inferior or less challenging than those
developed for other purposes. Many valued social and
political models are not defined precisely. The model of
the relationships among the executive, legislative, and
judicial branches of government, for instance, is often
described as a system of checks and balances. Most
informed citizens could generate examples of how that
system works and would probably know if it was not
working properly. Yet few (perhaps none) would be able
to define this system precisely. The fact that it
involves three, rather than two, entities increases its
complexity enormously. The special education system may
involve even more elements. In addition to parents,
children, school systems, and researchers, it includes
prevailing theories regarding effective strategies for
services, community attitudes toward the handicapped,
state laws regarding services to handicapped children,
and the immediate histories of individual school
districts, such as their traditional strategies for
serving handicapped children, their experiences with due
process, and their experiences with the research and
development community.

Nor are social systems like mechanical systems.
Models of social systems cannot be expected to have the
clarity or lasting quality of models of simpler mechanical

systems. Social systems are not closed; they do not start and stop as mechanical systems do. And because they are in perpetual motion, models must account for several kinds of mutual or circular causal relationships. A new federal policy influences individuals the way a wave influences sand. Each grain moves in a slightly different direction, so that the total effect might be better presented by a general description of the beach than by summing up the movements of all the grains of sand.

The construction of models of Congress's picture of the social and educational systems that affect handicapped children will allow researchers to determine in a general way which aspects of a system influence the quality of programs that young handicapped children receive and which appear to influence parents' abilities to exercise their rights. Already, investigators are finding evidence that special education mandates are not being readily implemented in schools (Kirp et al., 1976; Stearns et al., 1980; Weatherly and Lipsky, 1978). Their evidence suggests the need for understanding the entire system in order to determine how mandates can influence it. To provide such information to policy makers, the researcher should engage in close, continuous study of the system--study that will yield not quantified measures of outcomes but narrative descriptions of the inter-actions of all parties involved in the social-educational process, descriptions that would provide policy makers with an understanding of how the system is functioning overall, how the various parts interact, and what aspects would need to be changed to make it function differently. To learn these kinds of things investigators would have to observe the naturally occurring dynamic operations of special education systems.

Many investigators are reluctant to conduct case studies because they feel that the small number of cases involved in such investigations do not permit general-izations to the full population. The concerns expressed by these researchers reflect a number of scientific assumptions that are almost as vague as many of the congressional assumptions underlying these two enactments involving handicapped children. Larger samples are presumed to allow generalizations partly because the statistics describing the sample can be used to estimate the parameters of the population. Statistical inferences about the population are based on these estimates, and analytic tools have been developed that permit researchers not only to estimate a population value but also to

estimate their confidence in that value. The argument
that case studies involve too few cases from which to
generalize is based on the assumption that the method of
generalizing will be a statistical one, that the generalized statement must be precise, and that the "fact" that
is to be generalized is a quantitative fact. But the
kind of statements that are needed to describe the effects
of such programs as the Handicapped Children's Early
Education Program and the Education for All Handicapped
Children Act do not require such precision; and the facts
to be generalized about their effects are not quantities,
but dynamic interactions among individuals and institutions. What is estimated for the population is how, not
how often, these components can influence one another.
And if researchers use case studies to develop reasonable
models of how the system functions, their models will
specify the sources of variation among cases that are
relevant, so that sound, nonstatistical, general statements can be made (Kennedy, 1979).

Although these investigations may provide an understanding of how the system works, continuous, intensive
study of any particular system, aside from being expensive, is impractical. Automobiles are driven on the
assumption that they are functioning properly. Motorists
do not stop every mile or so and tear down the engine to
see whether all the parts are synchronized. Instead,
they wait for signs of trouble, a clank or rattle,
perhaps. Where federal policies are concerned, Congress
hears these clanks in testimony, in letters, and from
lobbyists, so there is no apparent need for researchers
to report them. But researchers can, like mechanics,
interpret these noises. They can inform Congress when
the noises are merely part of the normal functioning of
the system (and do not necessarily imply a dysfunction)
and when they are indicative of needed repairs.

Researchers can do more than wait for the clanks.
They can independently measure certain aspects of the
system. The quality of an automobile's functioning can
be estimated by such indicators as miles traveled per
gallon, the amount of oil being burned, or the quantity
of its noxious emissions. Measures such as these can
provide useful estimates of the extent to which the
automobile is functioning properly. In addition to
creating a model of the social-educational system,
researchers could devise a second, complementary form of
outcome measure, one that indicates the status of the
system at regular intervals. Since the special education

system is a part of a larger social-educational system, it will influence and be influenced by the larger system, so that regular spot checks of its operation are required over time. Already, studies initiated during the first two years of implementation of the Education for All Handicapped Children Act, such as Newkirk et al.'s survey (1978) of state definitions of handicapping conditions and Kotin's survey (1977) of state due process procedures, are outdated. Given that it is impractical for researchers to provide continuous descriptions of dynamic effects of the policy, these status indicators offer a cheap, effective alternative for monitoring global changes in the social-educational system.

There are many measures already at hand or that could be developed easily to indicate the status of the special educational system. Some of the following measures might be pertinent to the Handicapped Children's Early Education Program:

· The distribution of projects reflecting different theoretical orientations.
· The number of contributions to the professional literature that derive from the projects.
· The number of graduate students or teachers who receive in-service training in these projects.
· The distribution of projects serving different ages of children or children with different handicapping conditions.
· The distribution of projects across geographic regions.
· The number of projects housed in public schools versus university laboratories or experimental units in hospitals.
· The number of projects that continue to operate after federal funds are removed.

The measures given below might be relevant to the Education for All Handicapped Children Act:

· The proportion of children served as handicapped.
· The proportion of those children served who are being served with nonhandicapped children.
· The proportion of minority children served as handicapped.
· The proportion of educational decisions that are appealed.
· The proportion of appeals that are re-appealed the following year.

When the Education for All Handicapped Children Act was
passed in 1975, several of the findings used to justify
the need for it were based on such indicators, and a
recent report criticizing the administration's enforcement of the act was also based to a large extent on these
kinds of indicators (Education Advocates Coalition, 1980).
In many cases, the issues raised on these two occasions
were similar. For example, in 1975 Congress found (P.L.
94-142, Section 3) that "more than half of the handicapped
children in the United States do not receive appropriate
educational services which would enable them to have full
equality of opportunity," and in 1980 the critics charged
(Education Advocates Coalition, 1980:4) that "children
are frequently denied related services, such as physical
therapy, occupational therapy, school health services,
and transportation, essential to enable them to benefit
from special education." In 1975 Congress found (P.L.
94-142, Section 3) that "one million of the handicapped
children in the United States are excluded entirely from
the public school system and will not go through the
educational process with their peers" while in 1980
critics claimed that "children remain unnecessarily
segregated in special schools and classes for the
handicapped."

These measures are often called "atheoretical" by the
research community for two reasons. First, they are
value-free, in the sense that they merely describe certain
aspects of special education systems. Second, they are
hard to interpret in the scientific sense of attributing
their causes to particular events. But they are not hard
to interpret in the social-political sense; tremendously
important values are embodied in these data. While the
indicators themselves may be value-free, their interpretations are not.

The importance of these indicators does not lie in
their status as measures of "outcomes" in the traditional
meaning of the term. Indeed, no one knows what the right
proportions for many of these measures should be. The
outcomes of interest are in the system itself, and the
indicators are important because they provide some clues
as to how the system is working. That policy makers
interpret these indicators according to presumed relationships between the system and the measure means that the
value of the indicators depends less on their technical
precision than on the extent to which their relationship
to the rest of the system is understood. The debate and
discussion following from the 1980 critique of the

183

administration of the Education for All Handicapped
Children Act included much of what might normally be
considered the job of the research community, i.e., to
infer causal relationships responsible for these
numbers. Rather than drawing these inferences from
controlled studies, a forensic process was used to
generate rival hypotheses; these in turn were tested
either by reference to findings from case studies, if
these are available, or by alternate analyses and
displays of the available numerical indicators of
different aspects of the system.

In fact, the forensic process is similar to the
critical process often used by researchers following the
release of findings from a large-scale impact study--with
two important differences. First, the debate following
an impact study usually centers on such issues as the
relative merits of different statistical treatments of
the data or the validity of certain outcome measures,
whereas the debate following the recent critique of the
administration of the Education for All Handicapped
Children Act centered on the relationships among the
federal, state, and local education agencies. Second,
the debate following an impact study is often restricted
to members of the research and development community,
whereas this recent debate included members of interest
groups, lawmakers, and federal administrators.

Many researchers will find this forensic process
disturbing in part because it deprives them of an aspect
of their trade in which they take great pride--the process
of drawing inferences from data. The relationship between
data and decision making that has been described here
brings into question the appropriate role of researchers
and their unique skills in social problem-solving: To
what extent can or should the researcher interpret, either
in the scientific sense or in the social-political sense,
the data that he or she may be gathering for policy
makers?

In the example given here, the most appropriate
contribution for that group would be to provide two kinds
of data: intensive descriptions of the processes by which
the social and educational system operates and quantitative atheoretical indicators of the special education
system's functioning. Such a contribution would be
similar to that provided by economists; they regularly
produce a variety of economic indicators for policy
makers, who in turn find these indicators useful because
the economists have also developed a reasonable,

if imprecise, model of how the economic system operates.
Models of the special education system must be developed
if special education indicators are to be useful. Yet
even the combination of these two kinds of data is not
sufficient without a forensic process to provide the
causal interpretations necessary for policy modification.
The information ultimately used by policy makers results
from a three-way interaction among descriptions of
processes, indicators of processes, and the forensic
process itself.

This process need not exclude researchers from causal
interpretations. Indeed, researchers could be in the
center of the forensic process, conducting ad hoc analyses
and searching through extant data as alternate hypotheses
are raised. Such a role would not preclude them from
raising and testing their own hypotheses, nor from
maintaining a role of objectivity or neutrality. The
particular posture that researchers take with respect to
the forensic process is as much at their discretion as it
is when they debate the meaning of large-scale impact
studies.

The mention of large-scale impact studies brings up a
second objection that researchers may have to the kind of
interaction between data and debate that has been
suggested here. The data involved in this debate do not
define the particular kinds of program effects that most
researchers are accustomed to measuring and that most
researchers feel are of paramount importance: the
cognitive and social development of handicapped children.
Shouldn't these outcomes be a part of the debate about
the effectiveness of Congress's programs for handicapped
children? Our analysis of the Education for All
Handicapped Children Act and the Handicapped Children's
Early Education Program has not suggested that Congress
lacks interest in these outcomes. Rather, we suggest
that Congress has indeed recognized those outcomes as a
national issue. We also suggest that Congress itself has
limited its participation to one of creating a forum in
which other concerned parties can exchange ideas and
evidence about these outcomes. Federal policy makers
probably assume that studies of cognitive and social
outcomes will be carried out and that the results will be
discussed and debated among service delivery agencies,
parents, advocacy groups, and researchers. The quality
of educational programs, while it is the concern of all,
is not a federal policy issue; what is an issue is who is
involved in determining these programs.

The situation is analogous to a division of labor. If
other groups will concern themselves with methods of
improving programs, Congress can then address itself to
the best ways of distributing funds. Those researchers
who think such a division of labor is inappropriate may
try to persuade Congress to attend more to questions of
treatment efficacy. But in so doing they will be entering
the forensic process, not as impartial researchers but as
advocates.

REFERENCES

Brightman, A., and Sullivan, B.
    (1979)   Disabled children and their families, progress
           report 1-9. Cambridge, Mass.: American
           Institute for Research in the Behavioral
           Sciences.
Craig, P. A., and McEachron, N. B.
    (1975)   Whom do teachers identify as handicapped?
           Studies of Handicapped Students (Vol. 1).
           Menlo Park, Calif.: SRI International.
Education Advocates Coalition
    (1980)   Report on Federal Compliance Activities to
           Implement the Education for All Handicapped
           Children Act. Washington, D.C.: Children's
           Defense Fund.
Goldstein, H., Arkall, C., Asheroff, S. C., Hurley,
O. L., and Lilly, M. S.
    (1976)   Schools. In N. Hobbs, ed., Issues in the
           Classification of Children. San Francisco,
           Calif.: Jossey-Bass, Inc., Publishers.
Kennedy, M.
    (1979)   Generalizing from single cases. Evaluation
           Quarterly 3:661-678.
Kirp, D. L., Kuriloff, P. J., and Buss, W. G.
    (1976)   Legal mandates and organizational change. In
           N. Hobbs ed., Issues in the Classification of
           Children. San Francisco, Calif.:
           Jossey-Bass, Inc., Publishers.
Kotin, L.
    (1977)   Due Process in Special Education: Legal
           Analysis. Cambridge, Mass.: Research
           Institute for Educational Problems, Inc.
Newkirk., D., Block D., and Shrybman, J.
    (1978)   An Analysis of Categorical Definitions,
           Diagnostic Methods, Diagnostic Criteria and

Personnel Utilization in the Classification of
Handicapped Children. Reston, Va.: Council
for Exceptional Children.

Stearns, M., Green, D., and David, J.
(1980) Local Implementation of P.L. 94-142: First
Year Report of a Longitudinal Study. Menlo
Park, Calif.: SRI International.

U.S. Congress, House
(1968) Hearings Before the Select Committee on
Education, Committee on Education and Labor,
on H.R. 17829. Washington, D.C.: U.S.
Government Printing Office.

U.S. Congress, House
(1963) Hearings Before the Special Subcommittee on
Labor, Committee on Education and Labor, on
H.R. 6013 and H.R. 6025. Statement of
Lindley J. Stiles. Washington, D.C.: U.S.
Government Printing Office.

U.S. Congress, House
(1968) H.R. 17829. 90th Congress, 2nd Session,
Section 2(a). Washington, D.C.: U.S.
Government Printing Office.

U.S. Office of Education
(1979) Handicapped Children's Early Education
Program. Bureau of Education for the
Handicapped. Washington, D.C.: U.S.
Department of Health, Education, and Welfare.

Weatherly and Lipsky
(1977) Street-level bureaucrats and institutional
innovation: implementing special education
reform. Harvard Educational Review 47:171-197.

Preschool Education for Disadvantaged Children

David P. Weikart

A continuing problem in American education is how to curb the widespread failure in school of children from disadvantaged backgrounds. Many programs have been developed in response to this problem, a large number at the preschool level. Although it seems fairly certain that preschool intervention may facilitate a child's adjustment to and progress in school, participation in these programs does not ensure them. This paper discusses some aspects of the history of early childhood education, describes some exemplary programs, describes methods used to evaluate their effectiveness, and presents some alternative methods of evaluation.

The social pressures for general reform in society and especially in education produced one of the most enduring Great Society programs, Head Start, in the summer of 1965. Based on a few adventurous programs established in the early 1960s, this eight-week effort was to accelerate disadvantaged children and allow them to enter school at an intellectual and academic level equal to their middle-class advantaged peers. The fate of these expectations is well known. The Westinghouse-Ohio University study (1969) of longitudinal findings on Head Start recorded the lack of any long-term intellectual or academic impact from Head Start participation. These findings all but eliminated Head Start from a political point of view. In 1970 the program itself was saved only by the direct lobbying efforts of parents of Head Start children, who had learned their skills in local Community Action Project battles, and by the Office of Child Development (now the Administration for Children, Youth, and Families). The program's rationale was converted to the delivery of social and health services. As such, Head Start limped along with level funding for almost a decade, written off

187

by news media as well as politicians, carefully nursed by
staff at the regional and national levels, dedicated
professionals in early education, and by parents who
could see in their own families the benefits that Head
Start provided.

EARLY EDUCATION PROGRAMS

While these changes occurred in the nature of the Head
Start program, a quiet revolution was under way regarding
the effectiveness of early education programs in general.
Information on the effects of preschool, which had been
accumulating from a range of studies initiated in the
1960s, were becoming available to the public and to policy
makers. Before discussing assessment issues, it may be
useful to summarize the state of those data. One source
of information is a collection of articles reviewing the
problems, issues, processes, and successes of Head Start
over the years (Zigler and Valentine, 1979). One of the
major sources of information is the Consortium for
Longitudinal Studies (1981). The consortium represents
an effort by 14 early childhood education researchers to
pool data from the early 1960s with more recent follow-up
information to evaluate the impact of early education
experiences on disadvantaged children. Although the
studies differ greatly in terms of sample, rigor of
research methodology, geographic locale, instrumentation
used, etc., they represent a major body of information on
effectiveness of early childhood education. This paper
draws extensively on several of these studies, conducted
by the High/Scope Foundation, because of their pivotal
role in the design and collection of family-based data,
cost data, and postschool records used by other studies.

The Ypsilanti Perry Preschool Project: Preschool
Years and Longitudinal Results Through Fourth Grade
(Weikart et al., 1978a) is a study of the long-term
effects of preschool education on a group of "high-risk"
disadvantaged children as they progressed through the
early elementary grades. Grounded in a rigorous methodological framework, the study provides evidence that
preschool made a different in these children's lives.
The impact of the preschool experience on their school
achievement and grade placement, compared with the control
group, has been positive and sustained. (See Schweinhart
and Weikart, 1980, for a follow-up of these children
through ninth grade.)

The Ypsilanti Preschool Curriculum Demonstration
Project: Preschool Years and Longitudinal Results
(Weikart et al., 1978b) presents and analyzes data from
an experiment designed to compare the impact of three
programs, which represent the dominant approaches to
preschool education during the late 1960s. The principal
findings were that (1) the programs were equally effective
both during and after preschool and (2) the children's
cognitive gains were still being maintained five years
after they entered elementary school.

An Economic Analysis of the Ypsilanti Perry Preschool
Project (Weber et al., 1978) is a study of the social
rate of return (the return to society) of public investment in the Ypsilanti Perry Preschool Project. The
benefits and costs for the experimental group were
compared with those for the control group using the human
capital approach of economics. In the analysis the
economic benefits of the preschool program were quantified; then, by comparing the costs of the educational
program with these economic benefits, the rate of return
on the investment was calculated. Although these results
are primarily illustrative, because they are based on a
small sample and because the computations required some
broad assumptions about the applicability of census data
to the studied cohorts, the results appear to show that
the costs of the program were more than compensated by
benefits to society. The economic benefits were derived
from (1) less costly education (i.e., less special education and institutionalized care) for the experimental
group, (2) higher projected lifetime earnings for this
group, and (3) time released from child care responsibilities for the mothers of this group.

It is important to examine the methods used to
determine outcomes of education programs. Standardized
tests, indeed, any measurement of immediate or intermediate outcomes, are merely approximations of real-world
goals that education purports to reach. Educators in
particular and the public in general have long been
enamored of tests of short-term outcomes as though they
stood for something real. Early grade achievement
correlates with twelfth-grade achievement "somewhere
between .75 and .95" (Bloom, 1964:97), but what such
correlations mean in terms of actual adult performance is
unclear. The functioning of adults includes such factors
as job performance capacity, ability to relate to peers,
willingness to learn from experience, interest in being a
contributing member of a group, capacity to earn one's

own way in the world, and ability to manage as an effective family member. These general goals are little predicted by the type of short-term tests available to
educators at this time. Yet these are the goals that make
a difference to both the individual and society at large.

MEASUREMENT OF OUTCOMES

Measurement of outcomes in early childhood education
programs occurs at three points. First, assessment
during the program itself guides the staff as to the
development of the participating child and the effectiveness of the program. Second, at the end of the program
summative measures are used to assess immediate program
outcomes. Third, assessment after completion of the
program is used to study its long-term validity.

Formative Program Evaluation

Assessments made during the program use several
methods. Typical procedures include staff observation
and ratings of a child's progress, focusing on the
child's development and facilitating interaction.

Not only can the progress of the child be rated along
the theoretical dimensions demanded by the curriculum,
but the classroom system or organization and management
can also be appraised. Central features of program space
and operational needs are arranged in checklist format so
that each can be studied for presence or absence in the
program being evaluated. Such evaluations can be done by
trainers or by the staff itself.

In addition to various checklists for teacher (and
parents) to use in evaluating the progress of program
development and the path of child growth within the daily
experience, there are other, more systematic methods.
Observation scales have been carefully developed to give
a time sampling of the actual behavior of teacher and
child in the classroom. These can be genuine outcome
measures when the goal is to document how children spend
their time in learning-teaching situations and how the
life of the child in one curriculum compares with the
life of another. Perhaps the best known approach is that
of Jane Stalling's study (1975) of classrooms in Follow
Through.

The problems involved in using observation schedules are sufficient to daunt even the most enthusiastic supporter. Constant supervision is necessary to obtain reliability in observations. This problem of reliability is usually solved through rigorous training, vigorous onsite supervision, and careful development of the final instrument to be used in the field. Thus, almost all observational schemes are tailored to specific programs. In addition, most observation instruments must reflect the theoretical nature of the program observed. Innovative preschool educational programs differ greatly, and procedures to capture the basic goals of a particular program do not necessarily generalize to other situations. A final issue is the cost of training, observing, scoring, and reporting the findings from observation procedures. (Generally such costs are prohibitive, except for well-financed research projects.) While some cost control can be achieved by carefully selecting the youngsters to be observed through small-sample, random selection procedures, keeping the use of the method to a minimum, systematic observations are then for program validation and not for individual child diagnosis.

Other methods exist for evaluating a program during its actual operation. Practitioners skilled in the curriculum used in a classroom can be employed to give a professional assessment (see Miller and Dyer, 1975). Weikart et al. (1978b) used a system of professional consultants to summarize opinions of classroom operation based on direct observation. Parent committees, operational standards, licensing officials, etc. all offer some means of gaining information on immediate operations. The more general the method, however, the less valuable the outcomes.

In short, immediate information from daily operation is possible through the use of checklists and rating forms, direct time sampling of ongoing classroom operations, and general opinions of those who have contact with the classroom. Such information is most useful to those responsible for the daily operation of the program and the quality of opportunity provided to the children. In addition, information can be gained on the "quality of life" the children experience, and such information may be the primary basis of recommending one curriculum or another for specific children. Research has not yet related these different experiences to performance as children progress through school or to adult performance.

Summative Program Evaluation

When programs are complete, a summative evaluation is often undertaken, although the emphasis historically given to this type of evaluation in early education projects has been questioned recently. Several issues are involved. Should early childhood programs have to defend their contribution to the child's development through careful evaluation if first grade or third grade, for example, have never been so evaluated? The need for summative and longitudinal data for validation of preschool has been raised only in connection with disadvantaged children. Middle-class parents seek experiences for their children and judge their effectiveness on their own impression of their child's progress and happiness; disadvantaged groups, some feel, should have the same prerogative. From another viewpoint, others have stated that long-term outcomes are what are important and end-of-project information is irrelevant (Smilansky, 1979). Although the timing of the evaluation is an issue, instrumentation raises the most questions.

Assessments of preschool effectiveness have used two major types of instruments: standardized, individually administered intelligence tests, typically the Stanford-Binet (S-B), and standardized achievement tests, such as the Metropolitan Achievement Test or the California Achievement Test. These instruments have been used because of their power to predict performance in the elementary grades and their reliability.

The use of these two types of instruments has generated considerable political and social debate. Whether these instruments measure the "true" abilities of disadvantaged children in general and disadvantaged minority children in particular has been at issue essentially because of the failure of disadvantaged children to "do well" on these instruments upon completion of intervention programs. Many thoughtful commentators have seen the problem as one of bias in the instruments and have questioned their cultural relevance. Legal proceedings in California have proscribed the use of individualized intelligence tests as the basis for placing youngsters in special education programs. Some viewers have seen the problem as a lack of congruence between the program goals and the specific content of the measurement instrument. For example, experience-based approaches to reading do not employ or teach the standard vocabulary list that forms the basis of the reading sections of most achievement tests. The book by Jensen (1979) on mental testing is likely to accelerate this debate.

Figure 1 illustrates the classic pattern of a successful preschool intervention with a nontreatment control in terms of standardized IQ testing. The data are from the Ypsilanti Perry Preschool Project (Weikart et al., 1978a).

While the youngsters start with nearly identical S-B scores, in the spring of their second preschool year (S2Y) the average score of the experimental group reflected a gain of 15.3 points from the fall entry year (FEY), 10.3 points more than the control group (Figure 1). One year later, in the spring of their kindergarten year, the experimental group reflected a gain of 11.7 points from FEY, only 4 points more than the control group who had gained additional points upon school entry. Although differences between the two groups remained significant through the first grade, the performance of the experimental group gradually declined once they entered elementary school.

The pattern of performance in the control group merits consideration in its own right. Since the children in the sample were selected specifically because of their low socioeconomic status (SES) and low S-B scores, it was anticipated that their S-B scores would increase somewhat--"regressing toward the population mean"--upon second testing, regardless of treatment. The change in IQ of the control group from initial to second testing at the end of the first project year was +4.8 points. This gain is the best estimate of the regression toward the mean in S-B IQ for children in this sample. It seem unlikely that testing procedures or acclimation to the test situation accounts for this gain since procedures were unchanging and closely resembled Zigler and Butterfield's (1968) "optimizing" conditions. Although a practice effect might be confounded with regression toward the mean, this too seems improbable given the nature of the test and the length of time between test administrations. Assuming that the regression effect was of the same magnitude in the experimental group, then perhaps only 10.5 points of the experimental group's 15.3-point gain in S-B IQ over two years of preschool represents the impact of treatment. This estimate of "true" gain is approximately equal to the actual difference in mean IQ between experimental and control groups measured at the end of preschool.

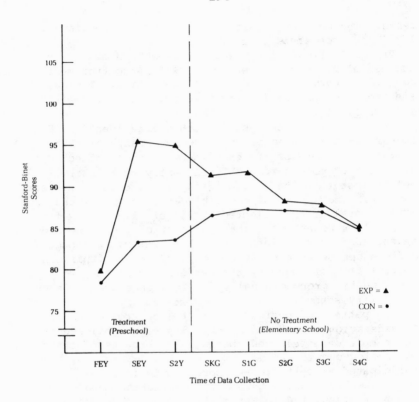

Arithmetic Means, Standard Deviations,
Number of Subjects, and Significance Levels of F Tests
on Group Comparisons at Each Testpoint

		Time of Data Collection							
		FEY	SEY	S2Y	SKG	S1G	S2G	S3G	S4G
EXP	Mean	79.6	95.5	94.9	91.3	91.7	88.1	87.7	85.0
	(S.D.)	(5.9)	(11.5)	(13.0)	(12.2)	(11.7)	(13.1)	(10.9)	(11.3)
	N	58	58	44	56	58	55	56	57
CON	Mean	78.5	83.3	83.5	86.3	87.1	86.9	86.8	84.6
	(S.D.)	(6.9)	(10.0)	(10.2)	(9.9)	(10.2)	(10.7)	(12.5)	(11.2)
	N	65	65	49	64	61	62	61	57
Significance of F tests		N.S.	<.01	<.01	<.05	<.05	N.S.	N.S.	N.S.

F tests presented here were obtained in three-way analyses of variance (Group x Sex x Wave) reported in the *Statistical Supplement*, Part A, Tables 1a-1c.

FIGURE 1 Average Stanford-Binet intelligence scale scores for experimental and control groups. (Source: Based on Weikart et al., 1978.)

The upward inflection in the control group's performance curve upon enrollment in kindergarten deserves
comment. On the average, children in the control group
gained 2.8 points in IQ during kindergarten and another
point during first grade. It seems likely that gains of
this magnitude might be expected for any group of disadvantaged children confronting a new and challenging
educational experience. Bloom (1964) uses the term
"freshman effect" to describe this impact of new environment and new demands on individual intellectual performance. By the end of the fourth grade, however, this
school-related effect was no longer evident, and the
control group's performance had dropped to the level
attained at the second testing.

Preliminary analyses of the Wechsler Intelligence
Scale for Children (WISC) full-scale IQ scores obtained
on eighth-grade children confirm the finding of no
difference in measured aptitude obtained at the fourth-
grade level. By this point the performance of both
experimental and control children was indistinguishable
from entry-level performance on the S-B.

The gradual attenuation of intelligence test gains
following preschool intervention in the Perry project
parallel the findings of most other compensatory preschool
studies. The erosion of preschool effects once children
enter regular public school is now a familiar pattern in
educational evaluation. Explanations of this loss include
the shift in the content of the test items to include more
verbal and abstract concepts and the understimulation of
children as a result of the increasing isolation from
ideal learning environments.

Two apparent exceptions to this pattern of vanishing
IQ gains are reported in the literature and should be
mentioned. Karnes (1973) reports on three programs that
maintained some small part (about 6 points) of their
initial IQ gains through the third grade. Weikart et al.
(1978b) report on three programs that maintained about 15
points of their initial IQ gains through the fourth
grade; children in the programs continued gains in IQ
through the eighth grade, a decade after intervention.

The findings of studies using data from the Consortium
for Longitudinal Studies on achievement tests tend to be
positive. Several projects report either continuous
achievement gains for experimental groups over control
groups or a gradually evolving significance of the
experimental group scores over those of the control
group. This latter phenomenon is often termed a

"sleeper" effect. However, it might more accurately be called weak program impact as the stronger programs show initial and continuing gains in achievement. In the Perry project, these gains become stronger each year, including the last test point at age 19, when a test of general competency was given.

ALTERNATIVE ASSESSMENT PROCEDURES

While it appears difficult to avoid the use of standardized assessment procedures for summative testing, two alternatives seem feasible. The first is the development of instruments that measure factors outside the confines of standardized tests. Efforts to create tests of emotional development, cognitive style, self-concept, etc. have had a history of failure in early childhood assessment; the examples of Follow Through and National Planned Variation Head Start are well known. There appears to be little possibility that psychometrically sound instruments could be developed, even with a massive infusion of funds. Other testing procedures have shown potential in programs such as the Educational Development Corporation's Project Torque to assess redevelopment of mathematical concepts and in High/Scope's efforts to assess the development of language competency through generative testing procedures. (In a generative test, students provide both questions and answers or have full control over the sophistication of their responses.)

The High/Scope Cognitively Oriented Curriculum is based on the idea that the child generates his or her own learning within a structure designed and supported by teachers. The dynamic learning situation is drawn from developmental theory, in part Piagetian, and includes materials for the child, encouragement by the teacher to use these materials, and questions by the teacher to extend the child's thinking or highlight underlying errors and contradictions in reasoning. The questions and activities initiated by the teacher are not meant to provide the "right way" but to allow the child to reason at the limits of his or her developmental level.

Given this orientation toward education, criteria for evaluating the program must reflect the experience of the child in the classroom, for to educate one way and assess another is hardly appropriate. The evaluation procedure should reflect important variables for adult success, yet it should be perceived in a broader way than simply as measurement of outcome variables. It should reflect the conditions under which the outcomes were developed. While classroom observations can be summative in nature when defined as necessary conditions for a curriculum or for specific operational goals, usually they are conceived as formative or process assessment. Basically, observation of the climate of learning is essential to determining the "cost" of whatever is learned.

In designing a "generative" testing situation, several additional criteria would have to be met. The instrument would have to allow the child to express what he or she knows in a functional way. The child should be able to construct answers so that they reflect his or her capacity to think and express concepts. The situation must be supportive of whatever the student produces so that the answers are not either right or wrong but simply an expression of his or her best ability. The situation should have supportive elements in it--friends or others with whom the student can work, familiar materials, opportunities to express the strengths of his or her educational career to date. This format does not call for a sampling of the universe of possible test questions, but rather for a situation in which the student can express strengths and weaknesses by generating original material. Generative assessment has the student convey his or her knowledge and abilities by constructing a response that indicates his or her level of development.

The High/Scope Productive Language Assessment Tasks (PLAT) is one example of a generative approach to curriculum assessment. Developed over the last seven years and used at the High/Scope Follow Through sites, it measures the capacity of the child to use language as an expression of conceptual ability.

One form of the PLAT battery incorporates two tasks, reporting and narrating. In the reporting task, children are given identical sets of unstructured materials and asked to make anything they want to make. After 20 minutes they are asked to write about how they made whatever they made and are allowed 30 minutes to complete their stories. The children are permitted to interact with one another during all phases of the task. In the narrating task, each child is given a set of relatively unstructured materials to "help you make up a story." After about 25 minutes of free (and usually dramatic) play on a carpeted floor, the children are asked to write a make-believe or pretend story. As in the reporting task, the children are permitted to interact with one another as they play and write.

While not a complete instrument, PLAT does represent
the type of assessment procedure that is being developed
by the sponsors of Follow Through, who represent child-
centered and open-framework types of curricula. Such an
instrument could be widely used to tap the abilities of
children not assessed by regular batteries, abilities
that in many respects reflect the highest goals of most
educational programs. Instruments that respect the
individual in the context of the culture offer a
promising area for further development.

A second alternative to standardized tests is to
employ direct measures of success. These are more
meaningful measurement methods than either IQ scores or
achievement test results, which represent success only
indirectly. Such "hard" measures as placement in special
education classes or other special service programs and
grade retention are important because they reflect actual
decisions by schools to manage youngsters and have very
real cost consequences. Each year of school that a child
repeats increases the costs of total education by at least
8 percent. Placement in a special education program often
quadruples the cost of education each year that the young-
ster remains in such a program. Once assigned to such
programs most youngsters remain in them until leaving
school.[1] These costs are the direct costs of education
and not some delayed future expenditure.

Using the High/Scope economic cost study as a model
(Weber et al. 1978), the Consortium for Longitudinal
Studies pooled the information from several of the older
and more complete studies of special education programs
(see Figure 2). These findings demonstrate the ability
of early education to affect public expenditures; they
present a powerful assessment procedure to judge early
education effectiveness.

On the whole, summative measures generally depend on
intellectual and achievement test results to assess the
outcomes of early education programs. While the

---

[1]While the Education for All Handicapped Children Act
of 1975 (P.L. 94-142) increases the likelihood of service
for youngsters who qualify, the pressures on schools to
be responsive to disadvantaged children with learning
difficulties without resorting to special education
placement means new--and no doubt costly--alternatives
must be provided.

199

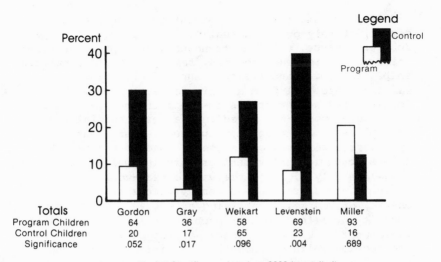

FIGURE 2 Percent of program and control children in
special education. (Source: Consortium for Longitudinal
Studies. Lasting Effects After Preschool. Final
report. HEW Grant 90C-1311 to the Education Commission
of the States. 1978.)

appropriateness of these results for either the assessment
of children or the program may be questioned, they are
widely employed as a means of judging a specific program--
against other programs or against its own goals. More
effective criteria begin to be available as a longitudinal
study continues. When children are beyond the third
grade, broadly conceived economic measures, which produce
data that are meaningful to both the educator and the
taxpayer, can be used as a very effective means of judging
long-term outcomes. Indeed, cost-benefit findings are
sufficiently powerful to directly affect public policy
regarding early childhood education. Their power exceeds
either IQ scores or achievement records in the final
analysis.

LONG-TERM SUMMATIVE MEASURES

Long-term summative assessment of early education
effectiveness is only now taking place as the passage of
time makes such studies possible. Measurements made 10

and 15 years after an early education experience focus
almost entirely on the actual performance of the subjects.
Job performance, college attendance, receipt of welfare,
crime and delinquency records, family formation, relationship with family and friends, supervisor ratings,
earnings, etc. all form a basis for evaluation. The
longitudinal follow-up has now left the general field of
child development and moved into a dozen specialized
disciplines. All assessment procedures are characterized
by concrete performance indices. Gone is the need to
assess academic achievement or intellectual ability.
These are only signs on the way to real-world performance.

There are special assessment problems at this level.
One is, of course, identifying effective indicators of
"quality of life." Another problem is income. Earnings
indicators must differentiate participants as to those
who receive welfare, those with legitimate jobs, and
those "on the cash economy." Another assessment issue is
the categorization of the manner in which young adults
approach economic decision making. Benefits paid to
workers such as sick leave, emergency leave, unemployment
compensation, etc., reflect an ethic of assistance.
Young adults today make financial decisions to maximize
income and personal purpose. How are young adults to be
"scored" who work the economic system to maximize personal
gain, taking sick leave when not ill, etc.? Thus the
breakthrough to real-world measures does not simplify the
assessment problem. Complex issues remain to be resolved.

On the whole, long-term longitudinal assessment must
move from academic "place marker" variables into the
world of hard performance and economic measurement. High
priority should be given to establishing baseline data
for the economic performance of adults from nonmainstream
backgrounds and to closer monitoring of the later performance of children who experience various interventions in
early childhood. This requires the involvement of
disciplines outside educational psychology.

REFERENCES

Bloom, B.
(1964)   Stability and Change in Human
          Characteristics. New York: John Wiley &
          Sons, Inc.
Consortium for Longitudinal Studies
(1981)   Lasting effects of early education.
          Monographs of the Society for Research in
          Child Development.
Jensen, A.
(1979)   Bias in Mental Testing. New York: The Free
          Press.
Karnes, M. B.
(1973)   Evaluation and implications of research with
          young handicapped and low-income children. In
          J. C. Stanley, ed., Compensatory Education for
          Children, Ages 2 to 8. Baltimore, Md.: The
          Johns Hopkins Press.
Miller, B., and Dyer, J.
(1975)   Four preschool programs: their dimensions and
          effects. Monographs of the Society for
          Research in Child Development 40:5-6.
Schweinhart, L. J., and Weikart, D. P.
(1980)   Young children grow up: the effects of the
          Perry Preschool Program on youths through age
          15. Monographs of the High/Scope Educational
          Research Foundation (Series No. 7).
Smilansky, M.
(1979)   Priorities in Education: Preschool: Evidence
          and Conclusions. World Bank Paper No. 323.
Stallings, J.
(1975)   Implementation and child effects of teaching
          practices in Follow Through classrooms.
          Monographs of the Society for Research in
          Child Development 40 (7-8, Serial No. 163).
Weber, C. U., Foster, P. S., and Weikart, D. P.
(1978)   An economic analysis of the Ypsilanti Perry
          Preschool Project. Monographs of the
          High/Scope Educational Research Foundation
          (Series No. 5).
Weikart, D. P., Bond, J. T., and McNeil, J.
(1978a) Ypsilanti Perry Preschool Project: preschool
          years and longitudinal results through fourth
          grade. Monographs of the High/Scope
          Educational Research Foundation (Series No. 3).

Weikart, D. P., Epstein, A., Schweinhart, L., and Bond,
J. T.
    (1978b) Ypsilanti Preschool Curriculum Demonstration
          Project: preschool years and longitudinal
          results. Monographs of the High/Scope
          Educational Research Foundation (Series
          No. 4).
Zigler, E., and Butterfield, E.
    (1968) Motivational aspects of changes in IQ test
          performance of culturally deprived nursery
          school children. Child Development 39:1-14.
Zigler, E., and Valentine, J., eds.
    (1979) Project Head Start, A Legacy of the War on
          Poverty. New York: The Free Press.

Comprehensive Family Service Programs: Special Features and Associated Measurement Problems

Kathryn Hewett, with the assistance of Dennis Deloria

INTRODUCTION

A few years ago a team from the Denver, Colorado, U.S. General Accounting Office (GAO) visited a child development demonstration program in Gering, Nebraska, as part of a routine review of such federally funded programs in the region. At this Child and Family Resource Program, the GAO team was surprised and impressed with the many types of services provided and with the program's approach to planning and delivering services to each family. Intrigued, they looked at 3 more of the 11 demonstration programs in other areas and subsequently produced a glowing report on the comprehensive family service model as implemented by the Child and Family Resource Program. Their report called attention to several aspects of the model that distinguished it from most traditional child development programs: the emphasis on families rather than children, the approach of developing with parents a distinct plan of service and activities for each family, and the program's role as a coordinator of services in the community for each family. So enthusiastic was the GAO team about the model that they recommended it to Congress as a prototype for future child development program legislation (GAO, 1979).

The Child and Family Resource Program is one of several research and demonstration programs developed by federal and private researchers that attempt to influence the development of children working with families. A number of demonstration programs funded by the Head Start Bureau of the Administration for Children, Youth, and Families (now part of the U.S. Department of Health and Human Services) have been delivering comprehensive family services for nearly a decade (15th Anniversary Head Start

Committee, 1980). Among these programs are the Child and
Family Resource Program, Home Start, the Parent Child
Centers, and the Parent Child Development Centers. Most
of these programs had roots in child development intervention programs developed by researchers such as
Levenstein, Weikart, Gordon, Klaus and Gray, Lally and
Honig, White and Watts, and many others. Initiated as
experiments in providing basic Head Start services, these
programs showed the influence not only of the child
development philosophies of Head Start but also of
philosophies about parent involvement and community
political action that characterized Head Start in the
late 1960s and early 1970s.

At the same time other researchers were developing
family oriented programs with the aim of enhancing child
development. Such programs as the Brookline Early
Education Project, the Syracuse Families Project, and the
Family Networks Project at the Merrill-Palmer Institute
resulted from these efforts.

In general these programs combine early childhood
intervention and family support in various degrees,
providing them directly by program staff and indirectly
through coordination of other service agencies in the
community. It is the combined emphasis on child and
family and the broad array of available services that
makes them "comprehensive." The federal demonstration
programs, and some of the private ones as well, provide a
full range of health, nutritional, and educational
services similar to those available to children in Head
Start, along with broad social and educational activities
for parents, such as job counseling, child care assistance, health screening, housing improvement, and legal
and other services. They go beyond Head Start and other
early intervention programs in enabling greater parent
participation in determining the direction of the program,
in emphasizing both child development and family services,
in assuming a greater role in coordinating services in
the community for participating families, and in improving
family services in general for the community.

This paper emphasizes the federal demonstration
program models, particularly the Child and Family Resource
Program and Home Start. Of course, this paper represents
only one approach to issues affecting families. It does
not survey the range of policies and programs that currently affect family life. For example, this paper does
not focus on entitlement programs, such as Title XX,
which legislates broad services for low-income families

(e.g., day care, homemaker service, family planning, etc.) Nor does this paper consider policies and programs affecting family life in countries other than the United States. Some of the provocative implications of policies in Europe and Asia can be found in the writings of Kahn and Kamerman (1975). There are also important single service programs (such as those for day care or health) that influence the quality of family life (see Travers et al. and Levine and Palfrey, in this volume).

The set of models discussed in this chapter were selected to illustrate important issues in measuring the effects of family programs. First, these models have been implemented in a variety of urban and rural settings nationwide and have served many different subcultural groups of families: Appalachian, urban white, black, Hispanics (both Puerto Rican and Chicano), native Americans, and many other regional groups.

Second, they have attempted to implement a personalized, direct approach to delivering services that involves the establishment of relationships with families. Compared with an entitlement program that theoretically serves all eligible families, these programs have a more intensive approach, serving fewer families in greater depth. Their approach is similar in some important ways to a clinical community mental health model of family service and in many other important respects is different, too.

Finally, all of the federal and private family service programs mentioned were conducted simultaneously with a research program; thus, these programs and the evaluations associated with them represent the most recent attempts to grapple with the research problems inherent in family service programs. Thus far the research suggests that however promising the comprehensive family service models may be, they pose conceptual and practical problems for research that are not yet solved.

In this paper the problems posed by family service programs and the efforts to grapple with these problems are organized around three features common to most of the programs mentioned. These features, in turn, have major implications for measurement:

· the mix of support and intervention;
· the emphasis on individualized treatment; and
· the role of integrating community services for families.

Throughout this paper the discussion of programs and measurement issues rests on a broad general assumption that it is necessary to consider not only measurement but also the social context in which programs operate and the values of different groups who may have a stake in the program. Several researchers have observed that research questions and measures concerning child development have historically reflected the values of individuals and of society at any given time (Kagan et al., 1978; Kessen, 1979). While this observation may apply to all research about children and families, it is particularly true of research concerning social programs that have diverse constituencies. This is not merely a philosophical stance. Because of the comprehensive and individualized nature of the programs, a great many domains of family life might be affected by program participation. The challenge to the researcher is to adopt a framework for research that helps to make explicit the different values, adopt or impose some priority among the effects of interest, and select measures capable of both detecting effects of primary interest and describing other possible effects of interest to other constituencies.

OVERVIEW OF FAMILY POLICY RESEARCH

Trends in Family Research

Family research has roots in many disciplines: rural and urban sociology, economics, and many areas of psychology—developmental, educational, and clinical. Until recently, research in these areas proceeded in parallel, with little exchange across disciplines. Generally, policy research concentrated on outcomes for children and on defining program treatments that children received, but it largely ignored outcomes for family members other than the mother, for families as a whole or for social groups, institutions, or communities.

A review of family and family-related policy research published in 1978 concluded that although more than 26,000 studies of the family had been conducted since 1974, the questions posed by family-oriented research represented "new questions for policy, and for behavioral science as well" (Newbrough et al., 1978:85). The "new" questions were concerned with the reciprocal influences among family members, the relationships between families and other social organizations or institutions (extended families, schools, and social programs) over childrearing, and the intended and unintended effects of intervention programs.

Overall, the questions signal a broadening of concern, from the child as primary focus of research and policy to the family and the social groups and institutions that are intertwined with family life. Because this broadening of concern is reflected in federal and privately sponsored research, it is useful to summarize the more general views that are often associated with it.

• Families remain important units for the socialization of children, and outcomes for families as well as children must be the concern of social programs and policies.

• Families are characterized by a dynamic process of development as a group that is similar to but not the same as the development of its individual members. In addition, certain states in the normal course of family development are likely to be sources of stress, as are the extraordinary events of family life (Hill and Mattessich, 1977).

• Families are both social and psychological units with various sizes, memberships, and values, which reflect subcultures, regions, and ethnic and religious backgrounds (Hill, 1971; Nobles, 1976).

• There is an "ecology of human development" (Bronfenbrenner, 1977) in which the family is an important one of many interrelated social groups and institutions which overlap in the care and socialization of children (Hertz, 1976).

The Newbrough report summarizes the work and findings of many researchers when it suggests moving federal policies away from programs of categorical services (i.e., programs that provide only health or only child development services) toward providing support in many forms to families based on varying needs from family to family. Furthermore, the report suggests that such programs of support should include mediating structures in social environments (churches, kinship networks, and others).

Optimal development of children depends on an ever-broadening circle of influences. These influences begin with the child's individual ability and temperament and move to the immediate family and household, to the extended family, its history and social place, and beyond, to the informal groups and formal institutions of society.

It is clear that such views about the interdependence of
families and social institutions imply a complex conceptualization of family policy that must be reflected in
research.

Assumptions About Family Policy

The foregoing summary of family research implies that
measures of program effects are influenced by assumptions
concerning values and social and personal responsibility.
Such issues will provide discussion and disagreement
among policy makers and researchers. Neither policy nor
research, however, can be made without recognizing the
importance of such values. Consequently, we present some
of the assumptions we make about current family policy.

First, we assume that a climate of belief persists
concerning the value of providing some types of service
or support to American families, although models and
systems of service delivery may vary from agency to
agency. Second, equity among different income and class
groups will continue to be important in determining
policy, although the political and economic mood of the
country in mid-1981 raises questions about the differential effects of budget cuts on poor, working-class, and
middle-class families. While the limitations of program
eligibility for low-income families have both desirable
and undesirable consequences, those families will continue
to receive some types of federal support.

Third, we assume that the federal government will
maintain some distance from direct intervention in family
affairs but will continue to exert indirect influence on
families through the types of financial and service
structures adopted (services, programs, and stipends) and
the types of coordination required between agencies,
schools, courts, etc.

Fourth, we assume that there is some awareness and an
acceptance of the diversity of family types and life-
styles in this country. If we accept the integrity of
various family types and ways of functioning, we can also
assume that it is difficult to agree on a single treatment, attitude, or behavior that is the "best" way to
enhance child and family development. What is ideal for
children and families may vary by region, community,
subculture, or developmental stage.

Finally, we assume that most policy decisions are
political and may not directly reflect the use of

research. Traditional outcome research is only one of
several types of information that policy makers use,
depending on the timing and political issues surrounding
the decision. However, it is the responsibility of
researchers to be aware of the assumptions and
implications of the research questions asked and the
methods used (Weiss, 1976).

COMPREHENSIVE FAMILY PROGRAMS

Program Descriptions

In 1973 the Administration for Children, Youth, and
Families (formerly the Office of Child Development)
initiated the Child and Family Resource Program as part
of the Head Start Bureau's research and demonstration
program. There are 11 of these programs across the
country, 1 in each of the 10 regions and 1 representing
the Indian and Migrant Division. Each program receives
approximately $130,000 per year to serve a minimum of 80
families; some programs serve as many as 350 families.
    The Child and Family Resource Program is a family
oriented child development program, providing support
services to families with children from the prenatal
period through age eight. It meets children's needs by
working through the family as a unit and provides
continuity in serving children during the major stages of
their early development. This is accomplished through
three program components: (1) an infant-toddler component
serving parents and their children in the prenatal period
through age three; (2) Head Start, for families with
children ages three to five; and (3) a preschool-school
linkage component, to ensure a smooth transition from
preschool into the early elementary school grades.
Another distinctive feature of the program is its
emphasis on a comprehensive assessment of each family's
strengths and needs and the development with the family
of an individualized plan for services. There is much
variation in the structure and staff rules from program
to program. Some programs have separate staff providing
child development services, social services, and health
services to families; in others a single person has
primary contact with the family, although this person is
backed up by specialists in the three areas. All programs
provide a mix of home visits and center activities for
mothers and children. All have a variety of educational

and recreational activities for parents in addition to child development education. Recent information and evaluations of the program can be found in Nauta (1981), Nauta and Johnson (1981), and Johnson et al. (1980).

Home Start operated actively as a demonstration program from 1972 through 1975; it was designed to demonstrate methods of delivering comprehensive Head Start-type services to children and parents for whom a center-based program was not feasible. Much of the program--parent education, social services, and child activities--took place in the home. All of the 16 programs also had center meetings, where children and parents got together two or three times a month. Many of the programs were in rural areas; guidelines were explicit in the intention to provide services as families identified them. In 1975 six Home Start programs became regional training centers for providing assistance to Head Start programs that wanted to adopt a home-based component. Like the Child and Family Resource Program, Home Start emphasized the whole family and not just children; unlike the Child and Family Resource Program, Home Start served only families with preschool-age children and enrolled them for two years at most. Information about Home Start can be found in Hewett (1978) and Love et al. (1976).

The Brookline Early Education Project is a privately developed and funded experimental program in a single service site, Brookline and Boston, Massachusetts. Initially based on the child development philosophy and research of Burton White and the work of White and Watts at the Harvard Preschool Project, the program sought to provide support and parent education to mothers of children from the prenatal period to age three. The program provided a physical center and educational materials on a lending basis; families were encouraged to use the resource center and to take material home with them. Each family also had a visitor who helped the family acquire educational information and practical experience in playing with and teaching their own children. The visitors also provided assistance to mothers in need for coping with everyday family problems. The program also included comprehensive health screening and treatment referral services. Both low-income and middle-class children were enrolled in the program. Three levels of service were offered, and families were randomly assigned to the levels for purposes of research. (Information about the program and its evaluation can be found in the paper by Levine and Palfrey in this volume.)

Program Features

Three characteristics common to family service program models[1] were selected for discussion in this paper: the mix of support and intervention in the structure and content of family service programs, the use of individualized treatment for families, and the program's role as coordinator of services for families in the local community. These features were selected because they illustrate important aspects of family service programs that distinguish them from the more traditional child development intervention programs. These same features also constitute difficult problems for measurement of program outcomes.

We noted earlier that the broad goals of comprehensive service programs and their individualized treatment of families create a long list of possible outcomes of potential interest in evaluating the programs. Effects may be anticipated in health and in educational, psychological, and social functioning for children, parents, and other family members. There may also be effects on the ways in which families and individuals in other social groups or institutions interact as well as effects for the services generally available to families in the site of program operation. Possible effects can be organized into three broad groups.

The first set of effects are those for individuals within the family household itself. These may include effects on child development, adult development, parent education, parent-child interaction, and intrafamily relationships (e.g., marital or sibling). Child development intervention programs have traditionally concentrated on studying effects on the cognitive and

---

[1]Throughout the paper "model" is used to refer to a specific program that was created by federal or private research with a particular set of guidelines and goals (e.g., the Child and Family Resource Program, Home Start, the Brookline Early Education Project). The term "program" refers to the local project(s) implemented under those guidelines according to a specific model. There are 11 programs following the Child and Family Resource Program model; 16 programs following the Home Start model. For the privately developed models, one project represented the program model.

212

physical development of children and on parent-child
(especially mother) interaction.

Another set of effects are those concerning the
relationships between families and the informal
organizations (social groups, extended families) and
formal institutions (schools, agencies) of society.
Effects of this sort might be observed in the role of
parent involvement in the child's public schooling or the
ability of parents to obtain regular income for the
family.

A third set of effects are those for the service
delivery community at the site of program implementation. Since some program models have as their goal
improvement of services for families in the community,
examples of these effects are improved prenatal care or
new links between agencies serving families in the
community.

The researcher must decide which set of effects is
most important and, within each set, which particular
outcomes are of greatest interest. The different groups
interested in family programs have different views of the
priority among these effects, which is suggested by many
aspects of a program's philosophy and practice. Each of
the three features and the measurement problems associated
with them exert influence on the type of effects selected
for study and the methods selected for measuring them.
In the discussion that follows the potential effects and
values of different constituencies, which are mentioned
but not emphasized, are provided primarily as a context
for the discussion of measurement problems.

The Mix of Support and Intervention

The family programs described in this paper have been
influenced by many social programs and lines of social
and psychological research. Inherent in many of the
programs and research is a dynamic tension between
intervention in the lives of children and families and
support of their strengths and capabilities. The two
views have been characterized by some researchers as the
"deficit" and the "strength" models of family functioning.

Both support and intervention are implied by the very
broad guidelines that defined the Child and Family
Resource Program, Home Start, and other programs funded
by the Administration for Children, Youth, and Families.
Support was implied by the wording of the Child and

Family Resource Program guidelines to build on the
existing strengths of families and to enhance the total
development of children, by working through the family
and by offering diverse social and psychological services
as needed by each family. Intervention was also implied
by the emphasis on educational activities for children
and parents and by the guidelines that limited
eligibility to low-income families.

Theoretically it is possible to see support and
intervention as two different, essentially philosophical
approaches to the operation of programs--philosophies
that influence program structure, content, and the nature
of the relationships between staff and families. It can
also be argued, however, that the two are inseparable--
that providing support to families can serve as an
intervention and that change, the primary goal of
intervention, is more likely to occur in an atmosphere of
support for parents. Because support and intervention
are intertwined in most programs, it is difficult to
distinguish them from each other. The list below
comprises somewhat stereotypical attributes of the two
approaches, as a way of contrasting the hypothetical
extreme for each approach:

INTERVENTION	SUPPORT
Change desired in children, mother	Change in children, parents, and other family members, social institutions
Change expected during or immediately after treatment	Change may be short term but more likely to take place episodically over years
Treatment provided for one period of enrollment, though this may be intense for one to two years	Treatment may be intensive at first but intermittent over years, as needed or desired by family
Standard treatment defined by professionals outside the family	Treatment individualized and determined by family and staff; emphasis on parent initative

Implied deficit model of family; family problems most important	Nondeficit model implied; strengths as well as needs important
Professional staff, often with educational and social work roles filled by different staff	Staff with multiple roles; mix of professional and paraprofessional staff
Emphasis on cognitive development for children and parent education, the latter focused on child development and educational topics	Child development and parent education important, but but other needs of family may take precedence; broader range of social and psychological services

In fact, none of the programs mentioned in this paper are solely interventionist or supportive in their approach. Programs with different mixes of support and intervention differ on many dimensions, thus influencing research decisions about:

• Who is expected to change (children, parents, or social agencies).
• What is expected to change (childrearing attitudes, coping behavior, the use of services, income, or quality of housing).
• When change is expected to occur (immediately, within months, or over a period of years).
• Who is responsible for initiating and accomplishing change (parents, professionals, or members of the extended family or social network).

The mix of support and intervention is the source of much ambiguity in the family service concept. The ambiguity in philosophy and program implementation encourages ambiguity in expectations by various concerned groups about what such programs do or should do and the criteria by which they should be studied. Understanding the mix in family programs should help researchers know how to look at the treatment provided by the programs as well as what effects and criteria for measurement may be most appropriate.

Three characteristics of programs are often implemented in different ways according to whether the program's philosophy is toward support or intervention in its approach:

• The relative emphasis on education and cognitive development versus a range of social, educational, and psychological services.
• The role of parents in determining treatment.
• Policies about family enrollment and participation.

The tendency for traditional intervention programs to emphasize cognitive and physical development for children rather than a range of developmental services has been mentioned. Support-oriented programs may have educational components and may place high values on certain types of education, especially for parents, but the child's school readiness or performance is not the primary aim of child development activities. Likewise, traditional intervention approaches emphasized certain aspects of maternal teaching behavior (such as verbal behavior or the ability to structure learning activities); a support approach may be more attentive to the affective quality of the mother and child relationship or the socialization aspects of childrearing as indicated by the mother's interest and need to know.

The role of parents in determining treatment can be observed directly by looking at their participation in planning or organizing activities. It can also be observed indirectly in the structure of the program and in staff attitudes toward family participation in program operations. The less formal the distinction is between staff as professionals and families, and the more parents have to say about the types of services and activities they get and the more a program leans toward support rather than intervention.

Policies concerning family enrollment and participation also illustrate philosophies of intervention and support. Although Home Start and the Child and Family Resource Program were intended for low-income families, there was variation in the types of families actually recruited as well as variation in program expectations for participation by families.

Some programs recruited families already interested in Head Start; others sought out low-income mothers with new babies through clinics and hospitals. Some programs limited the enrollment of families in crisis, believing that other agencies could better serve them. Others chose to emphasize enrollment of families of particular types (e.g., single parents, teenage mothers, and rural families).

Expectations for participation varied primarily in the length of time enrolled or the intensity or frequency of participation while enrolled. Home Start families were enrolled for two to three years and were expected to participate regularly: weekly home visits, group activities for children every other week, and parent group activities a few times a month were common. In the Child and Family Resource Program, however, there was more variation among programs in expectations for participation. Some required contracts with families specifying a schedule for participation similar to Home Start; others allowed great differences in intensity or frequency of participation. A family could be quite active (one or more contacts with the center and weekly home visits) or relatively inactive (monthly telephone calls initiated by the family). Variation depended on whether the family was new to the program (usually more active), was undergoing crisis, or was temporarily too busy with other familiy business to participate in program activities.

The variations in type of family enrolled and in levels of participation have far-reaching implications for the treatments delivered by programs and the outcomes expected as a result of the program. For example, gains in children's mental development in Home Start and the Child and Family Resource Program seem linked to regular participation over a fairly short period of time (less than two years); this finding is consistent with those from intervention-type programs in short-term effects for mental development. For longer-term gains, anecdotal evidence from the Child and Family Resource Program suggests that changes in family circumstances or the coping skills of mothers take much longer; program staff report changes in some families in these areas after two years and in others after four or five. Thus, different levels of participation may be appropriate for producing outcomes in different areas of family functioning.

Likewise, different levels of participation may also be appropriate for different types of families. Some individuals seem able to make a commitment to the program and participate regularly right away; others develop similar relationships of trust with program staff only after long periods of weeks or months. Many parents expressed the view that the appeal of the program was that "it was there when we needed it"--in other words, it functioned truly as a resource and support program.

Not only do programs often have different expectations for participation depending on the type of family or the area of greatest family need, but they also may vary in the intensity of service or in expectations for participation over time for specific families. Thus, one family may participate regularly for two years, then leave the program; another may participate irregularly at first for a year and then regularly for two; still another may participate regularly for two years, then decrease steadily in participation over the next three years, stepping up contact with the program in times of special crisis. All three families might be served within a single program. In fact, length of time enrolled and intensity of participation are major ways in which treatment has been individualized in these demonstration programs.

The Individualization of Treatment

Individualization of treatment is entirely consistent with, even inseparable from, the mix of support and intervention in family service programs. Because individualization is closely related to the mix of support and intervention and because it is central to the philosophy of these programs, we provide an overview of individualization, followed by a discussion of some attempts to study programs that provide such treatments.

Though something of a misnomer when applied to a family unit, "individualization" refers to the process of planning for and the resulting pattern of activities and services a family actually gets as a result of participating in a family service program. Most programs mentioned in this paper have some individualized treatment; the Child and Family Resource Program has the most, as treatment is determined to a large part by the parents in conjunction with the staff. To understand individualization it is necessary to understand the process by which plans for families are made and what aspects of the program are actually varied.

In the Child and Family Resource Program the planning begins with a thorough assessment to identify what parents want and children need. A specific plan is developed, recorded, and approved; the plan, which varies in detail from program to program, is reviewed and revised periodically. Areas considered in assessment include the health of all household members; needs for necessities such as housing, clothing, food, and utilities; arrangements for adequate income, which may include education, training, or job interviews; and needs for social services such as legal assistance, day care, or recreation. In many programs, less tangible personal goals may be considered, such as social activities, new skills training, or personal counseling. A developmental assessment of children and full health screening are also included; sometimes a nurse visits the home to conduct health inventories. The plan that results from this assessment is approved verbally or in writing. In some programs, parents meet with program staff and representatives of other agencies who provide services identified in the family's plan.

What is individualized? Structurally, one important source of variation is the mix of direct services (by program staff; e.g., informal counseling of health education by a program nurse) and indirect services, through referrals to other agencies. Another source of variation is the mix of center- and home-based activities that parents elect. In some programs the mother may choose to have monthly home visits from a teaching staff member and weekly sessions for her child at the center. In other programs all families are expected to participate in the same schedule of center and home activities; variation may occur with the grouping of certain types of parents (single mothers, teenage mothers) and activities tailored to their interests.

Another source of variation is the content of home visits and center group meetings. Which of the many aspects of child and family development (health, social and emotional relationships, etc.) are covered and how these topics are addressed (group discussion, role playing, etc.) are important determinants of program treatment.

Finally, variation occurs in the nature of the relationship between parents and staff. This variation is difficult to characterize but concerns the degree to which the parents are self-sufficient in identifying goals, interacting with children, and participating in program activities. Such variation in the relationship between staff and parents may reflect the style of the staff member, the program philosophy, or the circumstances under which the parents came to the program (e.g., court referral, interest in child development, desire for social contact).

In short, virtually all aspects of the program may be varied. A summary of common variation includes the following:

- The mix of direct and referral services.
- The mix of center- and home-based activities.
- The types of actions and goals identified for families.
- The time of participation (regular weekday, weekends for working parents).
- The involvement of other family members (grandparents, siblings, other care givers).
- The type of child development or parent education activities offered or the relative emphasis on child versus family services.

While these aspects can be used to identify the type and degree of individualization in a program, they are collected as either input or treatment variables in program evaluations. In most family service programs the number of dimensions on which treatment may vary is large, a fact that poses a fundamental problem for researchers.

Measurement Problems

The foregoing discussion pointed out the complex nature of family service program models that deliver individualized treatment--treatment that combines support and intervention in different degrees for specific families and in different proportions across programs. Several problems for measurement of such programs were mentioned.

First, comprehensive family programs are difficult to measure because they have broad goals for diverse effects on families and communities. These programs have many constituencies (parents and children, program staff, policy makers, advocates, taxpayers, researchers) whose values dictate different priorities for program goals and effects.

Second, the mix of support and intervention in an individualized program makes definition of treatment particularly problematic. In effect, there are as many treatments as there are families. Clustering families by the patterns of service they receive is difficult because

the combinations of potentially important treatment
variables are numerous.

Third, it is difficult to determine which of the many
variations in treatment might be the important ones.
Assuming that program goals might be agreed upon among
some concerned groups and treatment reasonably well
defined, there is still the problem of being unable to
determine which aspects of treatment were responsible for
the effects observed. Thus, replication of "successful"
program features would be impossible.

Finally, there is the problem of assigning value to
different patterns of treatment and outcome and of
determining whether the treatment and outcome make sense
for the individual child or family case for which it was
designed. The inability to evaluate the appropriateness
of treatment or of treatment-outcome relationships is a
fundamental problem in evaluating these programs; it
raises other questions about the nature of public and
private services to families:

• Whose values are more "right," parents or staff?
When do parents know what's best for their children?
What constitutes a staff member's "providing alternatives"
in childrearing, and what constitutes imposing one's
values on another?
• What are the costs to families and society of
substituting professional relationships with those that
were formerly provided by families, churches, or other
community organizations?
• What is the effect of providing role models in the
form of staff members who may have social or political
views different from the family members who enroll?
• What is the implication of providing support and
intervention only to low-income families or to mothers
who are not working full time?

Many of the problems described above are higher-order
problems of conceptualization, definition, and values.
Without clarification of these problems, however, no
methodological solutions are likely to produce the answers
to the most important research questions to be asked
about these programs. Many of the approaches taken by
researchers to minimize these problems are aimed at
clarifying such higher-order problems.

ASSESSING THE PROCESS OF INDIVIDUALIZED TREATMENT

The discussion of support, intervention, and individualization above was intended to illustrate the most important characteristics of the family service model: When implemented as mandated, these programs may determine a unique set of goals and treatment for each enrolled family. Theoretically, then, it might be impossible to evaluate outcomes for participating families except on a family-by-family basis.

In recent years, description and measurement of program treatment has been justified on the grounds that it is useful in interpreting patterns of outcome observed between treatment and control groups (Hewett et al., 1979). There seem to be many reasons why description and measurement of treatments are desirable in themselves: The general goals and philosophical mix of support and intervention may be different from model to model and community to community, the needs of families and communities that help shape local programs differ, the identities and views of different groups may be unclear, treatment is likely to be individualized, the expectations and relationships among staff and families also vary. In terms of evaluation research, the description or defini-tion of program goals and treatment are often referred to as the study of "process," as distinct from "outcome" (Rossi et al., 1979; Goodwin and Driscoll, 1980). At least three types of "process" variables have been distinguished that are appropriate in studying family service programs:

* Indicators that the program delivered the services mandated by guidelines or dictated by program goals (Zigler and Trickett, 1978).
* Indicators of how much (hours of contact, number of visits) or what type of treatment (education, one-to-one relationship) was delivered.
* Indicators of the dynamic relationships through which treatment was delivered (staff-family, parent-child, staff-community agencies).

All three types of process variables may be captured through quantitative and qualitative measures, although the nature of relationships lend themselves more readily to qualitative measures in general.

We believe that the nature of family service programs requires the flexible and selective use of many quali-

tative and quantitive measures to capture all three types
of program processes and treatment. Not all studies need
to collect data about goals, treatment, and processes in
equal proportions; the selection of types of process
variables and appropriate measures is dictated, of
course, by the types of questions to be answered by the
research. Three general questions, which should be asked
for any family service program, are important for
understanding and assessing such programs:

• What goals are expressed for this program, and
what constituencies (local and other) do the goals
represent?
• What actually goes on in the program, and what
measures of process (treatment) can be used to capture
it? Can any be used to relate treatment to outcome?
• What issues for policy or measurement are raised
by the study treatment or process? What anticipated
outcomes are suggested?

What goals are expressed for this program, and what
constituencies do the goals represent? The notion of
identifying program goals first is a basic tenet of
evaluation research. With regard to family service
programs, it is easy to see that broad guidelines may be
interpreted locally in different ways in response to
different local conditions. More difficult still, there
are likely to be different sets of goals that represent
the groups who have a stake in the program, both at the
community and the state or federal levels.

Policy makers may want to provide service and to learn
the forms a program may take if left to local implementation. Program directors may see their programs as social
advocacy groups, mental health facilities, vehicles for
individual self-help, or preventive and compensatory child
development programs. Parents may see the program as a
source of accessible advice about childrearing, an entry
into a community system of child care, or a chance to
make new friends and participate in social or educational
activities.

But these are not the only concerned groups. Evaluators and social policy advocates in academic and political
positions may see programs as laboratories for human
development studies, as threats to the natural order among
family members and groups in society, as platforms for
grass-roots political organization, or as models for
preventive community mental health.

Identifying goals may be a complex task, even for a single set of constituents. The Brookline Early Education Project emphasized the goals and expectations of the parents, collecting tremendous quantities of process data from parents about initial expectations, experiences with various program practices, and satisfaction. The Home Start evaluation compiled case studies of the historical and organizational roots of each local demonstration program and included a case study of the national program office and its development of the federal program model.

Eventually the evaluator or researcher must choose some goals as the basis for structuring evaluations; the choice of a set of goals (whether those of policy makers, other researchers, or program staff) represents an implicit stand about their relative importance. Disproportionate attention to goals can be a trap for evaluators (Weiss and Rein, 1979); it is important to recognize the limitations of the use of goals sets or other contextual data in defining treatment.

What actually goes on in the program, and what measures of process (treatment) can be used to capture it? Can any be used to relate treatment to outcome? What goes on in a program can be characterized both qualitatively and quantitatively--measured or described, according to the purposes of the research. Selection of a particular group or process within the program for in-depth study is dictated by the orientation of the evaluator and the goals selected for study.

Qualitative methods are often appropriate to compile a thorough description of the purposes and realization of the program. Especially for programs based on a new model or guidelines, the very process of compiling a description of the program is likely to be useful to evaluators and to new audiences for the program. For evaluators the descriptive qualitative study will help focus attention on the most important program features as well as those most difficult to measure. Preparation for such a study may identify descrepancies between goals and practice and raise questions about unanticipated outcome. The issues and questions raised in a good descriptive study may be useful in themselves for policy makers and may serve as a basis for subsequent decisions about study design made by evaluators.

In the Brookline Early Education Project the largely descriptive process study raised many important questions about the "appropriate" role of staff who visit homes in different subcultures served by the program. In the Child and Family Resource Program both descriptive and process studies were used. The descriptive study attempted to determine through interviews with staff and informal observation of program activities whether there were common models actually in operation among the 11 sites. On the basis of this descriptive study it was observed that although certain methods of delivering particular services such as health or infant and toddler services were common to several of the local programs, no overall models of program structure could be identified. Such observations might have bearing on guidelines for future programs of this type.

Another aspect of the evaluation of the Child and Family Resource Program used a different qualitative method--ethnography--to capture the interpersonal processes between staff and families. Evaluations of educational programs have used this method for studying certain types of questions (Stake, 1978); at present, an ethnographic study is under way in five sites. At each site, trained ethnographers who are familiar with the community are spending extensive time with families during a six-month period to understand the role of the program and other social networks or programs. Ethnographers are also observing among program staff the process that goes along with maintaining relationships.

With the exception of the ethnographic study, the descriptive studies described above relied on some forms of quantitative information (e.g., number of group meetings) in assembling the qualitative picture. In general, the qualitative and descriptive methods require continuous cross validation between the evaluation staff visiting the program and the program staff; these methods are both subjective and time-consuming. As an initial step in assessing such programs, however, the investment of time and the mix of subjective observation and simple quantitative data are necessary for a broad understanding of what actually takes place in the program. Because it attempts to assemble a whole picture of the program and its various meanings to staff and participants, a descriptive program study is one of the major sources of judgment about the quality and appropriateness of service.

Qualitative description is sometimes disregarded because it cannot be related to outcome measures. However, from studies of parent education programs up to 1978, Goodson and Hess (1978) observed that only the most global treatment variables were common across programs

and useful in relating treatment to outcome. Among the
variables were the presence of a structured curriculum,
the role of parents in decision making, the combination
of home and center activities, and the evidence of a
one-to-one relationship between staff and families.
Thus, even the most broad qualitative aspects of the
program can be useful in characterizing treatment.

Quantitative measures of treatment are also important.
Most of the demonstration programs and private family
service programs of the Administration for Children,
Youth, and Families used quantitative treatment measures.
Some were used simply to describe program operations;
others were related to outcomes for families.

We consider two types of quantitative treatment
measures: systems of records kept by the program staff
and systems of observations of program activities by
evaluators outside the program.

Systems of Records

Typically, systems of records include detailed records
of services and activities delivered to clients and are
maintained by program staff. They often record numbers
for referrals, transportation, home visits, center group
sessions, and other types of contact between staff and
families. In programs characterized by individualized
treatment, records are typically kept for specific
families. An evaluator may use records kept by the
program internally[2] (which may differ in detail,
regularity, and content) or require that a separate
system of evaluation records be kept.

Typically these systems of records attempt to capture
measures of participation, although some evaluations also
attempt to record family stress, motivation to participate, staff perceptions of families, and other characteristics of the family-staff relationship. In Home Start
and the Child and Family Resource Program, participation

---

[2]This was the approach used by the General Accounting
Office team in the review of the Child and Family
Resource Program described at the beginning of this
paper. They were not concerned with comparability of
treatment across programs.

measures were found to be useful as covariables to explain
different patterns of outcome for children in the program.
In Home Start, children's gains on cognitive and language
outcome measures dropped or disappeared when families
made fewer than two visits per month. In the Child and
Family Resource Program, children's outcomes on a developmental measure (Bayley, 1969) were related to a complex
measure of participation (rate over time of participation
in both home visits and center activities). These
findings suggest that there is an effect of participation
in program activities beyond mere enrollment in the
program, although there were no overall differences in
development between children in the program and a
comparison group not receiving program services. While
this is a successful use of treatment variables to
explain outcomes, it captures only the broadest aspects
of treatment.

Attempts to capture the more individualized nature of
treatment in the Child and Family Resource Program have
been made with the use of family-specific goal records
kept by staff as part of the program's study of treatment.
There are many technical problems with this approach, some
of which have been documented in evaluation literature
(Kiresuk and Sherman, 1968; Kiresuk et al., 1978).
However, as the approach has not been widely used in
family service programs and does provide useful descriptive information, we will describe some of the problems
encountered with this approach.

Goal setting and goal attainment have been used as
measures of outcome primarily in mental health settings
making use of certain types of treatment: short-term,
behaviorally oriented approaches in which there is
explicit agreement between client and therapist about
what they will try to accomplish, how long it will take,
and what each will be expected to do. These characteristics of the treatment process are similar to the
explicit goal-setting process that is common in the
individualized treatment of the Child and Family Resource
Program. The forms currently used record a description
of the goal, who it concerns (the mother, child, or whole
family), the type of goal (health, employment), and when
it is expected to be completed. At regular intervals,
the staff report on the status of the goals: completed,
changed, much progress, no progress, dropped. In this
spare format, goal records provide a profile for each
family of the focus of treatment, the types and sequence

of services used, and whether many goals are dropped or
changed--a possible signal of disinterest or mismatch
between staff and family. Aggregated over all families,
goal records can provide a rough empirical picture of the
program's overall treatment emphasis, whether on immediate
needs, such as housing, or long-range goals for mothers,
such as employment.

Problems with goal attainment as a treatment measure
exist at several levels. One is validity: Goal records
may not represent the family's true goals and private
reasons for coming to the program or the implicit goals
the staff may be pursuing for the parent (such as more
regular attendance at the program). Others include the
reliability of the records, the level of detail at which
a goal should be stated, the difficulty in distinguishing
between services that are part of treatment (like health
screening) and goals, and the incentives for staff to
maintain such records regularly. As outcome measures,
records kept by staff give an automatic advantage to
staff or programs that are already record oriented or
sufficiently practiced or educated to be able to translate
their work well into record form. In programs in which
former program parents often become staff members, they
may lack education, practice, or a "professionalized"
attitude toward recordkeeping, which serves to penalize
their families on that measure.

Aside from the many practical problems with goal
records as measures of treatment, there is a more
important conceptual problem with using them as outcome
measures. It is virtually impossible to assign values to
different clusters or sequences of goals. Are goals for
maternal employment and housing repair more important
than goals for participation in program activities and
group activities for a preschool child? Is limited
progress toward a goal such as "to settle custody rights
with the children's father" more or less important than
completion of a goal such as "to obtain hearing and visual
screening for the child"? Clearly, attainment can only
be considered in terms of a particular family, not as a
basis for aggregating or comparing outcomes among
families. There are no models of what is normative or
desirable for each family (except what will generally
enhance the development of the child); thus, the study of
goals and goal attainment describes the individualized
treatment but does not help determine whether it is an
appropriate treatment for the family.

Systems of Observation

Systems of observation, both in-person and videotape, have been used to capture treatment variables. In Home Start the observations were modest, carried out by field observers who accompanied home visitors to record the content of the visit, the focus of activity (parent or child), and a few other variables. While this information was not used to study outcomes, it did have immediate consequences for policy from the national program office. From these observations it became apparent that although the focus of Home Start was on the parent, most home visitors spent a majority of time interacting with the children. Subsequently, the national program office provided additional direction and opportunities for training to help home visitors work effectively with adults.

Videotaped observation systems have been used to capture process variables (as in the evaluation of the Parent Child Development Centers) or outcome (as in the Child and Family Resource Program). These systems are usually prohibitively expensive for large evaluations. In the Child and Family Resource Program they were used only at selected sites.

What additional questions are raised by the process measures? A final important function of process studies is to identify additional questions about the program under study. Researchers routinely suggest further research on the basis of their studies; less frequently, however, researchers try to identify how their methods failed to capture what they wanted and what that failure suggests for different formulations of the problems being investigated. Weiss and Rein (1969) undertook such an analysis when they observed that they could not detect the effects of a program's efforts to change communities because they looked primarily at changes in individuals. Furthermore, because much policy research is conducted to answer specific questions posed by policy makers, evaluators are encouraged to frame their research as answers to specific questions in order to be useful and effective (see Deloria and Brookins, in this volume). In addition to answering the questions posed, researchers must formulate and raise questions that emerge from research and the problems encountered in research. This view of research as hypothesis generating rather than hypothesis testing is one that has been identified by a number of psychologists and other researchers (e.g.,

Weiss, 1972). They maintain that research methods and strategies must be continously modified in order to capture and explain the phenomena they investigate.

Studies of treatment and process may take many different forms, using a variety of methods to answer or raise questions about programs. Process studies can furnish a basis for understanding what goes on in a program as well as a basis for selecting appropriate outcomes for study and the methods likely to capture them. And, on a more limited basis, process measures can help relate treatment to outcome.

ASSESSING OUTCOMES FOR INDIVIDUALIZED PROGRAMS

As elaborated above, family programs with broad goals and individualized treatments require good process evaluation in order to describe what the programs intended to do and what treatments they provided to children and families. Likewise, the goals and treatments of these programs pose problems for the evaluation of outcomes as well as process. This section discusses four such problems in evaluating outcomes:

- Assessing outcomes across multiple domains.
- Assessing multiple outcomes within a single domain.
- Selecting an appropriate unit of analysis.
- Selecting appropriate comparisons.

Although each problem has distinct implications for evaluating impact, all four are interrelated. These problems arise directly from characteristics of the comprehensive family service programs that we have used as illustrations throughout this paper--Home Start and the Child and Family Resource Program. The problems are best exemplified by reference to specific features of past and current evaluations of these two programs.

Features of the Program Evaluations

Evaluations of Home Start and the Child and Family Resource Program were conducted at different times during the past decade. The evaluation of the Child and Family Resource Program was able to build and expand on the design of the Home Start evaluation (e.g., by including an ethnographic study of process and outcome). In many

important respects, however, the basic design and analyses
of the two evaluations were similar and certain common
evaluation features help illustrate the problems selected
for discussion.

Both Home Start and the Child and Family Resource
Program evaluations were charged with investigating
multiple possible outcomes for families and children as a
result of the program. In choosing to emphasize the role
of the family in child development, federal program
designers implicitly accepted the assumption that a wide
range of outcomes could be addressed directly or
indirectly through program intervention or support.

In addition to the child's own temperament and
abilities, outcomes were expected in the behaviors of
parents and other members of the immediate household and
in the functioning of the family in relation to neighborhood support and social service resources. Programs were
also expected to mediate the influences of forces outside
the family; for example, opportunities for employment or
education in the local community or state regulations
concerning Aid to Families with Dependent Children (AFDC).
Furthermore, there was an explicit assumption that
programs could bring about gradual changes in community
institutions or child care policies.

There were three potential units or levels of analysis
in both evaluations: the individual (child or parent),
the family or household unit, and the institution level,
which could include outcomes for local service providers
or for broad (state or federal) program policies. The
institutional level was qualitatively different from the
other two and is discussed in the "Integration of
Service" section of this paper, which focuses on outcomes
for children and families only.

Evaluations of both Home Start and the Child and
Family Resource Program organized diverse outcomes into
study domains that correspond more or less to areas of
psychological or sociological research. Prior work in
each research area provided a basis for the selection of
variables and measures that would capture change in each
domain. Both evaluations eventually included outcome
domains representing child development, parent-child
interaction, maternal and child health, family
circumstances (income, parental education, housing
quality, and employment), and family-social interaction
(the use of informal social networks, social service
resources, and individual coping skills). Each domain
was represented by several variables. For example, in

the parent-child interaction domain for the Home Start
evaluation, there were variables representing such
constructs as maternal teaching style and frequency and
type of parent-child interaction.

Another feature shared by the evaluations was the use
of a treatment comparison group design with random assignment to groups at each program site included in the
evaluation. In general, outcome analyses compared mean
differences between treatment and comparison groups using
all variables in all domains for all families, and
further analyses related process and outcomes for
treatment families only.

All three features shared by the evaluations reflected
accepted practice in psychological and educational
research. They were implemented because they would
answer certain types of policy questions concerning
outcomes for families receiving individualized treatment
incorporating multiple services compared with families
participating in no such program (or receiving different,
unsystematic services).

Assessing Outcomes Across Multiple Domains

Essentially this problem is the inevitable consequence
of attempting to assess outcomes from individualized
treatment based on the family's expressed needs and
goals. From among the many services available in all
domains, a family might choose and receive services or
benefits in only two or three. There might be as many
treatments and as many patterns of outcome as there are
families. One family (or individual within it) may need
health services in addition to child development services;
another may need job training and child care in addition
to child development services. Since program emphasis
and treatments vary by domain over time for a family,
expectations for outcomes in the domains of treatment or
need can logically be expected to vary as well.

In both programs there was consensus among program
staff that outcomes in two domains--child development and
parent-child interaction--could and should be assessed
for all families. Nonetheless, there was no agreement
about which of the two child-related domains was more
important, nor which of the other domains, expected to
vary with family need, was most important.

This is a conceptual as well as methodological
problem. It reflects an important lack of integrative

theoretical models for many of the changes or interactions expected to take place within families or between families and social groups, including the Child and Family Resource Program. The problem is not an absence of models altogether. There are many models of cognitive and socioemotional development in children and of psychological and social functioning in families. There are also theories (and implied models) about the reciprocal influences in family-child development (Bell and Harper, 1977) and about how families and social institutions interact (see Newbrought et al., 1978, for a discussion and summary of recent research).

There are recent promising attempts to characterize the "ecology of human development" (Bronfenbrenner, 1977), linking the development of the individual child to the functioning of the family and to the wider social systems that support or inhibit that functioning. However, these new theoretical developments have thus far not been widely applied in program evaluation.

The competing models and the absence of widely accepted conceptualizations for unifying such models force continued reliance on analyses within outcome domains. It has another result as well. Without well-defined models of the relationship among outcomes in several domains, it is difficult for evaluators to justify emphasis on a particular domain or to fully explore relationships among domains on theoretical grounds. Inevitably, resources must be expended on collecting and analyzing data in each domain; the necessity to be broad in analyzing several domains often precludes in-depth analyses.

In the Home Start and the Child and Family Resource Program evaluations, the domains of child development and parent-child interaction were emphasized because of their prominence in the program guidelines and because of the expressed interest of policy makers. While such decisions were legitimate given the goals of the programs and the federal agency, they did limit resources that might have been applied to the problem of understanding outcomes for families as a whole, in different domains, over time.

Assessing Outcomes Within a Single Domain

Within-domain analyses, combining a number of separate variables, is a microcosm of the previous problem; within a particular domain it is also often impossible to combine variables in a meaningful way. The difficulty in combining them varies by domain, to the degree that previous research in that domain has provided theoretical models and empirical groundwork. There are numerous theories and studies linking specific features of child development to one another and linking features of parent-child interaction to one another. In contrast, in the domain of family-social interaction, theoretical and empirical work has been fragmented. For example, while there is descriptive work relating individual coping behavior to social and institutional supports (Belle et al., 1980), little has been done to develop a theoretical framework for explaining the dimensions of such relationships.

An example of a simple within-domain analysis illustrates the problems inherent in analyzing outcomes both within domains and across multiple domains.

In the Child and Family Resource Program evaluation, program families at six sites were compared with non-program families on some variables in the domain of family circumstances. One was employment status; another was family income. The findings showed no significant differences on employment status, although somewhat fewer Child and Family Resource Program mothers were employed. The findings also showed that non-Child and Family Resource Program families reported significantly more income than Child and Family Resource Program families. Taken separately these findings seem to show that the Child and Family Resource Program had no effect on jobs and an adverse effect on income. Yet if the two variables are considered together, a more complex picture emerges showing informative differences between sites. For instance, higher family income is reported in sites and groups with more working mothers. Since most Child and Family Resource Programs encourage mothers to stay at home so they can concentrate on parenting, the lower employment and reported income figures reflect this; but in some sites, the Child and Family Resource Program encouraged mothers to work, and the employment rates and reported income are higher in these sites.

To further assess the ultimate value of encouraging mothers to work or not to work, we would have to cross domains and examine the respective child development gains. Long-range child development gains resulting from mothers staying at home could conceivably offset the short-term losses in employment and income. Only with more complete within-domain and across-domain analyses can reasons for underlying differences be discovered.

The difficulty of combining variables within some
domains and of analyzing them into a comprehensive
picture of outcomes across domains creates several
problems. It makes impossible a view of status and
change in the family overall, either at a single point or
over time. It makes difficult the compilation of a
comprehensive picture for each family or individual in
relation to the individualized treatment received. And
it may cause evaluators to draw false conclusions about
the variables or domains they have studied because they
cannot interpret their results. Finally, in the absence
of models or methods for combining outcomes in diverse
domains, evaluators and policy makers may spend valuable
resources collecting data of marginal utility or analyzing
them in ways that do not prove to be useful or interpret-
able. Careful consideration of research questions and
the issues raised by the program must guide priorities
for analysis among variables in a single domain and for
combining variables across domains. When such priorities
have been set in the past, child development and parent-
child interaction have received the most emphasis;
perhaps it is not the time to turn additional resources
to the exploration of the complex issues of combining
outcomes within and across domains.

Selecting a Unit of Analysis

In Home Start and the Child and Family Resource
Program, two units of analysis were recognized as most
important: the individual and the family. Although the
program emphasis was on the family, analyses nonetheless
used the individual child or parent almost exclusively.
In part this problem is similar to the previous two.
That is, if it is difficult to aggregate outcomes for an
individual within and across domains, then it will also
be difficult to compile and analyze outcome data at the
family level, since this involves outcomes for multiple
family members. For example, health outcomes are
considered separately for children and mothers, rather
than for a family as a whole, which would be more
consistent with the program's approach. This is a
continuing problem because of the stated goals and actual
emphasis of the program on the family—not only the
family as a group of members at any one time, but also
the family as it develops over time. Here the lack of
clear developmental models seems most crucial, although a

number of family psychologists and sociologists have attempted to grapple with this lack (Duvall, 1977; Burr et al., 1979). For the most part, however, methods that combine information on several family members or on the family as a unit are those developed for clinical work or research with families (Jacob, 1975; Gurman and Kniskern, 1978). It seems appropriate that some of these methods be explored for their utility in evaluating outcomes for family programs.

Selecting Appropriate Comparisons

In line with the analysis of single variables or measures within domains, the use of treatment and comparison group designs has been the primary means of attributing impact or change to the program. While there are some problems with using only such designs in evaluating some types of compensatory education programs (Campbell and Boruch, 1975) and practical problems (e.g., attrition) associated with using such designs in longitudinal research, there are benefits in the approach (Cook and Campbell, 1979). It seems appropriate to retain such designs in future evaluations when questions are to be answered about families receiving one treatment versus another. However, a simple treatment-comparison group design does not preclude the use of other standards for assessing change in individuals and families. Treatment-comparison group designs might well be supplemented by other approaches to help answer such questions as the following:

• How is a particular child or family developing relative to its own prior status or functioning (the family as its own comparison)?
• How are program children or families functioning compared with selected national norms for similar populations?
• How is a particular pattern of outcomes related to specific aspects of treatment?
• How are patterns of outcome different by important family variables, such as age of mother or household type (e.g., single mother)?

Answers to these types of questions are important in evaluating outcomes because they help clarify how the programs work or do not work with different individuals

and families. Particularly when heterogeniety of both
treatment and comparison groups may make it difficult to
detect effects based on group means, it is important to
understand the relationships between treatment and
outcome. It is desirable to have such information in the
context of each family, as contextual information may be
crucial in interpreting results.

Recommendations

Taken together, these four interrelated problems
suggest that thinking about evaluation designs and
analytic methods must be broadened in assessing outcomes
for family problems. Additional approaches should
supplement, not replace, the experimental and quasi-
experimental designs using randomized treatment and
control groups now in use. We make three general
recommendations.

First, continuing attention should be paid to the use
and further development of theoretical models of family
development, family-child interaction, and family-social
interaction. Attempts to operationalize existing models
should be continued.

Second, current experimental and quasi-experimental
designs should be supplemented by studies or alternate
designs that use the family as a unit of analysis and
compare the family's growth with selected others and with
their own status at earlier time(s).

Third, additional exploration should be undertaken of
methods that might be used in supplementary designs or
analyses to capture outcome patterns at the family level
as well as the multidimensional quality of those patterns.
Thus, increased attention might be given to certain forms
of multivariate and profile analyses. These methods exist
but have not been fully explored for their utility in
capturing the multidimensional nature of family status or
change over time.

In addition, methods developed for assessing clinical
work with families should also be investigated for their
appropriateness in assessing both process and multidimensional outcome. Among these methods might be
single-case experimental analyses that have used primarily
clinical data (Hersen and Barlow, 1976; Kazdin, 1977) or
the case argument method described for children's health
measurement by Levine and Palfrey (in this volume).
Social anthropological methods using participant-observers

also might be useful; this approach has been used
successfully by the Child and Family Resource Program
evaluation to obtain qualitative data about treatment-
outcome relationships. The methods of data collection
and analysis are documented in Johnson (1981) and in
Travers et al. (1981).

INTEGRATION OF FAMILY SERVICES

The third important feature of family service programs
is their approach to coordinating services for families
within a local community. This approach has potential
effects both on the families themselves and their use of
services and, more broadly, on the services available at
the local, state, and federal levels. This section
describes how such integration works and what problems it
poses for measurement of outcomes.

Family services have proliferated during the past two
decades, posing difficulties for both families and policy
makers. The confusing array of services available to
many low-income families has created a need for programs
that can integrate disparate services, to make them more
readily accessible to families. We can call this
integration function a "linkage" or "brokerage" service
to families.

The linkage or brokerage service to families contrasts
sharply with the traditional single services provided by
service agencies, such as health clinics, day care
centers, job training programs, food stamp programs,
legal assistance clinics, and housing programs. Each
agency characteristically provides a narrow cluster of
related family services, and for the most part the
services available from each agency do not overlap with
those of the others.

The proliferation of single-service providers has
created a strong need for linkage services. It is not
uncommon for an urban, low-income family to have access
to several hundred services from a like number of
separate providers--with each provider having its own
office hours, eligibility rules, application forms,
contact persons, and separate office locations. This
bewildering array of options presents formidable obstacles
to families that are already sorely stressed by the
routine daily demands of running their households.

This creates a dilemma for families: They cannot
solve some of the problems facing them without outside

help, yet they cannot easily surmount their immediate problems to thread through the bureaucratic barriers to get help.

Comprehensive service programs such as the Child and Family Resource Program and Home Start fill a major need in this regard. They are designed to serve as brokers of services for familes, matching available community services to specific needs of particular families. When a family enrolls it receives help in identifying and contacting service agencies from among the spectrum of agencies available in their community. Not only does this limit the family's primary institutional contact to a single program but it also limits it to a single person. The Child and Family Resource Program uses a person called a "family advocate" for nearly all contacts between the program and the family, and this person typically goes to the family's home rather than requiring a family member to visit the staff office. In Home Start the home visitor serves a similar role. The family advocates and the home visitors are specially trained to identify pressing family needs and to link individual families to the proper program or agencies that can best assist them with these needs. In this arrangement the family members do not have to become experts themselves in the identification and use of community services.

We might point out that these programs are not merely brokers; they also provide many individual services directly. They do carry the brokerage concept considerably beyond that usually found in other service programs.

Once families are enrolled in a linkage program, such as the Child and Family Resource Program, they receive many kinds of assistance in obtaining services from other sources. The first assistance that families get is information. Nearly all linkage programs provide lists of locally available services, with telephone numbers of people to contact. The lists can serve as permanent reference sources for the families; they often include several hundred contacts in urban areas. Monthly newsletters are often used to explain individual single-service agencies to families in more detail.

Program staff often conduct a needs assessment to help families determine which of the many available services would be most helpful for them. The needs assessments are usually updated periodically as family circumstances change, and they serve the program staff as a plan of action for working with each family. The procedure involves either formal or informal discussions with

239

parents to learn their views and wishes and to discuss
suggestions of the program staff. The needs assessment
results in a joint agreement between the parent and staff
on priorities for services.

Once the assessment is completed, program staff may
either refer the parent to particular service agencies,
call the agencies to make appointments for the parent, or
actually accompany parents to appointments, arranging for
transportation and baby-sitting if necessary. If some
payment is necessary, such as for medical care, the
program may pay all or part of the costs. In many cases
the program follows up the appointment to ensure that the
necessary services were provided.

When services are withheld from families without good
cause or are of poor quality, program staff often serve
as advocates for promoting changes in the delinquent
service provider--either by organizing parents to
represent themselves or by directly petitioning the
agency, its board of directors, or the state or federal
funding source.

As a last resort, linkage programs may directly provide
services to families if no other community sources exist.

Assumptions About Integration of Services

Most linkage programs are based on several unstated
but clear assumptions. They first assume that a mismatch
exists between families in need and the available
services--since, if family needs and the available
services were perfectly matched, there would be no need
for linkage programs.

This assumption of a mismatch further assumes an excess
of services over families--that some services are available but unused because families are unable to gain
access to them. Where there are fewer services than
families in need, the assumption becomes somewhat
modified. In its modified form it assumes that more
services could be made available if proper advocacy
actions were taken.

As implemented, most linkage programs carry out
advocacy functions for the families rather than for the
service programs: They assume that some familes are not
getting the services they need, to which they have a
right. They seldom assume the opposite--that some
families are getting services for which they have minimal
need or little right (because they are not fully eligible,

for example). This latter function may be likened to that of a monitor, preventing the misuse of services.

This "monitoring" function is more than hypothetical, since many programs do it to a minimal extent under a different name. The realities of limited service availability and unequal distribution may actually permit monitoring activities to produce an overall increase in effective family benefits if some are shifted from less needy to more needy families. The mechanism in linkage programs for carrying out this monitoring function is the needs assessment, whereby the services a family needs most are distinguished from those needed least. Few if any families can receive all available benefits for which they are eligible, so priorities must be decided; fortunately, few if any families need all benefits.

In the best of all possible worlds, every family would always thrive on its own. When it is not so, social institutions can intervene--preferably by temporarily helping the family to become self-sufficient, but also by providing continuous, ongoing services if necessary. In our less than perfect world, most linkage programs assume that their primary role is to get services to families, and the more services the better. This has both desirable and undesirable consequences. It is desirable because the families served are often those furthest from the mainstream of society, with the fewest advocates of any kind, and in great need of assistance. It is undesirable, because easy access to services may prevent the growth of family self-sufficiency and independence. Some program critics maintain that many program staff deliberately promote family dependence to justify their own reasons for being, even if only subconsciously. The ultimate cost of this dependence may well prove high both to the family and to society.

We present a point of view close to that of the programs: that there are many families who are not getting the services they need and that in general the more they get the better. But we should recognize that the underlying problems are much more complex and that future evaluations may have to reflect the more complex viewpoints and conflicting values.

Integration of Services: Expected Program Effects

Many beneficial outcomes may result from the hierarchy of linkage activities; some affect the families, some affect the single-service agencies, and still others affect state and federal service programs.

Effects on Families

Comprehensive service programs filling a linkage or brokerage role can affect families by:

* Increasing family awareness of available services.
* Increasing family enrollment in services when eligible.
* Increasing the use of available services.
* Improving family circumstances because of services and reducing family stress.
* Improving "consumer" awareness--fostering better knowledge of the family's rights and of the service agency's responsibilities for providing responsive, quality services.
* Improving "consumer" advocacy involvement for upgrading the quality of services.

The first four (awareness, enrollment, use, and improved circumstances) must logically be considered together. They are sequentially dependent such that the first (greater awareness of services) must logically occur before the second (greater enrollment) can occur; like-wise, the second must precede the third, and the third must precede the fourth. Moreover, none of the four effects can occur unless "linkable" services are avail-able in the community in the first place. Rural areas, especially, may have so few services that comprehensive service programs must use most of their resources to provide services directly themselves.

In addition to the four sequential effects of aware-ness, enrollment, use, and improved family circumstances, there are also two "consumer" effects that may result from comprehensive service programs. One effect is an increase in the family's knowledge of its own rights and of the service agencies' responsibilities for providing responsive, quality services. The other is increased advocacy involvement for upgrading the quality of community services. We can consider these, too, to be sequential, since families are unlikely to become active advocates for service improvement unless they first know what the services should be, then note the shortcomings.

Effects on Service Agencies

In addition to effects on families, linkage programs such as the Child and Family Resource Program will often produce changes in the agencies that provide services. Possible effects include the following:

• Simplified service utilization (through standardized application forms, adoption of consistent eligibility criteria, or additional neighborhood centers, for example).
• Increased resources, such as additional funds or staff to serve more families or additional "found" resources to meet special family needs.
• Better coordination of services among local providers, leading simultaneously to less overlap of services and fewer gaps.

There are many ways that comprehensive service programs can encourage agencies to make single services easier to use. One way is simply by keeping them informed about the kinds of problems families encounter while attempting to use the services. For many conscientious single-service agencies, merely having a problem brought to their attention is enough to encourage action. Failing that, the comprehensive service program can actively petition the agency's head, the board of directors, or the funding source until improvement begins. Staff from an established program can often get results when parents alone cannot, because the staff can draw on wider community or political support and because the staff usually have better skills than parents for coping with bureaucratic resistance.

Comprehensive service programs can sometimes encourage single-service agencies to obtain more resources. For instance, by recruiting new families the comprehensive service program often overloads the single-service agency so seriously that the agency can then document the greater need to its board or funding agency. Or new wells of "found" resources might be developed--such as finding community volunteers who can provide needed professional services or establishing informal family support networks, such as other enrolled families, neighbors, community groups, and churches, to carry out functions formerly performed by paid staff.

One of the most natural functions of comprehensive service programs is the coordination of like services

across agencies, neighborhoods, and service domains.
Single-service agencies usually have some leeway to shift
the emphasis of their services, and the comprehensive
service program staff are usually well located to spot
such needs and bring them to an agency's attention.

Effects on State or National Service Programs

Sometimes a comprehensive service program can
influence the larger state or federal systems that
support the networks of local single-service agencies.
Such effects might include the following:

• Better coordination between services at the state
and federal levels (by standardizing eligibility requirements, application forms, referral networks, and funding
procedures).
• Increased resources to serve more families,
perhaps in more states and counties, or to provide a
higher level of services to families now served.
• Pooling staff or facilities to provide services
jointly that existing state or federal programs could not
provide alone.

These and other related effects tend to happen only
occasionally, but they do happen and may have substantial
impact. For example, family enrollment procedures became
simpler when Head Start managers ruled that AFDC or other
public assistance eligibility was sufficient evidence for
Head Start eligibility. Also, many states have adopted
the Head Start Performance Standards for Title XX Day
Care Programs, which opens the way for shared facilities
and shared child-recruiting procedures. In yet another
example, Head Start and the U.S. Department of Agriculture
have agreed that every Head Start center is eligible for
food program funds. This decision removes the need to
screen every Head Start program for eligibility (thereby
saving much time and effort) and frees Head Start funds
for other family needs (such as child dental care, for
which there are few funds).
Comprehensive service programs can sometimes help
increase federal and state resources. For example, when
a state either lacks a Title XX plan or has a weak plan,
local Head Start staff may use their knowledge of family
needs and federal law, and state officials may encourage
the appropriate state agency to prepare an expanded Title

XX plan (thereby qualifying the state for increased federal funds).

Comprehensive service programs can also help match complementary services. An example of pooling staff resources occurred when national Head Start managers and managers of the Early and Periodic Screening, Diagnosis, and Treatment (EPSDT) program agreed to operate a national experimental program that used local Head Start staff to find and recruit children eligible for these health services. This sharing enabled both programs to serve low-income families better: Head Start by freeing health funds for other family needs, and EPSDT by reaching families that it could not otherwise find without Head Start's established community recruiting network.

Evaluation Problems and Approaches

Evaluating Effects on Families

By measuring the first four family effects in sequence we can determine the success of a comprehensive service program for improving families' circumstances, perhaps its most important goal. But if a program has little effect on these circumstances, an examination of this sequence of four effects will also indicate where the program is falling short. Such information is useful to program managers in upgrading deficient local projects.

In measuring the four family effects, the sequence must be examined for each family individually. For example, it must be known that EPSDT child health services are not available in a family's community so that a comprehensive services program is not erroneously deemed ineffective because it did not inform the family about EPSDT or enroll it. Likewise, if EPSDT is available but a family does not meet eligibility requirements, the program cannot be held responsible. Or if the family does not need EPSDT services, as determined by their needs assessment, the program would not be expected to affect the family's use of EPSDT. These and other conditions must be examined individually, for each family, to preserve interpretability in an evaluation.

Multiple data sources are needed to determine a comprehensive service program's success at each stage. First, program staff should be asked about the avail-ability of community services; for thoroughness, their responses should be independently cross-checked against

other community information sources to minimize
inaccuracies and omissions. Many questions requiring
answers are so detailed that only the single-service
providers can accurately answer them: How many services
do they provide? What kinds? What areas do they serve?
What are their eligibility requirements? Are they
capable of serving additional families?

Then, following the sequence, we need to determine on
a family-by-family basis if each family is aware of the
single-service agency, if the family needs the service
(according to the individual family's needs assessment),
and if the family meets eligibility requirements.

Families can be asked directly if they are aware of
the services, but other people will usually have to be
consulted to determine whether a family is eligible. One
of the first activities the staff of the Child and Family
Resource Program and Head Start undertake each year is
determining which of their families are eligible for food
stamps, EPSDT benefits, and welfare assistance, so the
families can be enrolled immediately. A comprehensive
service program's apparent effectiveness for enrolling
families in services is limited, of course, by the number
of eligible but unenrolled families it receives in the
first place. Since the families themselves seldom know
whether they are eligible, the evaluators have to approach
other people for this information. Moreover, eligibility
rules are usually complex and vary by community or state,
even for many federally available services. The evaluators themselves may have to perform calculations of
income eligibility for each family and match them
individually to the requirements for each service, to
determine the potential new enrollments possible.
Increases in program enrollment can be measured without
matching the effects for individual families, but the
maximum percentage enrollable cannot; it is a vital
policy statistic because it reveals the overall need for
a service and the current degree of success reached in
meeting the need.

The services that families actually use can often be
determined by asking families to name them. However it
is usually necessary to determine the precise name of a
service program, its funding source, or its legislative
authority--details families seldom know. This information
must typically be laboriously gathered by directly
contacting the sources of service cited by parents,
although at times linkage program staff know. Rough
estimates of the extent to which families use a service

can often be obtained directly from them, but precise
levels of use are difficult to determine.

Improved family circumstances can sometimes be measured
by equating them to service use (as, for example, when
food stamps can be given a dollar value and counted as an
increase in family income), but usually indirect means
are needed to determine the improvement. When a family
change is drastic, such as finding a substantial job for
a previously unemployed father, little risk is faced in
inferring improved family circumstances. In searching
for subtler effects, the problems grow more difficult.
The effects of preschool on children are usually less
clear, although many people seem to agree that favorable
results from selected child tests often imply an improvement in family circumstances. Families can ultimately be
asked directly if they feel their circumstances have
improved or if they experience less family stress. We
can always assume (after the fashion of pollsters) that
if families say things are better (or worse) then they
are better (or worse), even though appearances may suggest
otherwise. In areas such as preventive health services,
improved status can be determined only by using complicated medical procedures that are simply not feasible in
most evaluations. Thus, apart from a few notable exceptions, the ultimate goal of improved family circumstances
is the most difficult aspect of program success to assess.

The effect of increased family consumer awareness and
advocacy usually results from rather obvious involvement
of the families and can frequently be determined by
direct questions to the families or program staff.
Typical questions ask about parent participation on
policy councils, school boards, task forces, political
organizations, or ad hoc groups.

Evaluating Effects of Local, State, and
National Programs

Few individual families are aware of changes in the
service providers over time (because, for example, a
family usually applies only once for a service and has no
way of knowing previous or subsequent application
procedures). Long-term staff employed by the linkage
program are often aware of changes and trends in the
providers they work with. Since they typically go through
service application procedures with family after family,
linkage program staff can frequently identify changes

that are subtle--all the more so if they actively
advocated the changes.

Most often, however, changes in the single-service
agencies can only be identified with any certainty by
direct longitudinal review of the agencies themselves.
This may involve a study at the community level or it may
involve a study of an entire national service delivery
network. Because the designs required for this type of
evaluation are different from ones for assessing family
impacts, it often becomes difficult to carry them out
concurrently with evaluations of family effects.

Approximate descriptions of changes in service
providers can be obtained by gathering anecdotes from
appropriate community residents about the kinds of changes
they remember seeing. This kind of study need not be
longitudinal, thereby considerably reducing the cost.
Lazar (1970) conducted such a study on the community
impact of Head Start.

Changes in service programs at the state and national
levels can be identified through changes in regulations,
funding levels, legislation, reorganization, staff time
allocation, and so on; these can be "measured" by examining official program documents; observing operating
practices; and interviewing federal, regional, or state
policy makers and managers.

Once measurements are taken at the state or federal
level there are so many prevailing influences that it
becomes almost impossible to attribute any changes found
back to a particular comprehensive service program. This
does not diminish the policy benefits of straightforwardly
describing the changes, however, even without scientific
support for the causes of the changes.

Evaluators should also be alert for unintended consequences of comprehensive service program activities. For
example, outreach and referral activities may be so effective that the single-service providers are inundated
beyond their capacities, eroding service quality and
exceeding available funds or staff capabilities. This
may create new problems at the state and federal levels
as well as at the local level.

CONCLUSION

Our discussion has focused on two of the comprehensive
family service programs developed as demonstrations under
the auspices of Head Start and the Administration for

Children, Youth, and Families. Three essential features
of these programs were described: the mix of support and
intervention, the emphasis on individualized program
treatment, and the role of the program in coordinating
community services. Each of the features was shown to
have particular implications for the kinds of evaluation
questions posed and the methods used to answer them.

The mix of support and intervention was seen as a
natural result of the programs' broad goals and of their
acceptance of the strengths and different values of
families and communities. Individualized treatment also
was an expression of the broad goals. Treatment was
varied by family along many dimensions, such as the types
of activities and services emphasized, the role of
parents in the program, and the length and intensity of
participation expected. Third, the programs' role as
"brokers" of services and advocates for families implies
both support or change for families as consumers of
service and change in the services or policies concerning
families at the local, state, and even federal levels.
Thus, the programs are designed to support and bolster
the development of the children, the functioning within
the family or household unit, and the ways in which
families and social institutions interact. This broad
concept of program action necessitates a broadening of
methods and perspectives in program evaluation.

One area of evaluation to be expanded is the use of
process studies to describe and characterize what actually
happens in the program between families and staff, among
staff, and between staff and community institutions.
Different types of process studies can and should be used
to identify and clarify goals and constituencies for
family programs, to describe what the programs do, and to
help relate what goes on in the programs (the process
and/or treatment) to what results from them (the outcomes). Process studies also help raise questions and
generate hypotheses about unanticipated outcomes and also
look at questions about the relationships among different
family and child programs at a federal administrative and
policy level.

We make several recommendations concerning the study
of outcomes in order to address the problems posed by
individualized treatments for families in several domains
of family life over time. One is to retain the quasi-
experimental designs currently in use but to supplement
them with additional, smaller studies or analyses to
enhance their interpretability. Exploration of methods

used in clinical work or educational psychology but less
commonly used in program evaluation is urged in order to
give a whole picture of outcomes in several domains for
families or groups of families over time. Increased use
of atheoretical indicators, ethnography, and descriptive
analyses for synthesizing different types of data also is
discussed.

Overall, while the programs and the methodological
problems associated with evaluating them are complex, the
endeavor is not overwhelming. It requires careful speci-
fication and rating of the questions that are to be
answered at any one time for any particular program. It
also requires the recognition that many questions
concerning the evaluation of family support programs are
ultimately questions of values and social policy.

Perhaps most important, the problems, as we have
described them, derive from the richness and complexity
of the programs, their goals, and practices and of the
families themselves. It would be a mistake for evaluators
merely to complain about such complexity or to adopt new
methods or perspectives that would eliminate important
variety for the sake of precision and manageability. At
this point in the development of family programs and of
research about families, it is important for evaluators
to try to capture this richness and variety in different
ways, using multiple methods and perspective. Understanding outcomes at the individual, family, and social
levels demands that we consider outcome to be (like
families and programs) multidimensional, multiply
determined, occurring within a particular context, and
changing over time.

REFERENCES

Bayley, N.
    (1969)   Bayley Scales of Infant Development. New
             York: Psychological Corporation.
Bell, R. Q., and Harper, L. V.
    (1977)   Child Effects on Adults. Lincoln, Neb.:
             University of Nebraska Press.
Belle, D., et al.
    (1980)   Lives in Stress: A Context for Depression.
             Cambridge, Mass.: Harvard University Press.
Bronfenbrenner, U.
    (1977)   Toward an experimental ecology of human
             development. American Psychologist 32:513-531.

Burr, W. R., Hill, R., Nye, F. I., and Reiss, I. L., eds.
    (1979) Contemporary Theories About the Family.
            Vol. I and II. New York: The Free Press.
Campbell, D. T., and Boruch, R.
    (1975) Making the case for randomized assignment to
            treatment by considering the alternatives:
            six ways in which quasi-experimental
            evaluations in compensatory education tend to
            underestimate effects. In C. A. Bennett and
            A. A. Lumsdaine, eds., Evaluation and
            Experiment. New York: Academic Press.
Cook, T. D., and Campbell, D. T.
    (1979) Quasi-Experimentation. Chicago, Ill.:
            Rand-McNally.
Duvall, E.
    (1977) Family Development. Philadelphia, Pa.: J. B.
            Lippincott Co.
General Accounting Office
    (1979) Early Childhood and Family Development
            Programs Improve Quality of Life for Low
            Income Families. Washington, D.C.: General
            Accounting Office. February.
Goodson, B. D., and Hess, R.
    (1978) The effects of parent training programs on
            child performance and behavior. In B. Brown,
            ed., Found: Long-Term Gains From Early
            Intervention. Boulder, Colo.: Westview Press.
Goodwin, W. L., and Driscoll, L. A.
    (1980) Handbook for Measurement and Evaluation in
            Early Childhood Education. San Francisco,
            Calif.: Jossey-Bass, Inc., Publishers.
Gurman, A. S., and Kniskern, D. P.
    (1978) Research on marital and family therapy:
            progress, perspective, and prospect. In S. L.
            Garfield and A. E. Bergin, eds., Handbook of
            Psychotherapy and Behavior Change. 2nd ed.
            New York: John Wiley & Sons, Inc.
15th Anniversary Head Start Committee
    (1980) Head Start in the 1980's: Review and
            Recommendations. Report by the 15th
            Anniversary Head Start Committee. Edward
            Zigler, Chairman. September.
Herson, D., and Barlow, R.
    (1976) Single Case Experimental Design. New York:
            Pergamon Press.

Hertz, T. W.
(1976)   The Ecology of Child Development: Research
         Issues. The Child/The Family/Environment/
         Services. A Report for Planners of Research
         and Development. Prepared for the Interagency
         Panel on Early Childhood Research and Develop-
         ment. Washington, D.C.: The George Washington
         University. December.

Hewett, K. H.
(1978)   Partners With Parents: The Home Start
         Experience With Children and Their Families.
         Office of Human Development Services. DHEW
         Publication No. 78-31106. Washington, D.C.:
         U.S. Department of Health, Education, and
         Welfare.

Hewett, K., Connell, D., Affholter, D., and Weiss, S.
(1979)   Evaluation of the Child and Family Resource
         Program: Volume I: Design Report Draft. AAI
         No. 78-111. Cambridge, Mass.: Abt
         Associates, Inc.

Hill, R.
(1971)   Strengths of Black Families. Washington,
         D.C.: National Urban League.

Hill, R., and Mattessich, P.
(1977)   Reconstruction of Family Development
         Theories: A Progress Report. Paper presented
         at the meeting of the National Council on
         Family Relations. San Diego, October.

Jacob, T.
(1975)   Family interaction in disturbed and normal
         families: a methodological and substantive
         review. Psychological Bulletin 82:33-65.

Johnson, L., Nauta, M. J., and Hewett, K. D.
(1980)   Evaluation of the Child and Family Resource
         Program: Phase III Program Study Report. AAI
         No. 80-91. Cambridge, Mass.: Abt Associates,
         Inc.

Johnson, L.
(1981)   Methodology for the Ethnographic Study: The
         Child and Family Resource Program Evaluation.
         Cambridge, Mass.: Abt Associates, Inc.

Kagan, J., Kearsley, R. B., and Zelazo, P. R. (with the
assistance of C. Minton)
(1978)   Infancy: Its Place in Human Development.
         Cambridge, Mass.: Harvard University Press.

Kamerman, S. B., and Kahn, A. J.
(1978)   Family Policy: Government and Families in

Fourteen Countries. New York: Columbia
University Press.

Kazdin, A.
  (1977) Methodological issues in single case analysis.
          Journal of Clinical and Consulting Psychology
          34.

Kessen, W.
  (1979) The American child and other cultural interven-
          tions. American Psychologist 34:915-920.

Kiresuk, T. J., and Sherman, K. E.
  (1968) Goal attainment scaling: a general method for
          evaluating community mental health programs.
          Community Mental Health Journal 4(6):443-453.

Kiresuk, T. J., Calsyn, R. J., and Davidson, W. S.
  (1978) A critique of goal attainment scaling. In
          T. Cook, ed., Evaluation Studies Review Annual
          3:700-715.

Lazar, I., Hubbell, V. R., Murray, H., Roche, M., and
Royce, J.
  (1977) Persistence of Preschool Effects: Final
          Report. Grant No. 18-76-07843, Administration
          for Children, Youth, and Families. Washington,
          D.C.: U.S. Department of Health, Education,
          and Welfare. Office of Human Development
          Services.

Love, J. M., Nauta, M. J., Coelen, C. G., Hewett, K. D.,
and Ruopp, R. R.
  (1976) Home Start Evaluation Study. High/Scope
          Educational Research Foundation and Abt
          Associates, Inc. Cambridge, Mass.: Abt
          Associates, Inc.

Nauta, M., and Johnson, L.
  (1981) Evaluation of the Child and Family Resource
          Program: Phase III Research Report.
          Cambridge, Mass.: Abt Associates, Inc.

Nauta, M.
  (1981) Evaluation of the Child and Family Resource
          Program: Phase III Executive Summary.
          Cambridge, Mass.: Abt Associates, Inc.

Newbrough, J. R., Dokecki, P. R., Dunlop, K. H., Hogge,
J. H., and Simpkins, C. G.
  (1978) Families and Family-Institution Transactions
          in Child Development. Final report. Contract
          No. 105-77-1045, Administration for Children,
          Youth, and Families, Office of Human
          Development Services. Washington, D.C.: U.S.
          Department of Health, Education, and Welfare.

Nobles, W. W.
 (1976) A Formulative and Empirical Study of Black
         Families: Final Report. San Francisco,
         Calif.: Westside Community Mental Health
         Center, Inc.
Rossi, P. H., Freeman, H. E., and Wright, S. R.
 (1979) Evaluation: A Systematic Approach. Beverly
         Hills, Calif.: Sage Publications.
Stake, R.
 (1978) The case study method in social inquiry.
         Educational Researcher 7(2):5-8.
Travers, J., Johnson, L., Lynnell, J., and Irwin, N.
 (1981) An Ethnographic Perspective on the Child and
         Family Resource Program. Cambridge, Mass.:
         Abt Associates, Inc.
Weiss, C.
 (1972) Evaluation Research: Methods for Assessing
         Program Effectiveness. Englewood Cliffs,
         N.J.: Prentice-Hall.
Weiss, R. S., and Rein, M.
 (1969) The evaluation of broad-aim programs: a
         cautionary case and a moral. Annals of the
         American Academy of Political and Social
         Science 385:133-142.
Zigler, E., and Trickett, P.
 (1978) IQ, social competence and evaluation of early
         childhood intervention programs. American
         Psychologist 1:789-798.

The Evaluation Report:
A Weak Link to Policy

Dennis Deloria and Geraldine Kearse Brookins

As secretary of the U.S. Department of Health, Education, and Welfare (HEW) from 1977 to 1979, Joseph Califano personally requested many of the evaluations that were carried out by the HEW Office of the Inspector General. Among the hundreds of department priorities, issues commanding Califano's direct attention were of greater than usual importance. Following his request, the evaluation staff of the Office of the Inspector General would spend six or eight months gathering data, often traveling to many regional offices and local projects across the country. When data collection and analyses were completed, the inspector general and his staff reported the findings directly to Califano. Califano stipulated that the findings be summarized in a written report not longer than 15 pages and summarized orally in 20 minutes, followed by 40 minutes for his questions. From this brief interchange he decided what action, if any, should result from the months of evaluation.

Some dearly held evaluation practices are called into question when the secretary of a major department permits but 15 pages and 20 minutes for reporting important findings, when evaluation reports about federal programs and policies often are 100 to 300 pages in length. Given this discrepancy, it seems necessary to reexamine their contents and organization. By doing so we may find ways to refocus them to better meet the needs of policy makers such as Califano.

Here we first discuss the work of policy makers and some reasons why evaluation reports tend to be long. We then examine three policy reports to determine their similarities in meeting the needs of policy makers.

Finally, we summarize 10 features that appear to make evaluation reports more useful.

POLICY MAKERS: PEOPLE IN A RUSH

Managers' activities are generally characterized by brevity, variety, and fragmentation, claimed Mintzberg (1973) in a broad review of studies examining the nature of managerial work. He pointed out that managers' jobs are remarkably alike, including senior and middle managers in business, U.S. presidents, government administrators, production supervisors, foremen, and chief executives. He found the brevity of managers' activities surprising: telephone calls averaged 6 minutes, unscheduled meetings averaged 12 minutes, and work sessions averaged 15 minutes. Brevity was also reflected in the treatment of mail. Executives expressed dislike for long memos and skimmed most long reports and periodicals quickly. Most surprising, significant activity was interspersed with the trivial in no particular order. Managers must be prepared to shift moods quickly and frequently.

Mintzberg found strong indications that managers preferred the more active elements of their work: activities that are current, specific, and well defined. Among written communications, they seemed to prefer those dealing with active, concrete, live situations. The managers typically received about 20 periodicals and many reports per week. "Most were skimmed (often at the rate of 2 per minute), and an average of only 1 in 25 elicited a reaction," stated Mintzberg (1973:39). From this it would appear that to be effective, or to be even thoughtfully considered, evaluation reports written for policy makers must make some carefully thought-out concessions to such a frenzy of executive activity.

EVALUATORS: PEOPLE CONCERNED WITH METHODS

Evaluators are typically social scientists, with extensive training in the scientific method. Central to that training is the notion that any statement of evaluation or research findings must be accompanied by a careful description of the precise methods used, so other scientists can replicate them to verify the findings. By training and scientific necessity, evaluators devote a substantial part of most reports to detailed descriptions

of the methods used. Such reports typically follow the
classical "dissertation" style, having chapters on background, purpose, hypotheses, subjects, design, measures,
data collection, statistical analysis, findings, and
discussion. The many variations of this style share one
essential characteristic: Their fundamental organization
emerges from the scientific method. Practically, this
dictates that the overall report format be organized
around the methods used, and findings are embedded as a
subsection within.

The dissertation-style report may contain facts needed
by policy makers, but they are usually fragmented because
of the need to respect the conventions of science. For
example, the details needed to answer a single policy
question may be scattered across several chapters—some
in the chapter describing the subjects, some in the discussion of child measure outcomes, some in the discussion
of parent measure outcomes, some in the discussion of
staff interview outcomes, and some in the chapter presenting overall findings. The burden falls on the policy
maker to locate the fragments and piece them together to
answer complex questions.

TWO REPORTS ARE NEEDED: ONE SCIENTIFIC, ONE POLICY

The methods-oriented evaluation report is necessary to
uphold the conventions of science, but a policy-oriented
report seems necessary to reach policy makers. Coleman
(1972) elegantly described the relationship. He said
that the original policy questions must be translated
into questions that can be addressed by the methods of
science; at the conclusion of the scientific process the
findings must be translated into the world of policy.
Viewed in this way, most evaluations stop short of completion if the final report is a conventional, methods-
oriented one. Only a rare policy maker would spend the
time and effort needed to extract policy information from
a methods-oriented report while being bombarded by the
dizzying activity described by Mintzberg.

An alternative would be a brief, policy-oriented
report that describes concrete action items in language
understandable to policy makers. Passages detailing
methods used to conduct the evaluation would be removed
so the policy maker would not have to sift through them
to locate passages with findings of interest. Policy
questions and their answers would form the major organiz-

ing theme of the report. The jargon of evaluation would be avoided. Policy makers might well consult such a report in making important decisions--at present a too-rare occurrence.

Three Sample Policy Reports

To explore our hunches we examine three policy reports that embody many of the features needed by policy makers. All three were written to directly inform or influence policy, and they advocate specific policy actions. The authors appear familiar with matters of policy and policy reporting. They are situated differently in relation to the policy makers they attempt to inform: Some work in a federal agency responsible for administering programs, some in a private research consulting firm, and some in a child advocacy group.

The reports are different in important ways. One report presents original data only, another presents findings from other studies only, and one presents some of each. One looks only at the process of implementing a major piece of legislation, another at the effects on children of existing school enrollment practices, and another looks at both program process and effects on children. One project had a budget of more than $7 million, another less than 5 percent of that, and one used existing staff in a federal agency. One was requested by Congress, another by a program administration agency, and one was undertaken solely through private initiative. This diversity makes their similarities even more significant.

Although the three reports have certain exemplary features, they are also not without faults, some of which may be serious. Whatever faults they possess, however, do not detract significantly from the policy-oriented characteristics we are interested in. This paper examines and emphasizes the strengths of these reports, rather than their faults, in the belief that this strategy can more directly contribute to future improvements.

This paper does not attempt to assess the actual policy impacts that these reports have already had, nor does it lay out a sequence of events to increase policy impact. Past experience suggests that policy reports, no matter how well written, will not have much influence without deliberately organized support of one kind or another. Such a topic lies outside the intent of this paper.

Our examination is based on simple inspection rather than quantitative analysis. It should be considered a search for hypotheses to be confirmed, rather than a confirmation itself. To the extent our conclusions appeal to common sense, we consider them sufficient. To orient our examination we looked to the reports for answers to four questions:

1. What policy perspective did the authors adopt?
2. What policy questions did they address?
3. What methods did they use to answer the questions?
4. What format of presentation did they use?

There are many smaller questions buried in each of these; the answers are implicit in the narrative. From this examination has evolved some guidelines that may be of use to others preparing policy reports.

Report 1: *Progress Toward a Free Appropriate Education*

Policy Perspective This report (U.S. Office of Education, 1979) is the first of a series of annual reports to Congress on progress in the implementation of P.L. 94-142, the Education for All Handicapped Children Act of 1975. The act requires reports to be delivered to Congress each January.

The Bureau of Education for the Handicapped (BEH, now located in the U.S. Department of Education), which prepared the report, is the agency responsible for carrying out provisions of the act. This, of course, gives the authors a vested interest in the findings, since their purpose is to report BEH's success or lack of success in implementing the act. Despite the potential for a conflict of interest, the report maintains an objective tone throughout; problems as well as successes in implementation are highlighted. The report does not stress future policy actions, but its discussions of problems often include descriptions of corrective actions initiated by BEH or references to the need for additional money or work.

Although BEH wrote the report mainly for Congress, the authors explicitly kept in mind many others who might use the findings, such as federal administrators in HEW, the Office of Education, and BEH; state directors of special education and state evaluators; leaders of professional

associations and advocacy groups; and members of the
academic community (U.S. Office of Education, 1979:77).

The report addresses issues of importance to federal
policy by virtue of the source of its mandate, the
position of its authors, and its stated audiences.
Depending on the nature and seriousness of its findings,
the report could influence many kinds of decisions:
federal legislative authorizations and appropriations,
federal regulations and guidelines, federal program
implementation practices, training and technical assistance, and similar state (and local, where appropriate)
decisions. Moreover, massive funds are involved for
implementing the act. For fiscal 1979 the federal
appropriation was $408 million, and the states projected
outlays up to 30 times as great, for a possible total of
$24 billion nationwide (U.S. Office of Education,
1979:113). The act affects every state and every local
school district, involving thousands of educators and
millions of children.

Policy Questions Six policy questions are addresssed
in the report:

* Are the intended beneficiaries being served?
* In what settings are the beneficaries being served?
* What services are being provided?
* What administrative mechanisms are in place?
* What are the consequences of implementing the act?
* To what extent is the intent of the act being met?

All six are closely tied to the concerns of Congress and
the requirements of the act. Their final wording was
arrived at by a task force, which invited consultation
and review from all persons directly concerned with
administration of the act. None of the questions
explicitly inquires about the changes in children
resulting from implementation of the act; instead, they
explore the process of providing required services and
whether the intended children are being served.

Each of these questions implies a host of subordinate
questions, which are discussed either directly or
indirectly in the narrative. For example, under the
question "Are the intended beneficiaries being served?"
the main issue appears to be "How many eligible children
are not being served?" Another subordinate question
examines inconsistencies among states in the percentages

of children served and the reasons for the differences. Another asks if <u>only</u> eligible children are being served.

None of the major questions directly mentions costs, although costs are prominently discussed in many of the subordinate questions.

<u>Methodology</u> This report summarizes data from other sources rather than presenting original data. Sixteen sources are cited, although the body of the report says little about the studies or their methods. Readers wishing more information are referred to notes, appendixes, or to the studies themselves; references to them are made mainly through the use of footnotes or credits under tables and figures. By thus removing most discussion of the supporting sources, the full emphasis of the report is place on substantive issues, producing a high ratio of substantive findings to supporting explanation.

The policy questions are stated in general terms, but each section of the report begins by clarifying the intent of its question. The clarifications are taken directly from language in the act or related committee print, and the authors provide additional interpretation when needed. They cite findings from previous studies or court rulings when specific problem areas need to be emphasized. This results in a thorough contextual description for readers, setting clear expectations for the kinds of findings needed to answer the questions. The authors present and discuss data from the appropriate sources. The report often points out discrepancies or conflicting findings and isolates these areas for examination in future studies.

Throughout the report the methodology is subordinated to policy considerations. For example, historical narrative and case examples are interwoven with statistical tabulations for answering a single question. This is an improvement on the frequent practice of grouping statistical results in one part of the report, historical background in another, and case examples in a third; such fragmentation forces the reader into several disconnected sections of the report for partial answers to a single question. The BEH report avoids this problem.

<u>Format</u> The BEH report addresses six policy questions; the questions are used as chapter headings to organize the entire report. This permits the reader to go directly to the questions of interest and find all the needed information in one place.

An executive summary, which can be read in about 15 minutes, provides an overview of the report. A reader wishing to follow up one of the statements in the executive summary can find the corresponding sections of the report fairly easily. Two improvements would have made it even easier to locate them: page references following statements in the summary and a more complete table of contents. Policy-related subheadings are used throughout the report and could easily have been listed in the table of contents.

Most topics in the report are presented in self-contained, well-labeled sections that are readable in 15 minutes or less. This permits rapid access to the authors' conclusions in any area of the report, eliminating the need to sequentially read the report from cover to cover for answers to specific subordinate questions. This vastly improves accessibility of information compared with more traditional evaluation reports and saves much time and work for the reader.

The readability of the report is lower than anticipated, measuring near the "very difficult" score of Flesch's (1949) readability formula. A close look at the language in the report shows that there is just as much jargon as in the typical evaluation report, but with one important difference: The jargon is that of policy makers, not of evaluators. Much of the language derives from the act itself and from related legislative processes; some originates in the discipline of special education; the rest originates in the federal and state processes for implementing the act. Most of this jargon, unlike evaluation jargon, is likely to be familiar to the policy makers who will read the report or its summary. The report could nonetheless benefit from more deliberate use of plain English.

Statistical presentations were kept simple throughout, and graphic displays were used frequently. No special training is required of the reader to interpret the statistical data. Only the most elementary statistics were presented: counts, percentages, ranks, and costs.

Any backup materials that did not directly assist in answering the policy questions were relegated to appendixes or referenced in other sources. Throughout the report, however, sufficient information was included to eliminate almost all need for reference to the appendixes or sources in order to understand the report.

Report 2: *Children at the Center*

Policy Perspective *Children at the Center* (Abt
Associates, Inc., 1979) is the final report of the
National Day Care Study (NDCS), a large-scale study of
the costs and effects of day care. NDCS was initiated in
1974 by the Office of Child Development, now the
Administration for Children, Youth, and Families (ACYF).
This large-scale research project was designed to "investigate the costs and effects associated with variations
of regulatable characteristics of center day care--
especially care giver/child ratio, group size, and care
givers qualifications" (Abt Associates, Inc., 1979:xxv).
These three characteristics are generally considered to
be central determinants of quality in center day care and
are key factors in state and federal regulations.
  One of the central issues of federal policy in subsidized day care is the relationship of day care costs to
its effects on children. Undergirding this issue are a
number of assumptions regarding the characteristics of
center care, the quality of care, and the developmental
well-being of children in day care settings. ACYF was
particularly committed to the assumption that ". . .
developmental well-being and growth of children (could)
be fostered in a day care setting" (Abt Associates, Inc.,
1979:xxvi). Hence it seems the NDCS was implemented to
determine whether federal regulations could be developed
to incorporate ACYF's commitment to quality without
nullifying the indirect economic benefits that have
motivated day care legislation.
  Although ACYF was the primary source that influenced
the structure of the study, there were also other sources
and issues. The Federal Interagency Day Care Requirements
lacked empirical evidence to support the assumptions upon
which the requirements were based, and this lack to a
large degree motivated the structure of the NDCS. There
were few data available on a large-scale basis regarding
characteristics, such as group size, staff/child ratio,
and care giver qualifications, their effects on children,
and the relationship of costs to effects--all of which
are policy issues. The NDCS combined some of the concerns
of ACYF and the needs of the Federal Interagency Day Care
Requirements into one study by examining the effectiveness of varying center day care arrangements while taking
into consideration such demographic variables as regions,
states, socioeconomic groups, etc. At least with respect
to center care, it was thought that the results of such a

study could provide essential information for policy
reformation regarding standards and regulations.

The report speaks to several policy audiences. It is
explicitly addressed to administrators within ACYF and to
those preparing the Federal Interagency Day Care
Requirements. It is also addressed implicitly to state
and local governments that regulate day care licensing,
monitoring, and standards. In addition, the report can
be viewed as being addressed to Congress, which approves
the appropriations for federally funded day care.

Policy Questions In this report, three major policy
questions were addressed (Abt Associates, Inc., 1979:13):

* How is the development of preschool children in
federally subsidized day care centers affected by
variations in staff/child ratio, care-giver qualifications, group size, and other regulatable center
characteristics?
* How is the per child cost of federally subsidized,
center-based day care affected by variations in
staff/child ratio, care-giver qualifications, group size,
and other regulatable center characteristics?
* How does the cost-effectiveness of federally
subsidized, center-based day care change when adjustments
are made in staff/child ratio, care-giver qualifications,
group size, and other regulatable center characteristics?

The answers to these questions were intended to play a
major role in decisions about current regulations and
practices that affect day care centers serving federally
subsidized preschool children. Adequate answers require
that the policy variables have a direct relationship to
the major policy issues and questions. Staff/child ratio
and care-giver qualifications were assumed to affect
children's cognitive and social development. These two
characteristics of day care were also known to have a
significant impact on the cost per child of day care.
Group size was specified in the Federal Interagency Day
Care Requirements and therefore was of interest. Given
the variety of issues regarding day care, federal involvement, and regulation, an attempt to deal with more than
three major policy questions would have merely diluted
the report's policy effectiveness. The policy issues are
clearly identified and, notably, so are issues that are
not a focus of the study. The authors' disclaimers are
significant because they further delimit the research

being considered and restrict the readers' attention in the proper context. By calling attention to issues that are not a focus, the authors demonstrate a recognition that there are other important questions that could be addressed.

Methodology One of the major challenges of a study with national policy significance is the selection of a sample. To this end the evaluators carefully and deliberately selected a sample with appropriate classroom composition, care-giver qualifications, and racial composition. Fifty-seven centers with such diversity were selected within three sites.

Selection of sites was based on four general criteria. These criteria required that the sites have a sufficient number of eligible centers, represent different geographic regions of the country, show different demographic and socioeconomic characteristics, and exhibit regulatory diversity. The actual selection of sites resulted from an analysis that grouped urbanized areas according to measures of socioeconomic status. The analysis yielded six prototypical cities within three regions--South, North, and West. On the basis of feasibility of study implementation, the final choice of sites was Atlanta, Detroit, and Seattle.

In one phase of the study, a quasi experiment was executed to compare three groups of centers: treated high-ratio centers, matched low-ratio centers, and unmatched high-ratio centers. The authors point out that the staff/child ratio was selected for manipulation because of its critical policy relevance. The quasi experiment included only 49 of the centers within the total sample.

Given the policy questions involved, it was important to employ measures of classroom composition and staff qualifications that were reliable and valid. Classroom composition was defined in terms of number of care givers per classroom, group size, and staff/child ratio. These particular variables were measured by both direct observation and schedule-based measures. However, only measures based on direct observation were used in the effects analyses. Information regarding care-giver qualifications was gathered through interviews with care givers. Measures based on direct observation were also used to determine teacher behavior and child behavior. In addition, standardized tests were used to measure the impact of center characteristics on aspects of school

265

readiness. Parent interviews were also conducted to obtain information on parental involvement and family use of center services. These measures were used primarily to assess quality of care at the centers--the outcomes.

The data were subjected to multivariate statistical analyses, but the findings that link classroom character-istics to measures of quality and measures of costs are correlational. The statistical strengths of the reported relationships are sufficient to be used as significant indicators of both quality and costs. The researchers in the NDCS used methodological procedures that were sophisticated and appropriate to the study's goals and mandate.

Format The authors present the policy-relevant findings at the beginning of the volume, allowing the reader to become aware of the major findings immediately. Policy recommendations, which stem directly from the findings, are concretely stated and provide a contextual framework that encourages the policy maker to consider actual policy decisions. The recommendations are grouped by area, providing the reader with a logical progression. For example, the authors present first the findings for preschool children, then the findings for infants and toddlers. After the findings, the authors recommend regulations and guidelines for both groups. The summary gives suggestions for fiscal policy.

Unlike the authors of many research and evaluation reports, the authors of *Children at the Center* do not assume that all readers are familiar with key terms used in the study and therefore provide a glossary at the beginning of the volume. This feature guards against misinterpretation of terms and results and, hence, of implications on the part of the reader. Since the glossary precedes the executive summary, the reader does not have to turn to a specific section of the volume to determine how the variables were defined in order to place the findings and recommendations within the proper context; thus, time is saved for the policy-making reader.

All information is presented in discrete chunks, each of which represents a whole in itself. Specifically, a reader can glean from the executive summary the major findings regarding day care and federal policy. Or, to gain some insight into the manner in which regulatory language should be constructed, the reader could turn to that section and obtain information in a few minutes.

Just as written information is presented in discrete
chunks, most of the data are presented in bivariate
tables that are concrete presentations of statistical
relationships. This kind of uncomplicated presentation
seems more likely to be retained by the reader than are
complex multivariate tabular presentations.

Report 3: *Children Out of School in America*

Policy Perspective *Children Out of School in America*
(Children's Defense Fund, 1974) is a national comprehensive study of the nonenrollment of school-age children,
conducted in 1973 and 1974 by the Children's Defense Fund,
a child advocacy organization. Inspired by a similar one
conducted by the Massachusetts Task Force on Children Out
of School, the study was initiated by the Children's
Defense Fund, rather than by any particular federal or
state agency. It was principally addressed to HEW's
Office for Civil Rights but has wide applicability to
other federal agencies, state and local governments,
school districts, and parent advocacy groups. The
findings are presented in three categories: barriers to
attendance, children with special needs and misclassifica-
tion, and school discipline. Specific recommendations
are set forth for the federal government, state and local
governments, and parents and children. Inherent in the
recommendations is a strong advocacy position. The
authors advocate that specific actions take place within
the federal government, state and local governments, and
among parents and children regarding the exclusion of
children from school.

Policy Questions The major issue in this report is the
denial of a basic education to any child by schools, by
either overt or covert practices and procedures. While
the policy questions are not explicit in the report, one
can identify at least one major policy question and three
subsidiary ones:

• How do exclusionary practices (overt and covert)
of schools and school systems affect the education of a
significant proportion of school-aged children?
• How does the lack of specific procedures for
individual assessment and placement affect the education
of all children?
• What is the relationship between school attendance
and various school charges for essential educational
services and material?

• How are suspensions and other disciplinary actions
of school mediated by the race, ethnicity, and
socioeconomic status of school-aged children?

The exploration of these questions provided a rich
data base for policy makers at the federal, state, and
local levels. Indeed, such exploration fostered more
specific questions to be answered by a number of agencies
within these levels of government. The study also
provided a basis for active advocacy for children being
excluded from school.

Methodology This report uses both 1970 census data on
school nonenrollment and survey data obtained via a
questionnaire developed by the Children's Defense Fund.
The survey instrument was used to augment the census data
as well as to address issues of special policy concern to
the researchers. More than 6,500 households were
represented in the study. The data were collected in 30
areas of the country within various geographic regions
that encompassed 8 states and the District of Columbia.
In addition, school principals and superintendents were
interviewed about nonenrollment, classification procedures, suspensions, and other disciplinary actions.
The data analyses include frequency counts and percentages, with comparisons being drawn between census data and
the Children's Defense Fund data. These comparisons are
presented in single, straightforward tables. Descriptions
of specific methodological procedures appear in an
appendix.

Format The major findings of this study are reported
at the beginning of the volume. This allows the reader
to immediately become aware of the major issues and the
scope of the work that is required to remedy the problems
at issue. Most of the information is organized in short
chapters that can be read quickly. In the case of longer
chapters, the subordinate sections can be read within a
short time, facilitating access to particular issues.
For example, to understand the ways in which children are
misclassified for special programs, the reader could turn
to that section in the chapter on exclusion of children
with special needs and thereby quickly become familiar
with the subject.
The document is written in simple, nontechnical
language and is basically organized around the three main
issues: barriers to school attendance, exclusion of

children with special needs, and school discipline and
its exclusionary impact on students. The role of
statistics in minimal; the technical information is
placed in appendixes. The interspersal of case history
and anectodotal data with survey and census data is a
particularly effective mechanism for holding the reader's
attention and focusing it on specific issues.

MEETING POLICY MAKERS' NEEDS

These three reports share a few features that set them
apart from methods-oriented reports. The similarities
are not fully consistent across reports, but for purposes
of discussion there appear to be about 10 from which we
can learn.

1. The questions addressed are clearly linked to real
policy decisions. In each report the principal questions
arose from a policy context: debates about day care regulations, progress toward implementation of new legislation, or inequities keeping children out of school.
Policy makers and people affected by these issues were
directly involved in formulating the questions in each
case. They participated in meetings to explore and define
the questions, and the questions determined the evaluation
methods used.
2. At least some questions in each report consider
the costs affecting policy. Nearly all policy decisions
involve cost (or other resource) trade-offs, either
directly or indirectly. When appropriate cost data are
presented in a policy report, its possible influence is
greatly increased. The cost data can be obtained in
different ways: In the National Day Care Study, cost
data were collected concurrently with the process and
outcome data; in the BEH report to Congress, cost data
were estimated from several outside sources.
3. Policy questions form the central organizing theme
of the report. The overall organization of these reports
contrasts markedly with methods-oriented reports. A
glance at the three tables of contents makes the policy
orientation immediately apparent. They list the policy
questions examined in a reasonably direct fashion,
immediately immersing the reader in the substantive
issues. This reflects the fact that each chapter
typically discusses a single policy question or a small
related subset of questions.

4. <u>The reports describe enough of the policy context</u> <u>to permit informed interpretation without outside sources</u>. All three reports went to great lengths to present readers with broad policy perspectives surrounding specific questions. This permits ready interpretation of the findings by readers who are not already familiar with the policy or decision-making context.

5. <u>Evaluation methodology is played down</u>. Evaluation methods used to answer the questions are scarcely mentioned in the three reports. This is not to say that the studies were not built on solidly crafted methods, for by and large they were; rather, the authors chose not to present details of methodology in these reports, which were intended for policy makers. Quite likely the omission is insignificant, considering the purposes of the three reports, since few policy makers possess the training to interpret technical methods. Moreover, the reports provide adequate references to other sources (often appendixes or other volumes accompanying the report) that detail the methods, so readers who wish to can learn more.

6. <u>Reports begin with a brief summary of essential</u> <u>findings</u>. Usually called an executive summary, it permits readers to quickly learn essential conclusions from the report and to decide which other parts of the report they want to read. It seems important for the summary to be brief (10 pages or less). Brickell et al. (1974) interviewed top-level officials from several government agencies and found they preferred 1- to 10-page reports to longer ones. They commonly requested a short report for themselves and a longer one for their subordinate staff; their subordinate staff in turn requested short reports for themselves and longer reports for <u>their</u> subordinates, and so on down the hierarchy.

7. <u>Backup narrative for the executive summary is</u> <u>"chunked" into easily locatable brief segments throughout</u> <u>the body of the report</u>. The reports are generally organized such that a reader who wants to learn more about something in the executive summary can find the backup narrative easily and read it quickly. Throughout most of the reports, information is organized into self-contained, short chunks. This lets a reader quickly follow up on one or two findings of particular interest, without requiring cover-to-cover reading. Authors can usually assume that none of the policy makers will read their report from cover to cover; rather, they will be selective, reading the executive summary and little else

unless it is of high interest, easy to find, and quick to
read. Every incremental improvement in accessibility and
readability increases the amount of the report likely to
be read by the policy maker and, hence, increases the
likelihood of policy impact.

8. <u>Only simple statistics are presented</u>. For the
most part, statistical presentations in the four reports
included only counts, percentages, ranks, averages,
ranges, costs, and bivariate tables or graphs. If complex
statistical findings cannot be reduced to these simpler
forms, they probably will have little meaning to policy
makers. Few of them are trained in advanced statistics,
and the elegance of advanced techniques may escape them.
Moreover, liberal use of statistics will often obscure
other information in the report because of the demands it
places on the reader.

9. <u>Where jargon is used, it is the jargon of policy
makers, not of evaluators</u>. We thought the three reports
would minimize jargon to achieve maximum clarity in
presenting findings, but to our surprise they did not--
they were cluttered with jargon throughout. In contrast
to methods-oriented evaluation reports, however, their
jargon was taken from policy makers' language, not evaluators' language. Policy makers are likely to comprehend
it easily. The use of policy jargon may even enhance the
credibility of these reports for many policy makers, by
implying that the evaluators understand issues well
enough to become familiar with the appropriate language.

10. <u>Concrete recommendations for action are based on
specific findings</u>. The reports encourage policy action
by presenting specific recommendations. These recommendations tend to be down to earth and specific, avoiding
abstract platitudes. This translation from findings to
recommendations not only relieves the reader of the burden
of interpretation, but it also helps ensure that the
authors' intended interpretation will not be misunder-
stood. The concreteness of the recommendations coincides
with the preferences Mintzberg observed among executives
for activities that were specific and well defined.

Our 10 observations are little more than hypotheses at
this time, but they begin to provide a framework for
distinguishing policy-oriented reports from the methods-
oriented reports that underlie them. To the extent they
are incorporated in future policy-oriented reports, we
feel the policy impact of evaluations will increase, even
without the further improvements in methodology that we
feel are also needed.

REFERENCES

Abt Associates, Inc.
    (1979) Children at the Center: Volume 1, Summary
        Findings and Their Implications. Cambridge,
        Mass.: Abt Associates, Inc.
Brickell, H. M., Aslanian, C. B., and Spak, L. J.
    (1974) Data for Decisions: An Analysis of Evaluation
        Data Needed by Decision Makers in Educational
        Programs. New York: Educational Research
        Council of America.
Children's Defense Fund
    (1974) Children Out of School in America. Washington,
        D.C.: Children's Defense Fund.
Coleman, J. S.
    (1972) Policy Research in the Social Sciences.
        Morristown, N.J.: General Learning Press.
Flesch, R.
    (1949) The Art of Readable Writing. New York:
        Collier Books.
Mintzberg, H.
    (1973) The Nature of Managerial Work. New York:
        Harper & Row, Publishers.
U.S. Office of Education
    (1979) Progress Toward a Free Appropriate Public
        Education. DHEW Publication No. (E)
        79-05003. Bureau of Education for the
        Handicapped, Office of Education, U.S.
        Department of Health, Education, and Welfare.